DO IT YOURSELF
BONEFISHING

DO IT YOURSELF
BONEFISHING

ROD HAMILTON
WITH KIRK DEETER

THE DERRYDALE PRESS

Lanham • Boulder • New York • Toronto • Plymouth, UK

THE DERRYDALE PRESS

Published by The Derrydale Press
An imprint of Rowman & Littlefield
4501 Forbes Boulevard, Suite 200, Lanham, Maryland 20706
www.rowman.com

10 Thornbury Road, Plymouth PL6 7PP, United Kingdom

Distributed by NATIONAL BOOK NETWORK

British Library Cataloguing in Publication Information Available

Library of Congress Cataloging-in-Publication Data
Hamilton, Rod, 1954– author.
Do it yourself bonefishing / Rod Hamilton with Kirk Deeter.
pages cm
Includes index.
ISBN 978-1-58667-127-3 (cloth : alk. paper) — ISBN 978-1-58667-128-0
(electronic) 1. Bonefishing. I. Deeter, Kirk D. II. Title.
SH691.B6H36 2014
799.12'4—dc23
2013030046

To my wife Kim and my son Matthew,
who have made my life a truly magnificent DIY adventure

CONTENTS

FOREWORD

There is a generally held notion that bonefish come very close to being the perfect sportfish: They are beautiful to look at, they fight superbly, and, let's face it, they are not really difficult to catch. Anglers on their first guided trip commonly catch a bonefish if the weather is good and they can cast adequately. It is just no big deal catching a bonefish.

If you buy into what I just told you, it's a pretty safe bet you have never tried to do what Rod Hamilton, the author of this book, has taught himself to do better than anyone I know—namely, catch bonefish on his own. And I don't mean just without a guide. I mean completely on his own with nothing but his own knowledge about where bonefish tend to hang out and his own skill at spotting them and then casting to them. Believe me, squaring off with bonefish on foot the way Rod Hamilton does is a completely different kind of activity than standing on the front of a boat while an experienced guide poles you toward fish, giving you the old hands-of-the-clock cry: "Bonefish at 10 o'clock. Sixty feet. Moving left to right."

Don't get me wrong: There are few finer experiences in life than a day of guided bonefishing, preferably at an elegant lodge. What I'm trying to do is draw a clear distinction between the bonefish as seen from the front of a well-guided boat and those seen from the perspective of a do it yourself bonefisherman on foot, often in a brand-new area. If the former is a four on the scale of difficulty, then the latter is a nine.

I'll let Rod Hamilton explain why that is so and then follow that up with advice on how and where to go bonefishing on your own. His where-to-go guide is worth the price of this book, by the way. It takes up the entire latter section of the book and gives you general guidance on where to bonefish on your own across the Caribbean and in a few places far from there, such as the island of Oahu in Hawaii. But back to the subject at hand.

Here, I want to address the central riddle of this book—namely, why a sane adult would want to complicate his or her life by electing to pursue bonefish without a guide. And don't jump to the conclusion that the reason is rooted in economics. It is just not true, Rod Hamilton tells me, that do it yourself bonefishermen are not cheapskates who want to avoid paying for a guide. Rod himself has retired well and so have a lot of his followers, who are growing by leaps and bounds even before the publication of this book.

Rod Hamilton tells me one of the largest single contingents of his followers is made up of men with young families who want to learn how and where they can slip off for a day or two, or just an afternoon, on a family vacation and wade a flat where there is an outside chance of encountering a bonefish. Those in another sizable contingent want to find a way to add a few days of on-your-own bonefishing to a trip devoted primarily to guided bonefishing. The smallest group includes the guys and gals who just can't afford a full week of guided fishing or don't want to pay the kind of fees that guides are asking for now. At least not day after day on a whole vacation. And who can blame them with guide fees cracking $500 in a lot of areas, and even doubling that in isolated places like Turks and Caicos?

You get the picture. There are all sorts of reasons why anglers evolve toward chasing bonefish on their own. But the thing I believe they all have in common is a yearning to get face-to-face with the challenge of bonefishing. Think about it: Millions of trout fishermen teach themselves to read streams, match the hatch, and make their own presentations. Why not bonefishermen? If you are a bonefisherman, why not you? Just be careful—on-your-own bonefishing can start as a way to add some personal pleasure to a family vacation or a trip dedicated mostly to guided fishing and turn into something akin to an addiction.

I know. It's happened to me.

Don Causey
Editor, *The Angling Report*

ACKNOWLEDGMENTS

A book like this is an accumulation of knowledge learned from an untold number of people willing to share what they know about the world of bonefishing with an inquisitive angler from British Columbia, Canada.

I have picked up useful tips from hundreds of helpful souls over the last 20 years, but the first guides I had, like Dexter Simmons in the Keys and "Dubs" Young in Belize, helped to fuel the fire that became my passion for saltwater angling.

Thanks to the many lodges where I've visited, including Turneffe Flats, Two Boys Inn, Fedel Johnson's Outback Fishing Adventures, and The Long Island Bonefishing Lodge, to name a few. It's at the lodges where you make lifelong friends while being shown the beauty of the flats by professionals.

Since this is my first book, I need to thank those who helped me through the process. First, thanks to Don Causey and Kirk Deeter who convinced me that I could and should write a book. To Brian Chan for his early guidance in understanding the publishing world. To Nancy Buan for her help as my "grammar coach" and for proofreading when I just couldn't bear to see the word *bonefish* again.

I owe a fishing trip to Davin Ebanks for his expert help on where and how to fish the Caymans and to Captain Rick Lee for his help putting together the section on Oahu, Hawaii. Both Captain Rich Smith in Marathon and Jim Bernardin of the Pines & Palms Resort were instrumental in piecing together the section on the Florida Keys. Thanks to

ACKNOWLEDGMENTS

my fishing buddy John Andrew for his information and insight on Great Harbour Cay.

A debt of gratitude to those who provided photographs for the book, including Pat Ford, Vince Tobia, Glenn Pittard, Marta Morton, David Lambroughton, Melissa Maura, and Sam Root.

Thanks to Ed Moody of Costa Sunglasses for his help in explaining today's technology embedded in a pair of quality sunglasses.

It was a pleasure working with Jason McGarvey while he built the maps used for each of the destinations.

Captain Rich Smith interrupted his busy guiding schedule to take my wife and me out for a wonderful day as we tested the Diablo Stand-Up Paddle Kayak, which turned out to be one of my favorite watercraft. Thanks to Howard Gibbons of Last Chance Kayak Rentals on North Caicos for allowing us to demo the new Native Watercraft Versa Boards in Bottle Creek.

Thanks to my writing partner, Kirk Deeter, whose professional guidance, encouragement, editing, and contributions kept the project moving in the right direction.

For many years I have traveled with the same fishing "gang." A better group of fishing friends you couldn't ask for. We each have our own idiosyncrasies, but somehow those individual quirks, when woven together, make a complete fishing tapestry. We don't walk as far as we used to, but the beer shared at the end of the day tastes better.

Lastly, my deepest gratitude to my wife, Kim, who has traveled the world with me. Whether it is wading a pristine Bahamian flat or bushwhacking through mangrove jungles, she always has that beautiful smile on her face, letting me know that we are exactly where we should be. When the idea of the book came along, her enthusiasm and encouragement got me started. But her tireless work editing each sentence got me to the finish line.

Happy Tails

INTRODUCTION

The memory is as clear as a crystalline tropical flat under a bright blue sky. I took my first bonefishing trip 20 years ago out of Key West with one of the area's well-known guides. I doubt he remembers me because I was just another trout fisherman from British Columbia, Canada, who wanted to catch a bonefish, permit, or tarpon—preferably all three. A grand slam sounded good to me! And I had booked two days to make sure it happened.

I guess I don't have to tell you I didn't catch a tarpon, I was not even close to hooking a permit, and the guide says I saw three bonefish, but you could have fooled me. The fact is, I didn't do anything right. I couldn't see fish, I couldn't deliver a fly in the wind, and my strip set was a combination of yanking, lifting, and swearing. But the excitement, the adrenaline, and the anticipation when the guide said 70 feet at 11 o'clock—man, that felt different than casting to 16-inch rainbows.

I loved that trip, but the only thing hooked was a fisherman. How could someone who had been fly fishing for 20 years be so pathetic? How could saltwater fly fishing be that much harder than fishing for trout and steelhead in the Pacific Northwest?

I was humbled and humiliated by a foe much craftier than I, requiring skills I didn't possess, in conditions I had never faced before. Game on!

It must be my personality; I couldn't just be terrible and leave it at that. The challenge was intoxicating, so I threw myself into learning what I needed to know to be at least adequate, and the journey has been everything I hoped it would be.

After Key West, I began going to lodges in Belize, Mexico, and the Bahamas and consider myself fortunate that through the years I've fished with some of the best guides on the planet, true professionals that know their craft. They took this poor schmuck under their wings and slowly opened my eyes and mind to what I needed to learn and understand about bonefish, their behavior, and their habitat.

Within a few years, my development and education at Bonefish U reached a point where, as good as the guides were and as much as I loved going to lodges, I needed to see if I could do it on my own. I planned a trip and hired a guide for three days, then walked on my own for four. The days with the guide went well but the days by myself, not so much. My bonefish IQ went from 120 with the guide to 60 when fishing alone. I just didn't realize how much the guides contributed to my self-acclaimed hero status. Once again I was back in first grade, and there was a lot more I needed to know if I was going to drive down a dirt road, walk onto a flat, and catch a fish on my own.

After twenty years, I now feel confident I possess the two skills necessary for a self-guided fisherman to be successful: seeing the fish before it sees you and properly presenting a fly into the feeding zone.

I hope this book helps you become a better flats fisherman and find the same peace of mind and enjoyment that standing alone on a tropical flat has brought me.

Part I
DIY

CHAPTER I
WHY DIY

The evening could not have been more beautiful as the sun lazily dipped toward the fire-red horizon in what was surely the most glorious sunset I had ever seen. In front of me were dozens of glistening tails reflecting the last of the day's golden rays off the still waters of a Bahamian flat. That sparkle was more captivating than the Hope Diamond and was precisely the reason I had traveled 4,000 miles. Standing knee-deep in bathtub-warm water I reflected on my life's journey and how I got there.

I've been fly fishing for 50 years and casting bits of feathers and hooks at bonefish for 20. I started writing about my own self-guided bonefishing trips as an extension of my passion for fly fishing. My first venture was a website devoted to sharing with others what I'd learned through the years. That was followed shortly thereafter by a blog where I broadened the discussion to include my most recent trips, DIY tips and tricks, and topical reports on all things bonefish.

Those two media outlets have developed into a community of readers and subscribers. The more I communicated with the group, the more I realized that there were people from all around the world who enjoyed fishing on their own, and a book about self-guided bonefishing felt like the next logical step.

When news of the book's publication became public knowledge, I received an email from a well-known and prominent member of the angling community essentially asking the question, "Why on earth would anyone want to fish on their own when they can catch more fish with a guide?" And there is the question: why indeed?

A spectacular bonefish caught while stalking the flat (Photo courtesy of David Lambroughton)

Before venturing headlong into why DIY, let me be clear about one thing. It's my unwavering opinion that the best way to catch fish is with a guide. The quickest and surest way to learn how to bonefish is with a guide, and you can't have any more fun or be treated better than by staying at a lodge. I go to lodges for a couple of weeks every winter and hire independent guides virtually everywhere I go. But I target bonefish for around 100 days per year. Lodges and guides take up 20 to 30 of those, leaving me a lot of time to fish on my own. Whether fishing with a guide, staying at a lodge, or walking the flat on our own, we are all part of the bonefishing community with one intertwining thread of DNA connecting us: We love fly fishing for bonefish.

But back to the question: Why DIY? The answer depends on whom you ask; it's not black or white but hangs tenuously in the gray area between challenge, time, and economics.

Obviously, it's more difficult to catch fish on your own, so it can't be about numbers. It's much more physically demanding, so it's not about being pampered. The preparation is significantly more time consuming than booking at a lodge, so it's not simpler. So what is it about do it yourself bonefishing that draws more and more people each year?

For me, the answer lies in a complex combination of exploration, challenge, knowledge, ego, intimacy, and freedom. There is excitement in walking the next flat or wading the next creek; there's the opportunity to peek around the metaphorical corner and explore the unknown in hope of finding the greatest fishing "hole" anyone has seen.

When bonefishing on my own, I pit my experience and skills against the perfect example of evolution, Mother Nature's torpedo. I desire to learn everything I can about the quarry; I want to know how they live, what they eat, and where to find them.

There is the pleasure I get in catching a truly remarkable game fish by myself, knowing that to do so, I had to do a whole bunch of things right. And there is the serenity and intimacy of walking alone in a hidden creek to meet Mr. Bone on his own terms.

Add to this the freedom to fish where I want, when I want, and how I want, as well as the satisfaction of fishing the correct tide and understanding what a bonefish does before 9:00 a.m. and after 4:00 p.m.

I understand that not everyone wants to drive down nine roads to nowhere to find one road to somewhere. Or to walk a mile through swamps and mud to a flat that may not hold fish. Maybe I'm the only one that thinks catching two fish by myself is better than ten fish with help. But that's why I'm a DIY guy.

One particular episode and one special location embody everything I treasure about DIY trips. As with most of my adventures, this one started with a local's comment, followed by hours in front of the computer staring at Google Earth.

I fish a great deal with one particular friend, and it became our mission to find the place the local had mentioned. Typical of our wild goose chases, we drove down miles of what the rental car companies refer to as "impassable roads." Finally, on day three, we parked the car at the end of a two-rut track at the location we deemed to be as close as we were going to get. After testing our radios and checking our water supply we began to hike through the woods. That hike led us to a massive tangle of mangroves and mud, which led us to a thicket of casuarina trees and finally onto a beach that encircled the bonefish flat of all bonefish flats. This was the pot of gold at the end of the rainbow and the end of the yellow brick road. To me, that flat and its adjoining bonefish-filled creek are the reasons why DIY fishermen do it themselves.

I can say this with certainty: I have become a better fisherman because I walk the flats on my own. Fishing on your own forces you to improve as a scientist, fisherman, and philosopher. Catching fish on your own requires you to learn about bonefish behavior, their habitat, what they eat, and the effect of tides. You have to improve your casting, spotting, and wading skills, and there's plenty of time to reflect on your own life's questions.

Who Is the DIY Fisherman?

While DIY bonefishing is not for everyone, over the years the movement has grown as more and more fishermen find something appealing about hunting for bonefish on their own.

I have the good fortune of communicating with DIY anglers from around the world every day. When I first started my website, I assumed that most users would be like myself, hardcore fishermen looking for the next best place to fly fish for bones, but I couldn't have been more wrong.

In my experience, DIY fishermen broadly fall into three groups:

Fishermen in the first group, like me, enjoy the process of planning a trip and the gratification of ultimately subduing bonefish that they have

Fishing the roadside flats of Acklins Island, Bahamas (Photo courtesy of Vince Tobia)

found, stalked, and caught on their own. Like me, many of these fishermen hire local guides for part of the stay and walk on their own the rest of the time.

Fishermen in the second group love the sport, but economics dictates where they go and how they fish. If money were not a consideration, many in this group would stay at a lodge or fish with a guide.

Fishermen in the last, and by far the largest, group travel with family members or nonfishermen looking for a destination that combines a traditional tropical vacation with a few days of fishing. These fishermen tend to hire a local guide for a day and walk a flat for a few mornings or evenings on their own.

Expectations for DIY Fishermen

If you are a novice or intermediate fisherman, you will unequivocally catch more fish with a guide. You'll be fishing in the guide's home waters, and he knows where to fish, what tide to hit, and which fly to use. In addition, his flats boat allows for the ultimate in mobility with the capacity to reach flats that DIY anglers can only dream about. And perhaps most important, you get to ride on the coattails of the guide's experienced eyes.

As a DIY guy, you don't have any of those advantages and you have a whole lot of disadvantages. Consequently, success shouldn't be measured by the number of fish caught. The joy of fishing comes from the exploration of new waters, the hunt, the intimate nature of wading, what you learned during the day, and, oh yeah, how many fish were caught.

As the years have gone by and my skill has increased, my expectations for how many fish will be caught have grown. Though the pure joy of being out on the flat should be enough, at the end of the day with a beer in hand the conversation inevitably turns to "how many fish did you catch?"

Here is an informal "fish success" rating that my gang uses for our DIY days.

0–2 fish	a slow day
3–5 fish	a fair day
6–9 fish	a good day
10 + fish	a great day

The boys contemplating life after a morning on the flats

The more time you spend on the water, the better you get. One particular buddy and I fish a lot of days together and during the course of a trip will have many great days. Being a DIY fisherman doesn't mean you catch fewer fish, it just means you need to put in the time necessary to learn the craft.

How to Use This Book

This book is not a travel guide, so you'll find very few recommendations for restaurants, resorts, or tourist attractions. What I have included are those contacts and that information I think will help you pick the right destination while increasing your odds of having a successful fishing adventure.

In chapter 3, "How to DIY," you will find suggestions, tips, and tricks learned over the years and advice on how to plan a DIY trip which should shorten your learning curve.

Part II, "Where to DIY," encompasses 16 destinations with directions to more than 300 individual fishing locations. With the exception of a few places on Grand Cayman, Great Harbour Cay, and Oahu, I have fished them all.

The "Spousal Rating" is intended to help those planning a trip with nonfishermen to pinpoint a destination that is suitable for everyone.

The "Seven-Day Sample Trip" is designed to help build a fishing plan from home so you can hit the ground running.

The map that precedes each destination, which should be used in conjunction with Google Earth and local maps, is included to help you find the flats and creeks where bonefish are found.

Good luck on your adventures and remember that life is a DIY experience.

CHAPTER 2

EQUIPMENT

My views on equipment have changed over the years. Twenty years ago the premium rods and reels were so much better than anything else that it made sense to recommend the high-end products. But today, so many manufactures make equipment that works, it's hard to make cut-and-dried recommendations.

At the end of the day, the rod must be able to load quickly with relatively little line out, and the reel needs a smooth drag that can easily hold the fly line and 150 yards of backing.

Where I can be of help is with the equipment carried on the flat. Most of the books and articles I see regarding wading assume you are within minutes of a boat where you can readily replenish supplies. I am often miles from the car, so if I'm not carrying it, I won't have it for the entire day.

Rods. For bonefish I pack eight-weight and nine-weight rods. The eight is my "go to" rod in most situations, but the nine helps in big winds and for larger species and serves as my backup. I have certainly seen seven-weight rods work well for smaller bonefish in Belize and Mexico, but they don't cast as well in the wind. If I'm fishing from a boat or on a large flat requiring long casts, I prefer a fast-action rod. For close-in wading and short casts I prefer something with a little softer action.

Reels. I do a lot of trout fishing throughout western Canada and the United States. Let's face it, most of the time our trout reels are only used to hold the line. But saltwater flats fishing is different, and reels matter when you are fishing for bonefish. You need large arbor, anodized reels

Getting the gear ready before hitting the flats

that are simple in construction and have a sealed smooth drag that will stand up to both the rigors of hot fish and the issues caused by the corrosive nature of saltwater. Your reel needs to hold a minimum of 150 yards of 20-pound backing. Take a reel to match each rod and a spare if one breaks. I match each reel with a spare spool loaded with a different line. Bring a reel repair kit and the appropriate grease and oils recommended by the reel manufacturer with you.

Lines. You generally only need tropical floating lines matched to each of your rods. There are some great floating weight-forward bonefish lines out now. I lean toward the newer lines for shorter casts that load the rod quickly. For inexperienced saltwater fishermen or those who have trouble casting in the wind I am a big proponent of over lining. So if you have an eight-weight rod, bring a nine-weight floating line with you.

The new floating lines with clear tips work exceptionally well when confronted with spooky fish. I also load at least one spool with a slow-sinking clear intermediate line and bring interchangeable sink tips with a loop-to-loop connection. Bring one extra line for emergencies. I've cut lines on coral and had them crack in the heat. You need to clean the line at least every other day, so bring a line-cleaning kit.

You need a good quality saltwater reel with 150 yards of backing. (Photo courtesy of Sam Root)

Backing. Unlike in most trout-fishing situations, in bonefishing your backing gets used a lot. Make sure you have a solid connection between your reel and backing and between your backing and fly line. Test all connections before leaving home. The Internet is full of examples of how to tie each of these connections.

If your backing was put on your reel by anyone other than you, test the connection from the reel to your backing. Today's reels hold a lot of line, so there is no need to skimp on backing. As a rule, have a minimum of 150 yards of backing on your reels. As part of your pretrip routine, strip all the backing off the reel then wind it back on carefully so when that first fish takes off, the backing peels off evenly and doesn't pinch or grab.

Radios. Safety is the first concern when wading on your own or with buddies. We like to stay in touch with each other and report on the fishing. Through the years we have tried every imaginable device and have

The car loaded up with kayaks ready to launch into Chetamul Bay, Mexico

now settled on high-quality rechargeable, handheld, waterproof, floating VHF radios.

Kayaks and Inflatables. Inflatable kayaks are a pain to travel with and airlines charge extra, but I pack one with me to virtually every destination. They're invaluable when you want to cross a channel or paddle into a creek system or out to a cay a half mile offshore. Some of the rental properties may have hard-shell kayaks available, but make sure they are allowed off the property and can be safely transported by the vehicle being rented. There are a variety of kayaks on the market and I have tested many of them.

Rule #1: don't go cheap on the inflatables. We have had kayaks that blew apart, fell apart, mysteriously got holes in them on the plane. and experienced a variety of other disasters. I can guarantee that at some point you will puncture your kayak on coral, limestone, or mangrove roots, so make sure you take one that can be repaired easily. As a rule, I use the inflatable for transportation only, but lately I have been testing stand-up

A kayak can get you to areas that are otherwise unreachable.

paddleboards and kayaks. Where wind is not an issue, they allow you to cover more territory and see fish significantly better.

Packs. The pack you carry on the flat to hold all your gear, food, and water is an essential piece of equipment. I've experimented with a lot of packs and settled on the Fish Pond three-zipper fanny pack with a shoulder strap. Once you get all your equipment, food, and water for the day loaded, the pack is surprisingly heavy. Pick something you can wear all day with the weight evenly distributed. Backpacks work well for transporting, but they are a little inconvenient when you need something. Single-strap backpacks are good and actually hold more than a fanny pack. Of course, I learned this the hard way, but anything that needs to stay dry should be in a separate watertight bag.

Sunglasses. I talk about quality sunglasses at length in the section titled "Spotting Bonefish," but next to your rod and reel, this is the most important piece of equipment you use. Take two pairs of optical-quality sunglasses equipped with straps. Two different lens colors are always good, but you really need two so you have a backup.

Clothing. I like to travel as lightly as possible so I give my clothing selection some careful thought. The actual clothing for your trip is listed

Mangrove shoots waiting for the incoming tide (Photo courtesy of Sam Root)

in the "Travel Checklist" section, but there are a few things to consider when preparing for a DIY bonefishing trip. If there are laundry facilities at your location, it's nice to pack light and have your laundry done once during the week. On some trips we just walk into the shower at the end of the day with our shirt and pants on to clean them.

Shirts. Make sure the shirts you will be wearing on the flats are lightweight, quick-drying, long sleeve, flats-style fishing shirts. Everyone has a preference about this, but I prefer lots of pockets on my shirts. Remember, you don't have a boat to hold a fully stocked boat bag, so places to carry gear are at a premium. Be careful with your colors and avoid anything bright and flashy. I stay with neutral colors.

Pants. Pants need to be lightweight and quick drying. They offer protection from the sun and mangrove branches. They must have solid loops to hold a fabric belt. I've tried shorts, but I do so much bush bashing that I need the long pant legs for protection.

Flats Hat. It's important to have the right hat and to pack a spare. It should have a long bill, preferably with a dark underside with flaps or wide brim to cover your ears and neck. Remember that whatever hat you choose, you will most likely be in the wind, so it needs a way to button or tie down.

Belt. You need a fabric belt (not leather) that fits through the loops of your pants and has a solid closing buckle. You are going to hang your pliers and other items on the belt, so it has to hold.

Wading Socks. Coral, sand, shells, and small rocks somehow magically find their way between your boots and your feet. I like to use the Simms wading sock with a gravel guard attached; others use thin neoprene wading socks and separate gravel guards.

Flats Boots. You will be walking in the boots all day, so they need to be broken in and comfortable. On a DIY bonefishing trip you may walk six miles every day. If you have not broken your boots in, you will get blisters and be in agony for the rest of the trip. When wading the reefs in Belize you are around very sharp coral, so you will need substantial wading boots.

Resting the gear after a day fishing the salt ponds of Long Island

Outerwear. I know it is not supposed to happen, but it can be cold at times, so bring something warm like a fleece.

Rainwear. It's going to rain, which is what it does in the tropics. You need a quality lightweight, waterproof rain jacket with hood and waterproof rain pants. Trust me, don't go cheap on this gear; it will last you for many years and you will be thankful that it works when you need it.

CHAPTER 3
HOW TO DIY

Maybe you want to walk a beach in the evening to catch a bonefish or you're interested in being better prepared for an upcoming trip. That's the intrigue of bonefishing. No matter what the goal, there is always more to learn.

Over the last 20 years I have picked up a few things about self-guided fishing and hope that you may find a nugget of information in this section to help you in your pursuit of one of the world's great game fish.

How to Spot Bonefish

The old saying "even a blind squirrel finds a nut once in a while" doesn't apply to bonefishing. If you can't see the fish, you aren't going to catch them.

Spotting bonefish is part art, part science, and part intuition, but nothing takes the place of experience. Let's be clear: When I say spotting bonefish, that means seeing the fish before it sees you. Watching tails wave goodbye doesn't count.

My first real bonefishing trip was to the Turneffe Atoll in Belize, where I stayed for a week at one of the lodges. For the entire week I was paired up with a young guide who has become one of the best and most respected in the business. I have subsequently fished with him many times, and we now laugh at my "vision" during those early days.

I couldn't see squat. On day one, there could have been a bonefish gnawing on my boot and I wouldn't have seen it. On day two, I was a little

A single fish cruising the mangrove edges looking for breakfast (Photo courtesy of Pat Ford)

better, and I continued to improve throughout the week. I wasn't spotting dimes underwater at 100 yards, but I did see the occasional fish after the guide pointed it out. I can distinctly remember after seven days on the water wondering if I would ever be able to spot a single cruising bonefish. It seemed like alchemy to me. How on earth can anyone spot a two-pound bonefish weaving its way among the coral and grasses of a reef? My guide could, and I vowed that someday I would be able to as well.

Without question, the best way to improve and to shorten the learning curve is fishing with a *quality* guide. Standing on the front of a boat poled by a professional gives you a good vantage point. With an instructor to teach you how to scan the water, you'll have a chance to see plenty of fish throughout the day. The guide normally sees fish first and then directs your eye to where you should be looking. This is an important step in the learning process as it allows you to stop scanning and focus in a concentrated area and on a specific target. That's how you learn. You need to see plenty of fish in a variety of conditions over and over again.

Through the years I have asked every expert I could, "How do you see bonefish?" "What do you look for?" and "What is the secret?" Next to "What's my favorite fly?" that last question is the one I now get asked most often.

What follows is a compilation of information and advice I have received from others, mixed in with my own observations from 20 years on the flats.

It's a big leap from having a guide see and point out a fish to walking onto a flat by yourself and spotting a fish before it sees you. It's not unlike taking off the training wheels and riding a bike down the road on your own. You're pretty sure you don't need them, but you'll never know until you're on two wheels. In most cases a self-guided angler is not fishing the large open white-sand flats that are fished with a guide, but rather is walking a creek or shoreline scattered with rocks, coral, turtle grass, and mangroves. Large, expansive white-sand flats are the easiest places to spot fish, and mangrove creeks are not. The first time out on your own may be a little frustrating, but don't worry. I guarantee you will be better on day five then you were on day one.

The information included in this section is intended for a wading angler, so the tips and techniques are more relevant to a self-guided fisherman in knee-deep water than an angler standing at the front of a boat.

Look Where You Can See

All anglers have a window I call "the spotting zone," that is, the section of water in front of you where you can identify a fish. On one end of the spectrum is a seasoned guide who spots fish easily at 80 feet and on the other end is a newbie who sees fish at 20 feet. Most anglers' effective spotting zone is 30 to 50 feet (I know, you say 70 feet). Be honest with yourself, determine what your personal spotting zone is, and commit to seeing every fish within that zone.

Train yourself to spend 70 percent of your time looking where you can see, that is, in the spotting zone. Then 15 percent of the time swivel your head, looking behind and to the sides. The remaining 15 percent should be spent searching the surface, looking for nervous water, tails, and disturbances.

The eyes of a new saltwater angler are not trained. They typically wander indiscriminately, roaming from side to side, from close in to far out, and from the bottom back to the surface. My advice is to be honest with yourself, get in the water, and really determine how far out you can spot and identify a rock or coral head and stick to those limits. Let's say that's 50 feet.

Now do the same exercise while you are walking. I guarantee that drops your distance by a minimum of 10 feet. I'll discuss this more later, but the number one reason people don't see fish is because they are moving. Seeing a fish while walking is twice as difficult as spotting that same fish while standing still. It's a function of the way the brain works—it focuses better when it is only doing one thing.

Lesson 1: Figure out what your spotting zone is while walking, spend 70 percent of your time scanning that zone, and commit to seeing every fish within it.

How to Scan

It doesn't seem right that you have to learn how to use your eyes to scan back and forth and close in to far out, but you do. Generally

Surveying a classic Bahamian flat

speaking, we all have the same vision, either corrected or not. So why can some people spot bonefish at 100 feet while others are lucky to see them at 40 feet?

Your eyes need to be trained or else they will simply wander. It still happens to me when I first hit the flats after a summer of trout fishing. I know my eyes need to concentrate, focus, and see through the water, but they don't want to. They bounce all over the place. I continually catch myself looking in areas out of my zone, and my vision pops to the surface instead of staying trained on the bottom. It's what your eyes want to do. You have to work at making them see through the surface glare to focus on the bottom.

Once you have identified the distance where you can actually see a fish, slowly start scanning left to right. While scanning, you are asking your brain to memorize the bottom and identify what you are seeing, then scan back from right to left to see if your brain picks up anything different. Don't let your eyes dart from place to place or revert back to the surface. You are trying to determine if there is a green patch that wasn't there before, a little flash, an odd shape, or a horizontal line that should be vertical. But most of all, you are looking for movement.

This is where art, science, and intuition meet. Often your eyes see something your brain hasn't interpreted as a bonefish, but intuitively you know something is different. You need to trust that feeling and focus. What did my eye see that my brain didn't identify? Stop moving, focus, and determine what caught your attention.

Remember, 70 percent of your time is spent scanning within your spotting zone; 15 percent of your time is looking to the side, behind, and out to 70 feet; and 15 percent of your time is searching on the surface. The surface look serves two very useful purposes. First, it offers the opportunity to look farther away for surface disturbances, nervous water, pushed water, tailing fish, flashes, and large schools. Second, it relaxes and rests your eyes. I have had guides and experts tell me they take a relaxed view of scanning and don't strain to see through the water column, but it just hasn't worked for me. When I'm fishing hard and in the zone, I have a razor focus and am really concentrating. I rest my eyes and brain when looking to the side, behind me, and on the surface.

Lesson 2: When your eyes see something your brain can't identify, stop, focus, and evaluate.

What to Look For

I wish I could say that you will see a nice clear picture of an entire bonefish, but it just isn't true. It's much like my early days of bow hunting. I started out walking through the forest looking for a deer, but as my knowledge grew and I became more successful, I realized that what I was really looking for was a twitch or movement, a mismatched color patch, a piece of a tail or an ear, a vertical line where it should be horizontal. In other words, anything but a deer. That's how it is in bonefishing. As you get better you'll understand; you'll notice a movement, a patch of color, a spot that's there now but wasn't before, a flash, something that sets off your "Spidey sense" and makes you concentrate on a particular spot.

Movement. You won't see a whole bonefish; more likely the fish will appear as a darker spot that is moving. Focus on the movement and confirm that it's a fish, which direction it's traveling, and how best to present a fly. The current and wind make everything look as though it's moving, so the first thing to do is stop. Next, place the butt of your rod against your stomach and point the rod tip at the object to determine if it's stationary or in fact is moving.

Color. As we know, the color of a bonefish is silver. Well, not exactly. When you hold it out of the water it is, but in its natural environment the bonefish is a master of camouflage. Depending on the way the sun is shining, the direction it's swimming, the cloud cover, and the color of the bottom, its appearance can range from a dark green to a bright silver. I have stared at fish I could plainly see only to have them turn a certain way and simply disappear. This phenomenon explains why you can scan through an area and see nothing, then come right back to the same area and see a fish. Knowing a bonefish can appear as different colors can help by making you aware that it's not a silver fish you're looking for. Instead, you should be looking for a dark patch over a light-colored bottom, a mismatched color in green grass, or a moving shadow.

Horizontal Lines. The silhouette of a bonefish is generally horizontal as they swim along the bottom. The lines of grasses and mangroves tend to be vertical. Sometimes your eyes will see and your brain will pick up a horizontal line where everything else is rising vertically from the bottom to the top.

Flash. I've caught tons of bonefish as a result of seeing a flash. Generally, this is from bonefish feeding, turning slightly and reflecting the sun. It's not like a camera flash or a neon sign—it is much more subtle. Many times I have seen a flash and after stopping and staring still can't see the fish, but I know it's there. Often when fishing in deeper holes and slots, the flash is what you notice. You have to distinguish between a flash and a sparkle on the surface, but your eye will pick up the difference. It's crucial to trust your instincts.

Bottom. Everybody sees fish better on clear white-sand flats. The fish show up darker against the bottom, so it stands to reason that the more difficult it is for you to spot fish, the more you should lean toward fishing the whitest, clearest flats you can find. If you aren't fishing over white sand, then seek out those white-colored holes and easier places to see. The bottom can also be helpful by revealing locations where fish have been feeding. When bonefish are burrowing in the bottom after prey, they expel a jet of water that blows the sand away from the prey. These crater-shaped holes let you know that a bonefish has been there. Seeing the holes provides clues regarding how regularly bonefish use the area and confidence that you are in the right place.

Noise. Why is noise in a section on how to spot bonefish? Because bonefish make noise and when you hear bonefish you focus. I know lots of fishermen that have never heard a bonefish. Why? Because they make too much noise when they walk. You hear fish when you are still. They make noise feeding, splashing, and digging out food in the mangroves. If you want to hear fish, stop moving.

A couple of us had spread out over a large oceanside flat one day, and a novice saltwater fishermen came up to me and said, "It's been so long since I saw a bonefish—remind me what they look like."

I said, "Sure, you see those gray things?"

"Yep."

"Well, those are rocks. See those green things?"

"Yep."

"Well, that's turtle grass. The stuff you can't see, those are bonefish!"

Lesson 3: Look for small things—movement, color change, a slight flash, or horizontal shapes—and spend less time walking and more time looking.

Tips and Tricks

Sun at Your Back. You all know this one: You can see better into the water with the sun either at your back or off to the left or right over your shoulder. But I bring this up for an important reason. When you get out onto a flat, have the sun behind you and then look to the right and left. Somewhere in that view you are going to be able to see better. It may be right in front of you and it may not. It's important to figure that out because it will help you decide which way to walk.

Fish Early and Late. Typically, a guide will have you fishing between the key hours of 10:00 a.m. and 2:00 p.m. This is when the sun overhead is at its best for spotting fish. The same holds true for the wading fishermen. But I have learned over the years that some of my best fishing is early in the morning and late in the evening. The sunlight does not penetrate the surface of the water, which makes it easy to know where to look. You're scanning the surface hunting for tails, small disturbances, pushed and nervous water, and the sound of fish. It's a quiet time to be on the water.

You have to fish the tide. There is nothing more important than being on the flat when the tide is rising. If that happens to be at 7:00 a.m., then that is when you should be on the flat.

Wind. Optimum spotting conditions for me are when the water has a slight ripple on it. I feel as though I can see through the water column well enough to spot fish; at the same time, the ripple makes me less visible. Severe winds churning up the surface can impact your ability to see fish and, unlike with clouds, you can't even see tails and nervous water. But the beauty of the tropics is you can almost always find a location that is more or less protected. A wading fisherman should fish a creek system where the wind is cut down by the mangroves or find a cove protected by a point. Go where you can see.

Clouds. We would all like to fish on those picture-perfect bluebird days, but it doesn't always work that way. Cold fronts and clouds are the enemy, but some clouds and overcast conditions are better than others. In a weird way, a solid gray sky is better than either the high wispy white clouds or the big billowy clouds that cover the sun. Surprisingly, your eyes can adapt to a constant gray and you will have some vision. The challenge is when the clouds come in and out and turn the water from crystal clear to "who turned out the lights." Your eyes just can't adapt to the change.

On those tough, cloudy days, you have to take a different approach. Fish shallower areas where you can see tails and nervous water. Look for ambush points where the fish are going to be crossing in and out of a creek mouth or around a point. Look for large schools, not singles. Find a nice clear white patch of sand and stay there.

When a cloud turns out the lights, stop moving but continue fishing, noting two things. First, there will always be one direction that you can see better than others. Visibility will only be 20 feet, but concentrate there. If a fish crosses that spot, you won't have time for a cast so just use a quick flip. Second, spend more time working the surface looking for nervous water, tails, and surface disturbances. When the sun comes back, do a 360-degree check of your surroundings before taking the first step. Fish may have moved in while the sun was blocked.

Target Schools. It's far more difficult to spot singles and doubles than it is to see a large school. Maybe physically your eyes just aren't good enough, you walk too fast, you make too much noise, or you are just learning. If you are not seeing fish, adopt a strategy of either staking out an ambush point or finding the one or two larger schools that are sure to be in the area. The advantage is self-explanatory. You can see the fish farther away so you won't scare them if your wading style is loud. Adopting a strategy of hunting for schools means you can walk faster and cover more ground.

Ambush Points. Finding ambush points should be number one on the list of tips for the rookie. These spots are in the channels on large open flats or the openings in creeks and mangrove systems where the fish pass through on the incoming and outgoing tides. A deeper channel next to a flat or along the shoreline is ideal. This is a fish highway that they use to filter on and off a flat. Just stake it out; don't move and let the fish come to you.

Sandy Clear Points. I like fishing turtle grass and blotchy bottoms, but for the novice sight fisherman it's a nightmare. Picking out fish on that kind of bottom is like having someone pull out your eyelashes one at a time. It hurts. When you find yourself staring at a bottom that doesn't easily show fish, find a clear sandy spot and watch it for 30 minutes. You will be surprised how many times fish cross it.

Released Fish. Release a caught fish and follow it as it swims away. I promise you will be surprised at how far out you can see the fish. It may well be 100 feet. So the good news is that you can see fish at 100 feet. The bad news is that you aren't seeing fish at 100 feet. Now you know your eyes can identify a fish 100 feet away, but for some reason that is not translating to your brain recognizing it as a fish. All I can say is you need to convince your spouse you need more time on the flats.

Watch the Birds. Bonefish hate birds flying over them. If you've fished enough, this will have happened to you: You are just getting ready to cast to a group of happy fish when a bird flies over and its shadow scares the living $%&* out of the fish. Well, it's possible to use that to your advantage. Whenever you see a bird flying over the flat, watch the water underneath to see if it has scared a school of fish. It's like a secret weapon to actually see a school of fish spook 250 yards away. Now you know where they are.

Turn Around. As a rule, you pick the direction you are walking because of the tide and the sun. You walk in the direction to intercept fish coming on or off the flat. But sometimes you're wrong. If one school comes up behind you, OK, but if it happens twice, turn around because you're walking the wrong way.

Hunting Tails. There's nothing I like more than searching for tails, and no time in the day is better for tail hunting than dusk. Around 4:00 p.m. the sun gets so low in the sky that seeing through the water becomes difficult. The poor visibility forces you to spend more and more time scanning the surface. But after 6:00 p.m. the sun is low on the horizon and the tails really begin to show. You're looking for that "glint" as the sun reflects off the silver. Do an about-face and start walking toward the sun because that is when the gold glistens.

Stop Moving. Everyone sees better when they are not moving, and fish don't spook when you're standing still. When a cloud blocks out the sun and turns crystal clear water into a dark abyss, stop moving. When there are fish in the vicinity, stop moving.

Tide. Novice and experts alike know that the tide is the single most important environmental factor influencing the movements of bonefish. In general, they move out of deep water onto the flats or into the creeks during an incoming tide and off the flat and out of the creeks on the receding tide. Be in position to intercept the fish by being in front of them and waiting, not following behind trying to catch up.

Large school of tailing fish (Photo courtesy of Pat Ford)

Heads or Tails. There are two ends to a bonefish, but only one that counts. Take that extra three seconds to determine which way the fish is traveling and put the fly in front of the right end. I've yet to see a bonefish eat with its tail.

Sunglasses

Two good pairs of optical-quality polarized glasses properly tinted are as important as your rod, reel, line, and flies.

There are two skills that a self–guided angler requires to be successful. One is the skill to place the fly where it needs to be, and the second is the ability to spot fish. I can't tell you how many times I have seen anglers spend thousands on their equipment to support the first skill and then pick up any old pair of sunglasses to use for the second. Don't cheap out on sunglasses—they are critical to your success. Get two good pairs. Why two pairs? So you can have different tints to adjust for various conditions, and, just like your rods, so you have one as a backup for breakage. Make sure your glasses are polarized, provide 100 percent UV protection, are optically accurate with little distortion, have quality nylon frames, and are built with hinges to withstand the rigors of saltwater fishing.

Interestingly enough, you would think the same tint and lens materials would work identically for everyone. It's just not so. Much like fly rods, there are personal preferences for tints and lens materials, and you're going to have to try a few before settling on the one that's right for you. Whenever you are with a group of fishermen or your guide, try each others' glasses. You might find you can see better with a different tint.

Lens Materials and Construction

I'm oversimplifying the choices in lens materials available, but optical-quality sunglasses generally come in either glass or polycarbonate. Glass lenses have long been a favorite because of their clarity and scratch resistance, but over the last ten years, polycarbonate lenses have become virtually as good and have the added bonus of being lighter and shatterproof. I was a glass-lens guy for years but was convinced to try today's polycarbonate lenses. Honestly, I can't tell the difference.

Lens Color

The question about sunglasses I am asked most often is "Which color of lens works best?" Unfortunately, there is no single tint that works best in all conditions.

There are two base colors used by flats fishermen: gray and brown. The brown-based lenses come in a variety of tints including brown, amber, copper, rose, and vermillion.

The gray-based lenses are considered neutral, as they maintain the natural colors and tend to be easy on the eyes, but they don't provide the contrast that many anglers like. The brown-based lenses show more contrast and for most fishermen make it easier to see fish. For the wading DIY fisherman, contrast is good and helps separate the fish from the grass, rocks, and sand.

For low light conditions, yellow, vermillion, and rose brighten the landscape, so are good in the early morning and twilight hours.

With all those choices, let me tell you what I wear. On super bright days I switch back and forth between gray and amber lenses. Gray is softer on my eyes for those bright days, but the amber lenses help me to see fish better by providing more contrast. On days when there are a few clouds in the sky I wear the amber lenses to create the contrast that I like for picking out fish. I have tried a variety of the lighter tinted lenses in yellow and vermillion for dawn and dusk, but I normally just take my glasses off once the sun angle gets so low that my eyes can't penetrate the surface. I also believe that the glass polarization dulls the glint off tails flashing in the sun. I like the wide frames and wraparound style to cut out as much light on the sides as possible. Add a long-billed cap with a dark underside, a secure strap, and lens wipes, and I'm ready.

Walking the Flats

There hasn't been much written about how to walk a flat, but next to casting and seeing fish, walking the flats effectively is one of the most important skills for a self-guided angler to have.

I suspect that the topic gets cursory attention because most fishing is done from the bow of a boat, and wading is often secondary during the course of the day. But to the DIY guy, mastering this technique ranks pretty high on the skill-o-meter.

Almost everything in the ocean tries to eat bonefish. Consequently, they go through life with chips on their shoulders and are a little "uptight."

Getting ready to cast into a nice school (Photo courtesy of Pat Ford)

Wading the flats with a buddy (Photo courtesy of Pat Ford)

The shallower the water, the more nervous they are. Bonefish don't like noise, they don't like vibrations, and they don't like movement. Knowing the propensity for bonefish to bolt, your mission is to walk through the water quietly enough so that you see fish before they see or sense you.

Make no mistake; there is a direct correlation between how effectively you wade and how many fish you spot. The number one rule for wading is that you can only walk as fast as you can see!

The Correlation between Walking Speed and Spotting Fish

This is a difficult concept to describe in writing; as a matter of fact, I haven't been all that successful in person either, but here goes.

You have to be able to spot a fish farther out than the distance a fish can notice you. For instance, a perfectly still angler only needs to see fish 20 feet away because, in theory, at that distance a still angler won't spook the fish.

Conversely, the noisy wader transmits sounds and vibrations that a fish picks up 60 feet away. If your spotting zone is 40 feet, the fish is long gone before you ever knew it was there. There's the number one reason walking anglers don't see fish—the correlation between walking speed and spotting fish.

You must walk at a speed and noise level that doesn't scare fish within your spotting zone. The spotting zone expands and shrinks based on conditions. On a bluebird-sky day at 1:00 p.m. you may be able to see out 70 feet, but on a cloudy day the zone shrinks by half, which means you should walk at only half the speed.

Walking Speed

I've walked with a lot of anglers, and all but the most skilled walk too fast and make too much noise.

Here's the deal. We all see better when standing motionless than when moving. You see progressively worse the faster you move. That's the way your brain works. It processes information more effectively when it is focused on one task, such as scanning the bottom. When you combine multiple tasks, like taking the next step, managing a trailing line, and scanning the bottom, your ability to focus is compromised.

So if we can see better when standing still, then why are we moving? First, we have to find fish, which means exploring and searching. But once you are into fish, if you're being honest, it's because you're bored. Standing in one place isn't as much fun as hunting.

I fish with anglers all the time who wade faster than I do. I know how well I see fish, I know how far out my spotting zone is, and I know they see fish about half as well as I do. Math tells me that they should be walking at half my speed. But they might think, "Rod is successful at that pace, so that must be the right speed." No, your speed is a function of how far out your spotting zone is, not how far out mine is.

A better example was a conversation that took place with a buddy at the end of a day on the flat.

"Rod, why don't I see as many fish as you do?"

"Because you walk too fast and you're scaring the fish."

"But, I'm walking at the same speed I was walking with the guide yesterday."

"I know you are, but your guide can see twice as well as you can, he's spotting fish out to 80 feet. He is picking up fish farther out than his sound carries, hence his speed. You can only see out to 40 feet, which means you need to walk half as fast, then you will see the fish before they sense you are there."

If you admit to yourself that you see bonefish about half as well as your eagle-eyed guide, then walk at half his speed.

Over the years, I have developed a terminology for the speeds I walk so that I can communicate a little more clearly to those who are new to the sport. All experienced anglers do this intuitively and don't need a name for the speeds they walk, but if you're starting out or having difficulty seeing fish, knowing there are different tempos might help.

I use four distinct speeds while on the flats.

Prospecting. This is the speed I walk when scouting. I'm either trying to get to where I think the fish will be, or I'm in a searching mode, hoping to get a glimpse of fish moving away. This is not a fishing speed. If you learn nothing from this book, learn this—you are not fishing when you are prospecting.

Hunting. This is half the speed of Prospecting. Now you are in fishing mode. I know or think there are fish around because I know the area, I saw a fish, or my Spidey sense says, "It's time to start fishing." I am on full alert, in silent mode, expecting to see a fish somewhere in my spotting zone.

Stalking. I see fish or suspect I am about to see fish. Now I'm moving at half the speed of Hunting, barely moving at all. Picture how a heron or egret stalks the flats, quiet, virtually motionless, and ready. Nearly all of your energy is focused on spotting fish and only 5 percent on moving.

Still. This is the best speed of all. This is the speed 75 percent of wading anglers should strive for. If you are in an area of fish, stay still and they will find you. The beauty of bonefishing is that they move, so you don't have to. Your entire attention is focused on spotting fish and being in the ready position, prepared to execute the perfect cast. If you are motionless, you won't scare fish and your spotting skills are infinitely better.

How to Walk—the Flamingo Slide

Before reading this section, let me remind you where you're fishing. You're a self-guided angler. You're not three miles from shore on a perfectly white flat that allows you to see schools of fish from 100 feet.

Instead, you just parked the car and have walked into a creek system or are fishing a shoreline flat. This is a much more intimate place where stealth and skill is essential.

Probably nobody taught you how to walk on a flat. How hard can it be? Lift up your foot and place it in front of the next one? Nope, that's not how it's done.

Noise has a lot to do with seeing fish. The quieter you are, the more fish you will see. It's easy to know if you are making too much noise while in fishing mode. If you can hear any sloshing of water from your legs, pants, or boots, you are making too much noise. You are either walking too fast or walking incorrectly. Remember, Prospecting is not a fishing mode, so some noise is expected at that speed.

How should you walk? It's not a stepping motion, it's a sliding motion. I have dubbed it the Flamingo Slide. Picture the flamingo or egret: They balance on one leg and slowly slide the next leg forward. No noise, no ripple, no nothing. That is the Flamingo Slide and the motion to use while in fishing mode (Hunting or Stalking). Balancing on one leg, you gently slide your other foot along the bottom, then balance on that leg and gently slide the other foot along the bottom and forward. The motion is primarily sliding and very little lifting. If you are doing it right, there is no noise coming from the leg moving forward. If your forward-moving leg is making a sloshing noise, slow down. There you go—that's how you move while in fishing mode.

The Flamingo Slide works in depths from about knee deep to waist deep. Shallower water creates the most noise and is the most difficult to walk quietly in. In water less than 12 inches deep, it's necessary to pick your foot completely out of the water and reinsert it toe first.

Noise

Let me tell you, I've scared a lot of fish over the last 20 years, but one episode stands out. I was fishing Pigeon Creek on Cat Island, where Bonefish Highway 101 (a channel) ran alongside a rocky shore. I was at Hunting speed, moving along the rocks, and could clearly see a lemon shark and a small group of bones working their way down the channel toward me. All I needed was to send out a 20-foot cast in front of the approaching bones. On the last step, I placed my foot on a rock that moved,

I lifted my foot, one rock clanged on another rock, and you would have thought a gun had gone off. The shark took off as if it had been shot and the bonefish were gone faster than a pickpocket in Times Square. The point is, I was a spectator to the whole episode and saw what fish do when rocks clang, mangroves break, gravel scrapes, coral crunches, and water sloshes. They're nervous as hell and don't like unnatural noise.

Conditioning

Putting in a full day of wading is hard work, and you need to be somewhat physically fit. If the last time you saw a gym was when the first *Die Hard* movie was made, maybe you should ease yourself into it. Fish with a guide for four days and walk the flats for a few afternoons. On the practical side, I am much quieter on the flat the fitter I am. I am at my best as a fisherman when my core and legs are strong enough for me to do the Flamingo Slide all day.

What is waiting for you after a long walk and wade

Footwear

To be clear and unambiguous, let me say that safety comes first in any discussion about footwear. If you don't do a lot of wading or are unfamiliar with the terrain, wear a good sturdy pair of flats boots made by one of the major manufacturers. On places like the Turneffe Atoll where live coral is common, you have to wear heavy boots that won't cut. On the white flats of the Bahamas, your options are a little more varied.

The second consideration is comfort. You've been sitting in an office for six months; your feet are lily-white and so soft they would slice open if you stepped on a sponge. You need boots that you can wear for eight hours without getting rub spots, blisters, or cuts while covering three to five miles per day.

Your footwear has a lot to do with the noise made on the flat, and being quiet is the goal. We've all been with guides who wade barefoot, and they're as quiet as can be. A few years ago, I was walking with a guide I know well, wearing a pair of traditional wading boots, when he turned and said, "You're just never going to be quiet walking in construction boots."

It's a fact of life, the flats boots sold today are heavy and make noise, but on the bright side they protect your feet and ankles from injury.

I suspect that most wading boots sold spend 80 to 90 percent of their fishing time on the front of a boat with very little actual wading done. When you walk all day on the flats in conventional boots, you discover how heavy they really are. I guess they weigh between 2.5 and 3 pounds apiece, fully soaked. That's a lot of weight to be picking up and putting down for eight hours.

To enjoy a comfortable week of wading, your boots have to be broken in, to fit well, and to keep out all of the "crap" that can get in. None of the methods to keep out sand and other sharp objects is perfect, but some are better than others. I use a long neoprene wading sock with a built-in gravel guard. Underneath that, I wear a skintight neoprene diver's sock. This system works well at keeping out the sharp bits but has a couple of drawbacks.

The first is that it can get hot during the day. The second is that neoprene tends to develop a "sucking" sound over time when you walk. A slight variation to my system is to put on a light cotton sock first, the neoprene wading sock and gravel guard second, and then your boots. We have also had success with long woolen hiking socks that fold over the top of the boot, which is then topped with an independent gravel guard.

Personally, I seldom wear conventional wading boots anymore unless I'm fishing where there is coral or I'm going to be walking on the "death-rock" limestone outcroppings in the Bahamas.

In most places my standard footwear is a tight-fitting neoprene diver's sock inside a pair of hard-bottomed kayak boots. They are extremely light, keep all of the debris out, and are quiet as can be. When I get to those nice sand flats, I simply take off the kayak boots, Velcro them to my belt, and wade in the socks.

Tides and Bonefish

A basic knowledge of tides and the effect they have on bonefish behavior is critical to your success as a self-guided angler.

I would encourage you to read all you can about tides and the many ways they influence bonefish, but I'm taking a practical approach and simply covering the basics of what you need to know to prepare for the next

Fishing a creek opening on Great Inagua (Photo courtesy of Vince Tobia)

trip. Some of the classic bonefishing books like Kaufmann's *Bonefishing*, Chico Fernandez's *Fly-Fishing for Bonefish*, and Dick Brown's *Fly Fishing for Bonefish* are excellent references if you wish to learn more.

Understanding Tides

Tides throughout the world are much more complex than what I'll deal with here, but where I fish in the Bahamas, Florida, and Mexico, a tide cycle normally contains two high tides and two low tides, spaced approximately six hours and 12 minutes apart.

Neap tides occur with the quarter moon and exhibit the smallest difference between high and low tides. During neap tides, the highs are not so high and lows not so low, resulting in the least variation. This means you have more time to fish, as it takes longer for the fish to reach the protection of the mangroves and they stay there for a shorter period. During the neap tides there is less water flow, which is not typically as good for fishing, but overall it is the best time to plan a trip.

Spring tides are associated with full and new moons and create the highest high and lowest low tides of the month. This means that during the high tide the fish reach the mangroves faster and can stay out of reach longer. During the low tides many of the flats dry completely, moving the fish into deeper water. There is more current and flow, which is good, but overall the period when the fish are accessible is shorter during spring tides.

The distinction between spring and neap tides is important to the self-guided angler because your access to different habitats is not as far-reaching as it would be with a boat. The ideal situation is to have a tide that allows you the greatest amount of time when the fish are accessible during the incoming and outgoing tides. I remember a day on Acklins when the variation in the tide was very small and the fish couldn't make it back into the mangroves. I was able to spend a couple hours of quality fishing time walking the mangrove edges as the fish cruised the shoreline, waiting for the water to rise so they could get back into the feeding grounds and the protection of the mangroves.

When to Fish

As a general rule, the best times to be on the flat are the first two-thirds of an incoming tide and first third of an outgoing tide, preferably between the hours of 10:00 a.m. and 4:00 p.m.

Without question, the best time is the early portion of the incoming tide as the fish move from deep water back onto the flat or up into the creek. They are hungry and you know which way they will be moving.

The second most important time is the first third of the outgoing tide, when the fish are exiting the protection of the mangroves or moving off the flat into deeper water. This is generally not as productive as the incoming tide when the fish are hungry, but on the positive side you will normally know the direction they're traveling and where to intercept them.

Where to Fish

During the prime incoming tide, the fish are moving out of deeper water and onto the flats that were dry and now are coming to life. Position yourself to walk toward the fish, moving with the tide onto the flooding flat. The paths taken by bones coming into the creeks tend to be even better defined than the paths onto an open flat, as the fish normally swim in from the mouth and travel up a defined channel before spreading out in the upper creek.

During the first third of the outgoing tide, the fish are leaving the mangroves and moving off the flats, heading for the protection of the deeper water. When leaving the flats, the fish are spread out and their paths off the flat may not be easy to determine. What you do know is they will be filtering off the flat toward channels leading to deeper water. In creeks the exit strategy is much easier to determine. As the tide turns the fish leave the mangroves and move toward the creek mouth.

So what to do during the full high, complete low, and slack tides, when the fishing is not at its prime? During high tide, fish like to spread out and can be difficult to find on a large flat. In the creek, they will have pushed well into the mangroves and may be impossible to reach. This is the time to wade along the edges of the mangroves or on the rock shores where you can still find cruising fish.

At low tide, the fish have moved into deeper water to wait until the tide turns. This can actually be an effective time to fish if you give some thought as to where the bones might be. Walk the edge of the flat where it turns to deep water and look for muds and places where they have schooled up. They don't generally go far off the flat, so concentrate on deep spots adjoining the flats. They can also be in deep channels and deeper holes on the flat itself. Whenever I come across a deep hole or channel on a flat or in the creek during low tide, I always make a few blind casts.

One way to extend the prime fishing hours is to use the tide behavior in the local region. In many locations the tides vary considerably from north to south and from east to west. For instance, on Eleuthera the difference in tides between the Atlantic and Caribbean sides is two hours, which means you can fish a quality incoming tide on one side, then drive 15 minutes and fish the same tide on the other.

General Rules about Bonefishing and Tides

- Neap tides are generally better to plan a trip around.
- Bonefish use incoming tides to access prime feeding areas and outgoing tides to find deeper water.
- Fishing should be targeted around the first two-thirds of an incoming tide and the first third of the outgoing tide.
- Rising tides in both the early morning and late evening are good.
- On weak tides, bones may linger more around the edges.
- On strong high tides, they will move into the skinny water.
- Bonefish will often face or feed into a strong current.
- Bonefish are more aggressive and less spooky on the incoming tide as they head to and reach their feeding grounds.
- You have to fish the good tides, even if it is first thing in the morning or last light at night.

Planning around Tides

Once you have decided on a destination, find a tide table on the Internet corresponding to the destination. Unless you have specific information to the contrary from a local source, I normally book during a neap tide. Every destination is unique, but as a rule the neap tide provides the maximum fishing time during a one-week trip.

Make sure that when you are there, the incoming tide is occurring when the light is good and it's convenient for you to be on the flat. A quality incoming tide at midnight is not going to be much help.

To be sure about the best fishing tide for the destination, contact people who have fished there and ask which tide they prefer. That knowledge can come from the lodge where you are staying, the owners of the house you're renting, or the guide you've booked.

To the best of my knowledge, there is no scientific evidence that says bonefish feed particularly hard during the night of full moons. But most experienced fishermen and guides I know believe that bonefish feed heavily during a full moon and are less inclined to eat the next day. Don't book during a full moon if you have a choice.

Water Temperature and Bonefish

Understanding how bonefish react to water temperature can save a trip. One year we were fishing the southern end of Acklins and having very little luck. Fishing the normal tides and in those areas that traditionally contained lots of fish, we were coming up empty. The only success we enjoyed was with schooled-up "mudders" in waist-deep water. We would blind cast into the mud and often the four of us hooked up at the same time. Giggles and fun for an hour or two, but not the kind of fishing we had come to Acklins for.

It had been unseasonably warm and the water temperature in the shallows had skyrocketed to over 90 degrees. On the third day we moved operations to the central and northern part of the island where the water temperature was five degrees cooler, and the trip was saved.

I have been in situations where the water was either too cold or too warm, so I know it can happen, but in my experience water temperature rarely affects a trip because it tends to stay within a fairly narrow range. But if you are fishing during or right after a lengthy cold snap, the fish may have moved off the flats into deeper water, and the same goes for a long warm period.

My personal observations are that fish are happy with water temperatures between 72 and 88 degrees—80 degrees is about perfect. So if you find yourself facing nonoptimal water temperatures, my advice is to move either north or south or to the opposite coast in search of water closer to the optimum temperature.

In general, bonefish numbers on the flats are greatest when temperatures are moderate during March, April, May, October, and November. The numbers are fewer when temperatures are highest in August and lowest in January. This information can help you plan a trip, targeting destinations farther south like Great Inagua or Turks and Caicos in January and then northern islands like Grand Bahama in the heat of summer.

Casting

As I mentioned earlier, there are two skills a DIY fisherman has to possess to be successful. The first is the ability to spot fish and the second is the ability to present the fly in the feeding zone.

Casting into a 20-mile-per-hour wind is an art, and those that can throw a tight loop 70 feet into a gale are magicians. I don't happen to be one of those people. Over the years my casting has improved, but I am nowhere near as accomplished as I would like to be. But what I lack in technique I've made up for in strategies to deliver a fly on target in most conditions. It's getting the fly into the feeding zone that counts, not how it arrives.

I'm no expert, but let me pass on my number one tip for casting in the wind. It's from Lefty Kreh and it's simple: "Speed up and stop." Accelerate through the cast and then completely stop the rod at the top, don't drop the tip on your last cast, and don't let the rod tip drift—stop it. There, now you now know everything I know about casting.

Loading the rod into a stiff wind

A good guide does everything possible to put you in the best possible casting position. The boat's positioning tends to take the wind into account. I mention this because if most of your saltwater experiences have been with a guide, you may not have battled the wind as much as you think. When you are walking a flat, there is a good chance that you are heading right into the wind in order to keep the sun at your back or that the wind is blowing directly across your right shoulder, guaranteeing a hook in the back of the head. When you see a fish, you are going to have to present the fly to the feeding zone. Wind or no wind, there is not a lot of positioning that can be done.

Without giving casting tips, I think I can help you get the fly in front of the fish. When wading, most casts are shorter than they would be from a boat. They average more like 30 to 40 feet rather than 50 to 60 feet. That means your rod needs to load quickly with a lot less line.

To help you load the rod for shorter casts, here are a few tips. First, use a softer rod than those preferred in a boat. Over-line the rod one weight and buy one of the new bonefish lines that have moved the weight even farther toward the tip. Lastly, and this is the "biggie," build a leader that will unfurl to its full length in whatever conditions you face. In my experience store-bought leaders are too soft for the average saltwater fishermen to handle in the wind. If you are a good caster, stop reading; you can cast anything. But for the average trout fishermen, casting into a 20-mile-per-hour wind is usually a problem. Build leaders with long stiff butts, step down three times, and add some fluorocarbon for the tippet.

Over and over I see beginning fisherman arrive on the flat with 10-foot tapered leaders to which they add 3 feet of tippet for a total length of 13 feet. Then they head out onto the flat. The first cast into the wind, the line rolls out 40 feet and the leader unfurls all the way to 8 feet. It's tough to throw a 13-foot soft leader into the wind. The leader must unfurl to its full length because that's how you are connected to the fly and by extension know when a fish has got it. There can't be slack. This may hurt your ego, but it's important. If you can't unfurl 13 feet of leader, cut it to 9, and if you can't straighten 9 feet, cut it to 7. Nothing is more important than being able to get the fly to the fish with a straight leader. Seven feet straight is better than 13 feet with 5 feet of slack.

So my advice to help you improve casting in the wind is to use a softer rod, a brand-new weight-forward nine-weight line on an eight-weight rod, and a super-stiff nine-foot leader. Now you're ready.

Fly Delivery Tips

The objective is a quick, accurate cast, placing the fly in a hula hoop–sized target with one false cast. Here are a few tips to help make it happen.

Fish don't like false casts. Make sure your ready position prepares you for a quick delivery with a minimum of false casts. The more line and leader outside the rod tip in the ready position, the better prepared you will be for a one-false-cast delivery.

Cast low and to the side. I can't tell you how many fish I have scared with the fly line directly overhead.

There is a certain point in the day, around 3:00 or 4:00 p.m., when the angle of the sun behind you accentuates your silhouette to approaching fish. When you are between the fish and the sun, they almost always see you, either because of a reflection off the rod or the movement of the fly line. Let the fish move off to the side so the sun is not directly behind you before casting.

For those close-in shots, use the water to the rear to load the rod. This works well when you can't false cast for fear of spooking the fish. Just flip the line to the back, load on the water, and cast forward.

In the ready position with 10 feet of fly line and 10 feet of leader outside the rod tip, a roll cast is very effective, doesn't spook the fish, and can reach up to 20 feet.

When the wind is blowing from right to left, if you're a right hander, you need to deliver the fly from your left side. Practice casting across your body; it doesn't have as much power but is good up to 40 feet.

When you need to throw the line farther than 40 feet with the wind blowing right to left, turn sideways and cast backward to the target.

If you are a loud walker, you're never going to learn the flip cast because you won't get close enough to fish. But if you are a good stalker, you'll look down at one point and there will be a fish 15 feet from you as happy as can be. Obviously you can't move your body or rod without scaring the fish, so just flip the fly toward him. Don't strip the line; simply sweep the tip of the rod through the water until he is on it and then give one good sweep, with the tip buried, to set the hook.

Line Management

When fishing from a boat, your ready position and line management is pretty straightforward. For the ready position, have 10 feet of fly line and 10 feet of leader outside the rod tip and hold the fly between your thumb and forefinger. Strip out enough fly line to handle your maximum cast (plus another 10 feet), make a practice cast, and then strip the line back into the bottom of the boat. The only danger now is that the line gets caught under your feet or catches on something else in the boat as you cast.

For the walk-and-wade angler, multiply what can go wrong in a boat by ten. First of all, you are moving and your feet act like "fly line" magnets, mysteriously wrapping the line around your legs. The wind and tide dictate how and if your line trails behind you, and there are mangrove bushes, rocks, twigs, and coral for the line to catch on.

Typically the wading angler walks with 10 feet of fly line plus the leader outside the rod tip and a single continuous loop stripped off the reel, trailing behind. The amount of line trailing is based on a couple of factors: how far you cast and whether the wind and current will keep the trailing loop away from your feet.

The distance you need to cast is the lesser of how far you can physically cast and how far away you can spot fish. If you can cast 80 feet but can only see fish 50 feet away, trail 30 feet in the loop behind plus the 20 outside the rod tip to equal the 50 feet. It's a simple rule, but I see people who can cast 40 feet trailing 70 feet of line all the time. Nothing good can come of the extra 30 feet in the water; leave it on the reel.

The next issue is which direction the wind and current are moving the floating fly line in relation to the direction you're walking. If the line is holding in a nice long loop behind you, there is no problem. If the line is being carried into your legs and under your feet, you have to adjust. There are several ways to do that described in the section below.

Here is the last point on line management: The fly line must be clean; otherwise, it sinks and catches everything on the bottom. If you find the line is sinking, reel up more of the loop until the line behind you is floating.

Now that's line management. They actually landed a fish out of this mess.

The Ready Position

The ready position is determined by the conditions on hand. Sometimes it's just like you see in the magazines. You are silently walking along a beautiful Bahamian flat, there is no wind, and 50 feet of line in one continuous loop floats tangle free to the rear as you carefully move toward a group of tailing bones. It's a little like a *Sports Illustrated* swimsuit model jumping into your pool and apologizing for losing her top. It could happen, but it's just not that likely.

A more realistic scenario is this. You're a DIY angler, walking along a shoreline or deep in a mangrove creek. It's more likely you are stripping out line as you creep forward, trying not to get the loops wrapped around your feet.

What usually occurs is that some factors interfere with the perfect conditions. The wind is blowing hard, the tide is moving either across you or from behind, there are rocks and coral tops poking through the surface, or you are in tight to the mangroves. Whatever it is, your ready position has to be adjusted to fit the circumstance. No matter what, you need to deliver your fly to the target quickly in one or two easy motions.

Ready Position 1. This is the basic ready position, where you have 10 feet of fly line and 10 feet of leader outside the rod tip dragging on the water while you hold the fly between your thumb and fore finger. The amount of line trailing behind is equal to the maximum distance you need to cast minus the 20 feet already outside the rod's tip.

Ready position 2. This position is the same as above except the fly is in the hook keeper with the normal amount of line trailing behind. It's just hard to walk with the fly in your fingers for eight hours. Personally, this position has never caused me a problem.

Ready position 3. Because the tide or wind is causing the line to continually catch in your feet, trail half as much line as you require on your maximum cast. In this position you will need to make four or five full strips off the reel before a long cast.

Ready position 4. The hook is in the keeper and only 15 feet of line is outside the rod tip. The wind, tide, debris, grass, rocks, or mangroves don't allow you to drag any line behind you, so hold two loops totaling 15 feet in your left hand. This gives you a total of 30 feet ready to go. When you see a fish, throw the loops to the side away from your feet, strip off whatever length of line you still need, and cast.

Here is a piece of advice from someone who has screwed up in every conceivable way. It is quicker to strip off all the line you need and cast than it is to untangle the loop that is wrapped around your leg. Trailing less line is better than more, and you're better off focusing on spotting fish than worrying about clearing lines trailing behind.

The Retrieve

It's likely that most of your fishing is with a guide, following his instructions: "Strip, strip, faster, faster, stop." He's watching the fish and you are following directions. When fishing on your own, there are no instructions, and it's you watching the fish and adjusting as it reacts to the fly.

Most of the time a normal retrieve works fine for the self-guided angler. This is done with the rod tip in the water pointed directly at the fish, making strips of 6 to 18 inches and moving the fly away from the bonefish. A quick tip here: It's important that you watch the fish when

Beautiful flat on Acklins (Photo courtesy of Vince Tobia)

retrieving the fly. When a fish is following but won't take, stop the fly, let it sink completely to the bottom, and strike when you see his head dip.

The exception to using a normal retrieve is when you meet up with fish that have been pressured, have seen a lot of flies, and don't react well to normal retrieves, a reality that DIY fishermen are likely to encounter. The instant you strip the fly, they bolt. You'll run into them on Provo, Eleuthera, Abaco, and a host of other destinations where the flats are easily reached by car.

Those fish don't like a normal retrieve, so what to do? For super-spooky fish I've found that casting with flies made out of materials that pulsate on their own works well. Rubber legs, Finn Coon, rabbit, and marabou all have those qualities. Cast the fly to intercept the fish, then let it sit on the bottom and wait for the fish to get to it. Once all the slack is out of the line, watch the fish to see if it dips and picks up the fly, at which time you strike. If you can't just let the fly sit, then use a very slow hand-weave retrieve to keep some tension in the line and you connected to the fly. That is all the fly movement the fish will put up with.

Here are a couple of final thoughts on the retrieve. First, don't strip the fly toward the fish; they like chasing prey, not their prey chasing them.

Second, if you are casting into a strong wind, it is likely that your leader did not unfurl to its full length. Your first strip should always be long enough to take out all the slack in your line and leader.

Saltwater Leaders

I'll confess here and now that I am not the greatest caster in the world. In fact, I may not even be the best caster on my street. That means I need every advantage I can get when throwing a Crazy Charlie into a 30-mile-per-hour wind.

I've been casting into tropical winds for 20 years, so I have learned a thing or two about getting the fly in front of my quarry. One of the best ways to help an otherwise imperfect casting stroke is to construct leaders that turn over and straighten out, even in unfavorable conditions.

The knotless tapered leaders available from your fly shop have improved significantly over the last five years and work fine for competent casters. That being said, most of the good bonefish fishermen I know tie their own leaders and think that the store-bought leaders are made with mono that is too limp.

The following discussion about leaders is based on a DIY walk-and-wade situation. In other words, you are standing in 24 inches of water, there is a bonefish 45 feet away swimming from right to left, and you have time for one cast into a 30-mile-per-hour wind.

Leaders

It doesn't take a rocket scientist to figure out that the leader is a pretty important part of the equation when you're trying to catch a bonefish.

For walk-and-wade DIY fishermen, you must cast quickly, often in a cross or in-your-face tropical "breeze," and have the leader unfurl to its full length, gently landing at the target.

That describes what you are trying to do. What usually happens is five false casts that spook the fish, a final casting stroke toward the target 43 feet away, and an 11-foot leader extending all the way out to, ouch, 7 feet!

I'm not being snotty—I see this hundreds of times per season—the leader just doesn't unfurl to its full length. It can't fully turn over in the wind and collapses on itself.

Why do you need a straight, fully extended leader? First, a straight, fully unfurled leader is more accurate. Second, you can immediately start imparting movement to the fly. And, third, you are directly connected to the fly and can feel when the fish takes.

Like all of us, I learned this the hard way. Fishing with a guide in Belize, I cast where the guide told me, into a nice group of fish, and began my six-inch strip. Nothing. The guide said, "He took your fly." "No, he didn't, I didn't feel anything," I replied. The guide picked up my fly and showed me the bead chain eyes, which were bent 180 degrees. The fish had crushed the fly. What had I done wrong? My 11-foot leader was collapsing on itself and extending to only 8 feet. With my six-inch strips it took me six pulls before I even had contact with my fly. By that time the fish had picked up the fly, crushed it, and spit it back out.

So how does a properly constructed tapered leader help unfurl a leader to its full length?

It's all about energy being transferred evenly from the fly line through the leader's butt section to the middle section to the tippet and eventually to the fly. A good leader acts as an extension of the fly line, which is why the leader's butt section should be approximately the same weight and stiffness as the fly line. The leader then steps down in size, delivering the remaining energy to the tip and turning over the entire leader. One of the best descriptions of "leader logic" is in Chico Fernandez's book *Fly-Fishing for Bonefish.*

A leader you have constructed yourself also makes it simpler to add and subtract lengths and sections as conditions warrant. Shorten the leader for those really difficult conditions and lengthen the tippet when a stealthy presentation is called for.

Leader Length

In a perfect world you are better off with a 14-foot leader than a 10-foot leader. Your presentation is quieter and the large-diameter fly line is farther away from the fish. But realistically, an average trout fisherman is going to have a tough time in normal tropical conditions turning over a 14-foot leader. The length of the leader must match your casting ability. Start out with a properly constructed 10-foot tapered leader and add or subtract length as conditions and abilities warrant. I will say it again: Cast the length of leader you can straighten and unfurl to its full extension in the conditions you are facing. If it's 15 feet, I will be right over for lessons. If it's 8 feet, then that is the length of your leader.

Leader Material

Fishermen tend to describe leader sections by the weight of material used (e.g., the butt section is 40 pound) rather than what you really need to know, the material's diameter. Since every manufacturer's strength and diameter are different, it is important to make sure the diameters are stepping down and the diameter of the leader's butt section steps down slightly from the diameter of the fly line.

There are a lot of good monofilament manufacturers out there, and I have tried many of them while experimenting with handmade leaders. Each person's casting stroke and abilities are different, which makes it difficult to recommend one line over another. When considering which monofilament line to use, keep in mind that you want the same line from the same manufacturer throughout the leader, although the tippet can be different. Clear mono is best in most tropical situations, but stay away from soft, supple materials and lean toward stiffer lines.

My personal preferences are Trilene's Big Game for all-around use and Rio's Alloy Hard Saltwater for extreme wind or heavy flies. If you have relatively little experience casting in the tropics, you are much better off with something like the Rio product.

The tippet should be made of fluorocarbon and measure between two and four feet in length. There are a number of quality manufacturers of fluorocarbon tippet, and I don't have a preference as long as it is one of the premium brands.

Knots

For the connection between the leader and the fly line you can use either a loop-to-loop connection or a nail knot. I prefer the loop connection because it allows me to quickly change leaders when conditions change. For the loop in the butt section I use either a perfection loop or surgeon's loop.

For attaching the leader sections to each other I use a blood knot. Depending on the stiffness and thickness of the material, the number of wraps you use will differ, so experiment a little with that. The thinner the diameter, the more wraps you use. This is the weakest part of your leader, so make sure you use lots of moisture and seat each knot carefully.

For the connection to the tippet, I use a surgeon's knot.

Formulas

There are a number of different saltwater leader formulas to choose from. I have included four of the more popular ones for you to experiment with. Depending on your casting style and ability, one of the formulas will work better than the others.

Before getting started, here are a few things to consider. The more uniform the step down lengths (all equal), the more delicate the presentation. The longer the butt section, the better it turns over in the wind. If you have trouble turning over the leader in a normal tropical situation, shorten the leader to nine feet or less. Stiff monofilament turns over better in the wind than softer materials. Finally, if you are a good to excellent caster, it doesn't matter what you use.

Formula 1, Bruce Chard

Bruce uses equal lengths on all sections and the Rio Alloy Hard Saltwater tippet material.

- 30 inches of 30-pound test
- 30 inches of 25-pound test
- 30 inches of 20-pound test
- 30 inches of 16-pound test
- 30 to 48 inches of fluorocarbon tippet

This gives you a leader that is approximately 12 to 14 feet, depending on the length of your tippet.

Formula 2, Lefty Kreh

Lefty prefers a slightly softer material like Trilene Big Game.

- the butt section, usually 40-pound test, makes up half of the leader

- half that length in 30-pound test
- half of the prior length in 20-pound test
- 18 to 24 inches of tippet in 12- to 16-pound test

For a nine-foot leader, that is 54 inches of 40-pound test, 27 inches of 30-pound test, 14 inches of 20-pound test, and 18 inches of 12- to 16-pound test for the tippet.

Formula 3, Tim Borski

Tim likes to use fluorocarbon for the entire leader.

- 60 inches of 40-pound test
- 48 inches of 25-pound test
- 24 inches of tippet in 12- to 16-pound test

That is an 11-foot leader including the two feet of tippet.

Formula 4, Chico Fernandez

Chico prefers a soft to medium-stiff mono, has a couple of subtle changes for conditions, but generally uses a 50/30/20 formula. The butt section is 50 percent of the leader length, followed by a 30-percent mid-section and 20-percent tippet.

- 60 inches of 40-pound test
- 12 inches of 30-pound test
- 12 inches of 20-pound test
- 12 inches of 15-pound test
- 24 inches of tippet

This makes a 10-foot leader.

I have tried them all in a variety of conditions and found that the Chico Fernandez formula tied with Trilene Big Game and fluorocarbon tippet works the best for me.

The bottom line is this: If you are a good caster, any of the formulas work, but if you struggle in the wind, over-line your rod, shorten your leader, and tie them with stiff material.

What to Carry on the Flat

Over the years, I have been refining what I carry with me while wading and in most cases have come to the realization that less is more.

If you are new to DIY fishing on the flat, you won't realize how different packing for a DIY day is from a guided day until you give it a try. When considering what to take with a guide on his boat, storage capacity and weight seldom enter into the process. Even wading with a guide, most of your gear stays in the boat and you're back and forth throughout the day.

When I head out for a DIY day, I'm gone four hours at a minimum and usually all day. I'll walk between three and six miles, lots of times in muck up to my knees. Packing becomes a big deal. I bring one rod and a hip pack that needs to carry all my fishing supplies, photography equipment, food, water, sunblock, communication device, rain jacket, and other miscellaneous items. In the end you can't pack everything and have to make some concessions. I'm now down to one fly box that holds 58 flies. That's about 200 fewer than I used to carry.

Just taking a rest after a long day on the flats

I've tried a lot of waist packs and settled on a three-zippered pack with holders to carry two water bottles. It needs to have a padded shoulder strap, which helps keep the weight evenly distributed and off my hips. I'm experimenting with single-strap backpacks that are definitely an alternative. Conventional two-strap backpacks have the advantage of more space and comfort, but I find them a nuisance to access when I want something. Your pack, along with two shirt pockets, is all the storage you've got.

Here's a quick word of advice. Everything in a pack that would be damaged if it became wet needs to be in a waterproof plastic bag. Don't ask me how or why, but sometime during the day it's all going to get wet.

When creating the packing list below, I assume you are already wearing all of the clothing and equipment necessary to protect you from the sun, including buff, hat, sunglasses, and sun gloves. In addition, your rod is strung up with a clean fly line and new leader with tippet.

What to Pack on the Flat

- sunscreen and lip block
- extra leader
- 10- and 12-pound fluorocarbon tippet
- one fly box that holds 60 flies
- one 12-inch wire leader, two barracuda flies, two permit flies, and two heavy Clousers
- pliers
- glass wipes
- toilet paper
- reading glasses or magnifier
- small waterproof digital camera
- lunch
- two bottles of water
- eye drops
- aspirin
- rain jacket
- file, hook sharpener
- communication device, such as a walkie-talkie or VHF radio
- printed copy of Google map
- matches

- whistle
- thermometer
- GPS, if uncertain of area

Bonefish Flies

Through a variety of studies, it has been shown that bonefish eat over 100 species of prey. They dine on shrimp, crabs, fish, clams, eels, worms, and just about anything else that lives on or near the bottom. In my experience they are opportunistic feeders, and if something looks like food, they jump on it.

That said, you want to use a fly that imitates one of their major food groups, normally a shrimp or crab. There are a number of good general attractor patterns like a Bonefish Junk, but I normally start with a shrimp pattern similar to a traditional Gotcha or Charlie, colored to match the bottom and tied with rubber legs.

Gotcha

I have been tying flies for 45 years and have enough bonefish flies to last my friends and me for several lifetimes. I have spent every fall for the last 20 years tying flies and getting ready for the upcoming bonefish season. If a new fly or material hits the market, I have tied it and used it. So when I say I carry 58 bonefish flies when walking, you can imagine the mental anguish and gyrations I go through to make the selection. My preferences have been refined over the years to deal with most of the situations I might encounter.

Here are a couple of notes on buying or tying flies. First, don't cheap out on the hooks. Buy good saltwater stainless-steel hooks that are sharp. Your box is not residing in the dry comfort of a boat; it's in your pack or pocket and it always gets wet. I now use a waterproof box, which has helped, but when the inside of the box gets soaked, you need flies that don't corrode. Second, use materials that have life without being retrieved. Some of the fish you will cast to have seen more flies than a frog at a garbage dump. They can be fussy as heck and hate a fly moving unnaturally. It's enough to make you crazy, but in those cases the fly needs to sit on the bottom and let the current impart movement to the rubber legs or rabbit fur.

There are two things that I am super fussy about with my flies. First, the hook must be tacky sharp. Second, there must not be artificial scents on the fly. I can't tell you how many times I have failed to hook up because the hook wasn't sharp enough. They get dulled in more ways than I can count, so I make sure before I start and after each fish caught to take an extra 30 seconds and sharpen the point. As far as scent on my fly goes, I don't know if it matters or not. Scientists have told me there is no evidence to suggest that bonefish care about scent. All I know is that the most experienced guide I have ever fished with says bonefish hate sunscreen, lotions, and human smells, and that's good enough for me.

The DIY Fly Box versus the Boat Fly Box

Most of the guides like large, flashy, big-profile flies that can be seen from long distances and sink quickly in two to three feet of water. On a boat you have the luxury of carrying hundreds of flies in multiple boxes without worrying about weight or space. The fishing is normally done miles from civilization, and the fish are receptive to most flies when presented properly.

But when wading quietly through a mangrove creek or along the shore, the water is only 12 to 30 inches deep, the cast is 40 feet or less, and the targeted landing area is 2 to 4 feet from the head of a fish. Unlike on a boat, while wading there is only room to carry one or two small boxes. In addition, the fish are within reach of any fisherman with a car or kayak, which means they are cautious and require a subtle presentation.

Considering the conditions fished and the space limitations, the flies in a self-guided angler's box differ significantly from what is carried on a boat. In general, the flies are smaller, weigh less, and have a tighter profile with less flash. Within the 50 to 90 flies normally packed, you need to have patterns that imitate the various shrimp and crab species, as well as a handful of general attractors. They need to span sizes #2 to #10, from unweighted to heavy lead eyes, and you'll need a few equipped with weed guards. It takes some real thought to put together one box.

Selecting a Fly

When you are fishing with a guide, fly selection can be as simple as handing him two boxes and asking, "Which fly?" When alone on a flat, it's a little more difficult. How do I pick a fly if I've never fished the location before?

The first decision is whether to choose an imitator or an attractor. There are some great attractor patterns out there, the kind you look at and say, "Why on earth would a bonefish eat this?" But therein lies the magic. One of my favorite attractor patterns is Charlie Craven's Bonefish Junk.

If you go with a pattern to imitate either a shrimp or crab, first think about a color that matches the bottom. Then consider the weight, making sure the fly is heavy enough to sink quickly to the bottom. When picking the size, keep in mind that the presentations are normally made in close with the fish in shallow water. You need a few strands of flash to get their attention and some rubber legs to impart movement. The last thing to consider is the vegetation and bottom structure. Can you get away with a standard tie, or do you need a weed guard so the fly can move through turtle grass or over rocky shelves and crevices?

Bonefish Clouser

Generally speaking, the flies in a DIY box are smaller than those rec-ommended by a guide fishing from a boat. For the Bahamas, Caymans, Turks, and Cuba, my box is mostly made up of flies size #4 and #6. For Florida, I normally use #2 to #4, and in Mexico, #6 to #8. I always have six to eight flies outside the recommended sizes just to make sure I have all the bases covered.

When considering weight, you want the fly to reach the bottom quickly but with as little sound as possible when it lands. The depth of the water will average 12 to 30 inches, and a bead chain sized to fit the hook will usually suffice. My box also includes a row of weightless flies for delicate and super-shallow presentations and a few heavy lead eyes to fish the holes, pockets, and deep channels.

Another consideration is how often these fish see flies. For the self-guided angler, this is where the rubber meets the road. Since you have driven to the flat, it means that anyone with a car can cast to the same fish. It's likely that the fish are a little more sensitive to noise, movement, poor presentations, and common fly patterns. If you're faced with the highly educated fish of Governors Harbour or Savannah Sound in Eleuthera or the Town Flats and waters of Cherokee Sound on Abaco, you need to downsize and use a pattern that they haven't seen.

Bonefish Special

Raghead Crab

Refusals can be caused by a number of things, including an unnatural retrieve, a fly they don't like, smell, or a general unease. But if I'm casting to "happy" fish and they refuse the fly, I don't try to figure it out. I switch immediately to a different food group. If I was using a shrimp pattern, I switch to a crab, and that usually does the trick.

Last, you need to pick the fly you have the most confidence in. I'm not nearly as fussy as I used to be about flies; instead, I focus more on stealth, presentation, and retrieve. So start with your favorite fly in the right size, color, and weight. For me, that is generally a Greg's Flats Fly size #6.

My Fly Box

I now carry one fly box that holds 58 flies. I bring hundreds with me on the trip and adjust my box daily based on lost flies, local information, or lack of success on the previous day. Not included in the box but in a small plastic bag are two permit patterns, two large, heavy Clousers

My fly box ready for a day on the flat

for deep holes, and two poppers on a wire leader for barracuda. My box looks like this:

- The first row holds weightless flies, size #6 to #10, a few with weed guards.
- Row two is a mixture of Crazy Charlies in different sizes, weights, and colors.
- Row three is a variety of Gotchas, including a few with weed guards.
- Row four includes small-sized Charlies and Gotchas.
- Row five has Bonefish Junk, Peterson Spawning Shrimp, and Orange Butt Bunny.
- Row six has Sliders and Greg's Flats Fly.
- Row seven has Veverka's Mantis Shrimp, Bonefish Tailer, and Clousers.
- Row eight has Turneffe Crabs, Pop's Bitters, and Raghead Crabs.

My top six flies:

- Greg's Flats Fly
- Orange Butt Bunny
- Rubber-Legged Gotcha
- Bonefish Junk
- Tan-and-White Bonefish Clouser
- Pop's Bonefish Bitter

Here's my last word on bonefish flies. If you make a good cast to a happy fish, most of the classic bonefish patterns colored to match the bottom will work just fine.

Fishing Tips

Over the years I have developed for myself and learned from others a few tricks and strategies to use while wading the flats. I don't often fish those big open flats where the fish are visible from 150 feet and the water is crystal clear. Flats fitting that description and accessible by car tend to get pounded. The Town Flats and Cherokee Sound on Abaco or Savannah Sound and Governor's Harbour on Eleuthera are the reason scotch was invented. After a day on one of those flats, your self-esteem is shattered, and turning to the bottle is the only mature way to end the day's agony.

Rather than fishing the well-known flats, I look for creek systems, shorelines, and flats that aren't easy to find and require effort to get to. Many of the locations are small and the fishing situations more intimate than the wide-open flats a guide might run his boat to. In these areas, wading has to be silent because the fish are close, the casting is shorter, and the presentations more delicate. Often you are walking within casting distance of the mangroves, and there will be other obstructions where a fish can cut you off. With isolation and obstacles in mind, here are a few tips to help you when you're pursuing the ghost of the flats on your own.

Find the Fish

I don't have many zero-fish days anymore because I have finally learned a lesson the guides have been trying to pound into my dense Canadian head for years: You need to fish where the fish are. It sounds straightforward, but how many times have you been on a flat or creek and not found any fish?

This brings to mind a recent trip I had on Cat Island. I had found a creek after a great deal of effort, but the sun was setting when I got there. I could see hundreds of tails in front of me but only had time to catch a couple of fish before the light dimmed and I had to find the trail back out. The next morning I went back with my wife, positive it was going to be the best day of the trip. I couldn't find the fish. I spent 45 minutes looking and then hiked three-quarters of a mile to see if they were at the ocean mouth. They had to be somewhere, and there they were. My point is that if they aren't where you are, go find them. Something about your plan is wrong. They are in deeper water, shallower water, farther up the creek system, or maybe at the ocean mouth. The fish are elsewhere and you need to go find them.

Fishing a Creek

Fish enter a creek system on the incoming tide. It never ceases to surprise me how early in the tide the fish start pushing in, looking for food. They are anxious and don't want to wait.

Fishing a mangrove creek system on Exuma

At one particular system in Abaco I decided to walk up the creek to where the water met dry land. Thinking I was there ahead of the fish, I was surprised to see them already there, swimming in three inches of water, literally willing the tide to move the water closer to the mangroves. Don't be late on an incoming tide.

Conversely, on the outgoing tide you might think that the fish would wait until the last moment, but they don't. Once the tide starts retreating, the fish begin to head out of the creek into deeper water. Don't expect to find the fish deep in the mangroves halfway through the outgoing tide—they are already on the move.

My general plan for creeks is to fish the mouth and bay just before and during low tide to get those fish hanging around and waiting for the tide to turn. Then I walk back into the creek ahead of the fish, once the tide has turned. Often the creek itself will have channels and pockets of deep water where the fish will hang out at low tide. If so, they won't use the energy to go all the way out to the bay.

Casting to Tailing Fish

I love fishing for tailing fish, but they can be a little difficult at times. They tend to be in shallow water and very focused on the im-

A tailing fish hanging out on a flat in the Berry Islands (Photo courtesy of Vince Tobia)

mediate ground in front of them. They often don't have a pattern to their movement, so you can't necessarily throw the fly five feet in front of them predicting the fish will move to it. They may go in a completely different direction.

You need to cast closer to tailing fish than you do for traveling bones, but avoid spooking them. I set up with a 15- to 18-foot leader (depending on wind) and a much lighter fly, usually without a bead chain at all. The idea is to land the fly, softly without noise, very close to the fish or right on them, letting the weight of the hook sink the fly down the 12 inches it needs to go. It feels more like a dry fly presentation.

Spooky Fish

As a DIY fisherman, the fish you cast to may be spookier than those targeted from a guide's boat. A guide can run miles in any direction to find fish while you have to drive your car to the flat, the same as everyone else. I'm not saying you can't catch as many fish as in a guide boat because you can. I'm just saying this probably isn't the bone's first rodeo.

That said, there are certain basic tricks to keep in mind when fishing to the PhDs. Throw as long a leader as you can unfurl, with 15 to 18 feet preferable. The last four feet of tippet should be fluorocarbon and at least two pounds lighter than normal; start with 10-pound test. Use a lighter, smaller fly tied with materials like rubber legs and rabbit that have lots of movement when not retrieved. Make the strips, if any, very small and let the fly sit on the bottom for the take.

Noise and Other Things Bonefish Hate

Bonefish hate unnatural noise. Nothing sends them fleeing in the opposite direction faster than rocks grinding, boots scraping, water sloshing, mangroves breaking, people talking, or VHF radios coming to life.

I believe there are certain scents that alert them, such as sunscreen, hand creams, lotions, and bug spray. That's a personal opinion with no scientific corroboration. I put my sunscreen on right out of the shower, thoroughly wash my hands, and reapply throughout the day with a touch-free applicator.

Bonefish spook when a bird flies overhead, so you can imagine what they think about a fly line whipping over them, swimming under a floating fly line, or coming face-to-face with a leader that shimmers instead of blends in with the water. All I can say is they hate false casts. Kiss the bone goodbye if you land the fly line on top of its head and use fluorocarbon for the tippet.

They are not blind. Wear neutral colors on the flat and be aware that your silhouette really shows when the light is low and behind you. At certain angles the sunlight reflects off the rod and line when false casting.

Shrimp, minnows, and crabs don't swim at bonefish; they are trying to escape. Present the fly so that during the retrieve it's moving away from the fish.

Setting the Hook

If the two primary skills required to be successful are spotting fish and presenting the fly on target, then not far behind is properly setting the hook with a strip strike.

"Don't trout set, mon." If you were brought up fishing in British Columbia, Montana, Colorado, Pennsylvania, or anywhere else the number one species is trout, then you have heard your guide utter those words more than once.

The strip strike is not done by lifting the rod; instead, it's accomplished by a sharp pull on the line once the fly is in the bone's mouth. The rod tip stays in the water, pointing straight at the fish. Pull back swiftly on the line when you feel tension. Hopefully the tension is a fish, but if it's turtle grass, you're fine. The fly has just reacted as if it's being retrieved and the fish will still take it.

How to Turn a Six-Fish Day into a Two-Fish Day

My wife tells me to present "teaching moments" in a positive way. In other words, I shouldn't just say you screwed up but instead should explain in a gentle way how it could have been done a little better.

On a self-guided day you don't usually get that many shots at fish. Let's say that for one incoming tide you have ten quality chances. Of those ten chances I would expect to catch six fish. I've seen plenty of guys with the same chances catch between zero and two. Here's how they screwed up—oops, I mean how they could have done it a little better.

The number one reason for missed fish is poor casting. Often it's too many false casts, putting the bone on alert, or else it's the fly not hitting the hula hoop–sized target in front of the fish. Your first cast must be your best cast.

A group of spooked fish heading for deeper water (Photo courtesy of Vince Tobia)

Making noise, either with your feet or more likely by slapping the water with the fly line or "plopping" the fly right on his head, will spook the fish. Quiet, silent presentation with the fly delicately presented two to four feet in front of the bone's nose is what you are striving for.

For the beginning to intermediate angler, the lack of a good strip set results in losing at least two of the ten fish. When the fish picks up the fly and there is a halfhearted strip set and then a rod lift, the hook doesn't set in its mouth and, poof, it's gone. Keep the rod tip in the water, and when you feel resistance, give a sharp pull to set the hook. If you miss the hookup on a strip set, all you've done is moved the fly, giving the fish a chance to take it again.

Moving too fast and making noise are major obstacles to catching fish. You might still see some, but they are no longer "happy" and are aware of your presence.

Good line management is crucial. I can't tell you how many times I have seen a line caught up in legs and feet, pack straps, and belts at the exact moment it's time to cast.

General Tips

Walk in the direction the fish are coming from; in other words, walk into the fish. If one school of fish approaches you from behind, be alert. But if a second group comes up from behind, turn around and walk the other way.

I always carry lens wipes and eyedrops in my hip pack. You have to be able to see.

Even though it screws up the fishing, when I see a big barracuda I can't resist throwing a fly or popper at it. Be sure to have a 10-inch wire leader attached to a popper in your pack, not in the fly box. Hook your bonefish fly through the wire leader's loop and cast away. It only takes about 30 seconds to do, and if you have never caught a three-foot bar-racuda on a fly rod, hang on.

When close to the edge of the mangroves, completely loosen your drag before you cast. The fish might not go into the mangroves, at which point you can then tighten your drag. If it heads into the man-groves, let the spool run free, applying no tension at all. The fly line begins rubbing around mangrove limbs and gradually increases tension

Fish feeding along the mangrove edge waiting for high tide (Photo courtesy of Pat Ford)

on the fish, slowing the fish down. Eventually it can't go any farther and then it's time to follow the line through the mangroves until you reach the fish. I learned this from a guide in Acklins and found it gives me about a 50-percent chance of getting the fish.

When I'm close to mangroves, I cut off my 12-pound tippet and tie on 16-pound. Even though the drag may be off, use hand pressure to put the boots to the fish early and keep him out of the mangroves. If he makes it in, the tippet is strong enough to withstand some abrasion.

Here is a little trick that has served me well over the years. Wading along the edge of the mangroves, you can often hear the bonefish under the bushes splashing away and digging up prey. If they are less than 10 feet inside the mangrove line, I have put on a heavy fly and cast next to the mangroves into the open water so the fly lands with a loud "plop." On more than one occasion this has brought the fish out from the protection of the mangroves to investigate the noise.

Make sure your hook is sticky sharp. For some reason, walk-and-wade guys dull their hooks all the time. Take 30 seconds and touch up the point.

Think about what you wear on the flat and what your fly line can get hung up on as you are about to cast to the largest bonefish you have ever seen. Some things my fly line has caught on are pliers, a belt buckle, a GoPro, hanging sunglasses, coat sleeves, and the straps on my waist pack.

Planning a Trip

Preparing for a DIY bonefishing trip requires significantly more planning than booking at a full-service lodge. But it's not hard or complicated, and once you have done it a few times you will form your own checklist for packing and preparation.

When to Go

If you could choose, most people would go when the fishing is good, the weather is perfect, and the prices are low. The reality is that there are determining factors: work, vacations, school breaks, and statutory holidays. Keeping that in mind, here are a few thoughts. Try not to book during hurricane season, which officially runs from June 1 to November 30. If you book in December through February, the farther south you go the better chance there is of avoiding cold fronts.

What Kind of Trip Do You Want?

Every destination is different, offering advantages and challenges unique to the location. Before choosing where to go, it's important first to determine the type of trip you want and how you want to spend your time.

- Is it a trip where fishing is the main activity or a family vacation where fishing is secondary?
- Is it self-guided only or does the trip include some guided days?
- What is the skill level of the anglers?
- Are numbers of fish more important than size?
- Are the comforts of home important?
- Do meals need to be prepared, will you cook, or will there be a combination of meals?
- Is budget a primary concern?

Walking the shoreline looking for cruising fish (Photo courtesy of David Lambroughton)

The Different Types of Venues

Over the last five years, accommodation options for the self-guided angler have expanded.

If you want the planning to be simple, I suggest you go with lodges that offer combinations of DIY and guided days while providing all the meals. Some examples are Frankie's Two Boys Inn on North Andros, Long Island Bonefishing Lodge and their "assisted DIY" week, or Fedel Johnson's lodge on Acklins where you can fish out his back door. Alternatively, consider a hosted trip like those offered by Vince Tobia of Cattaraugus Creek Outfitters.

For those who want to rent a home, cottage, or condo, there are dozens of websites to search including the two I use, VRBO (www.vrbo .com) and HomeAway (www.homeaway.com). This way you can find the perfect home on the beach, support the neighborhood restaurants, shop at the local grocery store, and cook some meals of your own.

Choosing Where to Stay

Where you stay and the quality of the accommodations are almost as important as the fishing, so do your homework.

If booking a home or condo, ask the following:

- Does it come with a kayak and, if so, can I move it around by car?
- Is a car part of the rental package?
- Is Internet available and is there cell phone coverage?
- Do you know anything about bonefishing, have you rented to fisherman before, can I have a couple of references who are fishermen?
- Are there local maps in the home?
- Can you give the names of some locals I can talk with about fishing?
- How far is it to the grocery store?

If staying at a lodge that provides meals and purports to support self-guided anglers, make sure to ask about the following:

- Can I fish from dawn to dark and how will I be fed if leaving early or arriving back late?
- How many DIY places can you direct me to and are they flats or creeks?
- Do you have a kayak available and can it be transported?
- Can you help me with fly selection and steer me in the right direction if I'm having trouble hooking up?
- Do you provide transportation to DIY waters or do I need a rental car?
- Are maps available?
- Do you have Internet and is there cell phone coverage?
- Can you provide two references of self-guided anglers who have stayed at the lodge?

I mention this because I have had every possible scenario happen. If you book your own accommodations, you don't want to be an hour from the closest flat. I've stayed at lodges that said they accommodated self-guided anglers only to find out that if you weren't on a fully guided week, you didn't count.

Where to Get DIY Information

Supplement the information found here by going online and checking out fishing forums, social media sites like Facebook and LinkedIn, and the blogs and websites focused on saltwater fly fishing.

Once you have picked a destination, start spending your evenings on Google Earth, browse maps and books like those in the Explorer Chartbook series, and during the booking process talk with the accommodation owners, rental car companies, property mangers, and the local guide you book.

Where to Fish

Half the joy of what we do as DIY fishermen is finding spots on our own. But it's important that you find areas that are off the beaten track and not fished twice a day every day. Compounding the difficulties of catching fish on your own is casting to bonefish that have seen every fly known to man.

Keeping in mind that you don't want to fish where guides take their customers, go on Google Earth to look for flats, shorelines, and creek systems that are within a half mile of a road and no farther away than one mile by kayak. Look for areas that you think fish will move in and out of on each tide, like creeks emptying into bays, and are hard enough to reach to keep some anglers away. Print out the Google images you need and take them with you. I have found that many times Internet isn't available, even when advertised, and there's almost never a printer.

My advice is to always book a local guide for the first day, just to get a feel for the place, what flies work, and how to fish the tides. Make sure you tell the guide up front that you plan on spending a few days fishing on your own, then he or she can decide what information to share.

From home, plan where to fish for the first couple of days so you can hit the ground running. Once there, use the local "intel" to map out the rest of the week.

Don't book the dates until you know the tides. Just to be on the safe side, don't book during a full moon and lean toward neap tides rather than spring tides.

Things to Do before You Go

- Order the appropriate currency in the right denominations from your bank one week in advance.
- Call your credit card company and inform them of your travel dates and destination.
- Check that your inoculations are current.
- Be sure your travel and evacuation insurance is up to date, you have the appropriate cards and contact phone numbers in your wallet, and you have photocopies separately in your luggage.
- Prepay and organize financial commitments such as tax filings, bills, and children's tuition payments.
- Did you really book during your anniversary, a birthday, or another important special occasion? If so, you know what to do.
- Stop the mail and papers.
- If going for an extended period of time during the winter, confirm coverage with your house insurer, as you may need to have someone check the house and turn off the water tank.
- Provide your itinerary and emergency numbers to someone at home.
- List and copy all credit cards, driver's license, travel insurance, evacuation insurance, and passport and leave with someone at home, just in case your wallet is lost or stolen.
- Set up a Skype or FaceTime account with anyone you want to be in touch with.
- Check your equipment thoroughly. Take out each rod piece and make sure there are four pieces and they fit together, your reels are greased and working, the extra spools fit the reel you are taking, the reel seat threads work and hold the reel, your backing is secured to your reels, the backing strips off the reel for 150 yards without catching, and the connection between your backing and fly lines is solid.

Money, Credit Cards, and Currency

When you stay at a lodge, calculating the amount of currency to bring and how you will pay for the small items is relatively simple. But on a DIY adventure it is different. You are responsible for paying for everything, and most places do not take credit cards. Cash is king!

Plan ahead and determine how much you will need for food, liquor, guides, tips, gas, car, household supplies, and so on. You need to bring an emergency fund and plan on unexpected expenses. Don't count on either a bank or cash machine to help you out.

Once you have figured out how much cash to bring, make sure it is in currency readily accepted and in denominations that are common. Don't bring lots of large bills, as they are not easy for the locals to deal with.

Depending on the currency, you may be surprised at the size of the wad of cash you have to carry.

Documentation

Documentation is straightforward these days, but if you have forgotten something it can be a problem, so here are a few items to check:

- passport with an expiration date at least six months out
- photocopy of your passport located separately from where you carry your passport
- traveling visa, if required
- airplane, car, and hotel reservations in hand with correct dates
- copies of all of maps (road, Google Earth) you require to get around your DIY location
- emergency contact numbers, credit card information, and driver's license photocopied and placed somewhere other than your wallet, just in case it's lost or stolen

Travel Checklist

Over the years I have developed a travel checklist to help me prepare for a trip.

Miscellaneous Items

- airline ticket and itinerary
- passport and required visas
- confirmed travel insurance
- copy of passport in checked luggage
- medical insurance card and numbers
- accommodation and car reservations
- driver's license (if renting a car)
- fishing license
- alarm clock
- binoculars
- books, games, and cards
- cameras, accessories, case, lenses, tripod, extra batteries, and extra memory
- large and small ziplock plastic bags
- earplugs for plane and roommate
- emergency and contact numbers
- appropriate inoculations
- flashlight, headlamp, and extra batteries
- insect repellent and afterbite lotion
- sunscreen and chapstick (minimum 30 SPF)
- fanny or hip pack and water bottles
- maps or Google Earth printouts
- prescriptions that you always carry on the plane
- money, including small bills for tips
- toiletries
- duct tape, superglue, and Boeshield
- first aid supplies
- laptop, paper, and pens
- cell phone, charger
- waterproof boat bag
- small repair kit and screwdriver
- sewing kit
- converter from 110 to 220v
- guide gifts
- walkie-talkies, GPS, and VHF radio

- reading glasses, contacts and solutions, eyeglass cleaner, wipes, and eye drops
- mask, snorkel, and fins (if diving)
- soft-sided cooler
- mosquito netting
- rope, bungee cord, or straps
- garbage bag to bring home wet boots
- extra pair of shoelaces to fit wading boots

Clothes
- three to five long-sleeved, lightweight, ventilated, fast-drying flats shirts
- two or three pairs of lightweight, fast-drying wading pants
- wading shorts
- fabric wading belt
- T-shirts, underwear, socks, long-sleeved shirts, short-sleeved shirts, and shorts
- sandals and one pair of casual shoes
- flats hat with long bill, dark underside, and wide brim or flaps
- casual evening wear
- flats wading boots
- bandana, flats mask, or buff
- flats gloves (extra pair)
- neoprene socks, booties, and gravel guards
- rain jacket and rain pants
- fleece
- two pairs of sunglasses, strap, and lens cleaners
- swimsuit

Fishing Gear
- multipiece travel rods weight seven through nine
- reels to fit rods
- one spare eight-weight line
- backing
- leaders, 9 to 12 feet
- tippet, fluorocarbon (4×, 3×, 2×, 1×, 0×)

- flies
- fly boxes that can be carried
- pliers
- knife
- line cleaner
- nail knot tool
- nippers
- reel lubricant and grease/oil
- wire leader for toothy critters
- hook hone/file
- thermometer

First Aid

Many bonefishing destinations offer limited medical facilities, ranging from a simple clinic to nothing. I know of one island where you go to the vet for the best care. My advice is to make sure one member of your group has at least basic first aid training.

- first aid manual
- different-sized adhesive bandages
- moleskin/blister repair
- aspirin, acetaminophen, ibuprofen
- safety pins
- thermometer
- Imodium
- eye drops
- cold and allergy medicine/antihistamine
- sterile gauze pads of different sizes
- triangular bandages for the scalp or as a sling
- antibiotic cream
- calamine lotion
- medical gloves
- mild laxative
- Dramamine
- adhesive tape
- antiseptic wipes

- hydrocortisone cream (1%)
- sharp scissors
- alcohol wipes
- throat lozenges
- antacid
- aloe/sunburn remedy
- needle and thread

Insurance

Travel Cancellation. As I get older I have tended to buy the cancellation insurance to protect myself against surprises that tend to occur with more frequency.

Travel Medical. I buy an annual travel insurance policy and find that it is relatively inexpensive. This of course is not one of those items where you are shopping around for the least expensive deal. What you want is the best policy possible when you need it. If you are traveling to the United States, then travel policies normally perform fine. But if you are traveling to where the bonefish are, you need to make very sure you have the right policy. The fine print can bankrupt you—read and understand it.

Evacuation. This type of policy has become more and more important and is in addition to your normal travel medical policy. Do your homework and buy the coverage you can afford.

Rental Car. What can I say—rental car insurance is a pain. We all have credit cards and other coverage that say you are insured, but in some countries it's just not enough. Treat each situation differently and do what makes you comfortable. Driving in some of the countries where we fish can be an "experience" and is riskier even for those with good driving habits.

Travel Tips

Remember the golden rule of travel: #*&! happens!

If you are a regular traveler, you know that almost anything can occur and you need to be ready for lost luggage, missed connections, weather problems, or items stolen in transit, all of which have happened to me at one time or another.

My final two pieces of advice when planning, packing, and traveling on a DIY fishing adventure:

- Pack as if none of your bags is ever going to find you (believe me, it happens). Carry on the plane as much as you can, including all prescriptions, essentials you need in the sun (pants, shorts, hat, buff, wading shoes, sunglasses, gloves) and as much bonefishing gear as the airline will let you carry.
- Relax and stay calm—it will all work out. Consider surprises part of the DIY adventure.

Part II
WHERE TO DIY: DESTINATIONS

Over the last 20 years, I have had the remarkable good fortune to fish throughout the tropics pursuing my passion for fly fishing. The last 10 years I've concentrated on locations where at least half the time is spent wading without the benefit of a guide, and I've managed to find exciting fishing that is accessible with nothing more than a car or kayak.

Finding new locations and exploring the unknown is my motivation. Fortunately, I have a wife and friends who are willing to put up with my wanderlust, and every new adventure (no matter how crazy) is met with enthusiasm if not a little bravado. Catching more bonefish is no longer my goal, but finding them is the pot of gold at the end of the rainbow.

On the following pages are 16 destinations taking us from Florida to the Bahamas, Turks and Caicos, Mexico, and Hawaii, identifying close to 300 individual fishing locations. Except for a few on Grand Cayman, Great Harbour Cay, and a couple in Hawaii, I have fished them all.

Each destination begins with a map, pinpointing the highlights for the area and specific locations where you can find bonefish, followed by a brief description, places to fish, and pertinent fishing information. For planning, I have developed a seven-day sample fishing trip and, if you are traveling with a nonfisherman, a "spousal rating" based solely on my personal opinion.

By no means is the list all inclusive, but it's meant to represent the DIY opportunities available to the adventurous angler. Just so you know, there are plenty of locations I haven't listed, either because I made a promise or selfishly wanted to keep them to myself. That means there are plenty of bonefish swimming around on the flats and creeks, within walking distance of a road, waiting for you to find them.

CHAPTER 4
THE BAHAMAS

THE ABACOS

Lay of the Land

Situated two hundred miles east of Palm Beach, Florida, the Abacos are the most northerly group of Bahamian islands, exposing the 10,000 residents to cold fronts from November to March. Boasting the third-highest population of the Bahamian islands, the atmosphere is relaxed and friendly. The residents are primarily employed in commercial fishing, boat building, government, and tourism.

Named Abacoa by the Lucayan Indians who inhabited the island before the arrival of the Spaniards, the Abacos were settled by the Loyalists who left the British Colonies of North America after the War of Independence.

The island of Abaco is 130 miles long, stretching from Crown Haven in the north to Sandy Point in the south. The "mainland" is Great Abaco with a curve of cays a few miles offshore creating the protected Sea of Abaco. Though the majority of these tiny islands are uninhabited, the larger cays, including Green Turtle, Great Guana, Man-O-War, and Elbow, are worth a visit using the regularly scheduled ferry service.

In the north are the small settlements of Crown Haven (catch the ferry to Grand Bahama from here) and Fox Town. South of the Little Abaco causeway is Coopers Town, originally settled in the 1870s by the Cooper family from Grand Bahama, with 900 residents working primarily in the fishing industry. South of Coopers Town on the S. C. Bootle Highway is the Treasure Cay Airport, the Green Turtle Cay Ferry, and the resort area of Treasure Cay. Named for the fleet of more than 15 Spanish treasure galleons that sank off its shores in the late 1500s, Treasure Cay is Abaco's second-largest settlement. With a large marina, an 18-hole golf course, and some of the best beaches in the Bahamas, Treasure Cay is an ideal vacation spot for just about any traveler.

Thirty-five minutes south of Treasure Cay is the commercial center of Abaco, Marsh Harbour. Home to the island's only stoplight, Marsh Harbour is the Bahama's third-largest settlement with about 6,000 residents. Marsh Harbour offers a wide selection of comfortable and reasonably priced accommodations, the largest airport on the island, shopping, dining, banking, a medical clinic, and supplies for just about anything you might need, including an Internet café.

As you head south from Marsh Harbour, the population thins and settlements become smaller. Little Harbour, quiet even by Abaco standards, is worth the 45-minute drive south from Marsh Harbour. This picturesque settlement is known as the home of the acclaimed bronze and wood sculptor Randolf Johnston and Pete's Pub. Just a few miles from Little Harbour lies the charming settlement of Cherokee Sound, well-known for its extensive bonefishing flats. At the southernmost tip of Abaco is Sandy Point, a quiet commercial fishing village that has fuel and a grocery store.

Where to Fish

Though Abaco isn't known as a DIY location, it has become one of my favorite places in the world with dozens of locations that can be reached either on foot or by kayak.

Abaco is famous for its western shore flats, creeks, and mangrove cays known as the Marls. The Marls run north of Sandy Point, following the length of Abaco to Crown Haven. They hold a remarkable number of bonefish and should be fished at least once in your life with one of the island's experienced local guides.

While the Marls hold much of the allure on Abaco, the eastern shore and outlying cays should not be ignored, as they hold some of the largest fish I have seen in the Bahamas.

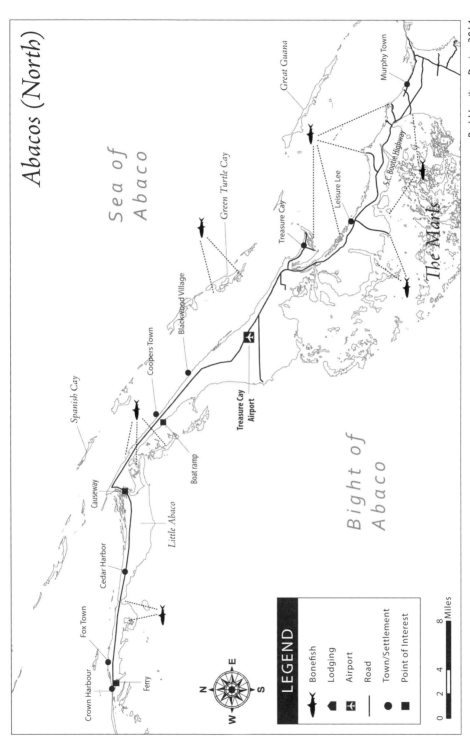

Abacos (North)

Sea of Abaco

Spanish Cay

Green Turtle Cay

Great Guana

Treasure Cay

Leisure Lee

Murphy Town

Coopers Town

Blackwood Village

S.C. Bootle Highway

The Marls

Boat ramp

Treasure Cay Airport

Causeway

Little Abaco

Bight of Abaco

Cedar Harbor

Fox Town

Crown Harbour

Ferry

LEGEND

Bonefish

Lodging

Airport

Road

Town/Settlement

Point of Interest

N W E S

0 2 4 8 Miles

Rod Hamilton Design 2014

Rod Hamilton with a bonefish from the Marls of Abaco

Everywhere we fish, tides are critical, and it is no different on Abaco. Though I have been unable to find a tide table for the western shore of Abaco, the tides on the east side (where tide tables are available) are significantly different than those on the west. My experience is that the tides on the west are approximately two hours later than the tides on the eastern shore, but even this changes as you move north to south.

There is very little DIY fishing on the eastern shore until you get south of Marsh Harbour, and other than Green Turtle, the outlying cays are best explored by renting a boat.

Marsh Harbour to Sandy Point

Use the Marsh Harbour Airport roundabout as marker 0 when measuring distances south from Marsh Harbour. This is the start of the Great Abaco Highway, which ends in the town of Sandy Point.

Eastern Shore. Located in Marsh Harbour, this housing area has to be mentioned since we caught some nice fish right out the front door

Landing a nice fish in front of our rental home

of the home we rented. This should not be considered a fishing location in the typical sense, but it's sure nice to be having a beer on the porch, your rod within spitting distance, and see three six-pound bones lazily feeding out front.

Broad Creek. The road to Broad Creek is 0.7 miles south of the airport roundabout. This is a smaller creek system on the eastern shore that has undergone some rehabilitation over the last few years. From the main highway follow the Broad Creek road 2.3 miles to the various parking spots from which you can walk and wade.

Snake Cay. The road to the garbage dump is 3.8 miles south of the airport roundabout. From the main highway it's 2.6 miles to a boat launch and parking area. Snake Cay is one of the better walk-and-wade fishing spots on Abaco and is located very close to Marsh Harbour. This is an excellent choice for a quick fish on an incoming tide or to hit tailing fish in the evening. The fishing can be a little technical but worth the effort if you hit the tides correctly. Don't fish the outside channels and lagoons; stay on the western shore, concentrating on the northerly half of the creek. You can walk and wade directly from the road where it first touches Snake Cay, kayak from the boat launch, or use the dirt road running parallel to Snake Cay.

Bight of Robinson. Accessed from Little Harbour, this beautiful bay with extensive creeks has enough fishing to keep a couple of folks happy for a week. When fishing here we stay at Joe Kirwin's home (VRBO listing #7018) and use his hard-shelled kayaks. There are plenty of flats to walk at low tide in the bight itself, and the creeks are enormous. To find Little Harbour drive 9.8 miles south of the airport roundabout and take the turn to Pete's Pub. It's another 8.7 miles to the turnoff to Little Harbour and then 1.5 miles to the left-hand turn to the Bight of Robinson.

Cherokee Sound. A few miles down the road from Little Harbour is Cherokee Sound, one of the better-known flats on Abaco. This is one of the most beautiful flats you will ever see and is in a picture-perfect setting. The people of the settlement are welcoming, love bonefish, and understand fishermen. There are numerous places to stay, a small grocery store, and some well-known guides. Take a walk on the long dock jutting out from the shoreline and keep your eyes out for cruising bonefish. I love fishing Cherokee Sound in October because over the summer the fish have forgotten that a "Charlie" is a bad thing. But by December they can be some of the toughest fish to catch in the Bahamas. You will find plenty of fish, but they definitely have an "attitude." The difficulty factor ranks right up there with the Town Flats on Green Turtle Cay and Savannah Sound on Eleuthera. We are talking long, light leaders; small, lightly weighted flies; and sophisticated presentations. When they get picky, I have found more success with weedless Pop's Bitters in the turtle grass than conventional bonefish patterns on the sand flats. If what I've described discourages you, don't let it. This area is worth a day or two simply for its beauty, and you could very well see the largest bonefish of your life.

Cherokee Sound Creek. Adjacent to and north of the flats is the Cherokee Sound creek system. We walk and wade this creek right off the road during low tide once we get discouraged by the PhDs on the flat. There are a number of places to ambush fish entering the creek, and a kayak doesn't hurt either. The creek system is massive, so print off a Google map before planning your attack.

Dock over the flats of Cherokee Sound, Abaco

Casuarina Point. Back on the main road, continue south from the Little Harbour exit for another 4.3 miles until you reach the exit to Casuarina Point. This community of two dozen homes resides on one of the most beautiful beaches and flats imaginable. It is a personal favorite not just for its fishing but for the beach, atmosphere, and housing options. The fishing starts directly in front of the rental homes and continues south along the deserted beach for a couple of miles. With a kayak or a small boat (many of the rental houses come with boats) it is a quick trip over to Duck Cay. Adjacent to the now-defunct Different of Abaco Resort there is a small creek system that is totally tide dependent. The fish enter the creek through the small entrance on the incoming tide and leave as the tide turns.

Boat Canal. Drive 6.3 miles south of the Casuarina Point exit to a dirt road heading west to the Marls and ending at a boat launch and man-made boat canal. If you reach Lelas Road you have gone too far south. This boat launch is used extensively by the local guides, so park out of the way and leave them plenty of room to turn around, launch their boats, and park their vehicles and trailers. This is one of the primary access points for flats boats to access the middle section of the Marls. It is well worth it to

Kim and Kerrie with a double from Cherokee Sound, Abaco

hire one of the local guides to fish this section of the Marls. For the DIY fisherman, there is some very good fishing both north and south from the boat canal's mouth. The creek system one mile south of the boat canal can be reached on foot or kayak, and the wading within the creek is fine. The fishing is good here, but the bottom is filled with sharp rocks, making it difficult to land the fish. The fish are not spooky, so go with 16-pound fluorocarbon, as they seem to know where every rock is. The creek system north of the boat canal can also be reached by foot or kayak, but the interior portions of the creek are soft and really tough wading. I prefer to fish the outside shoreline where the wading is excellent and ambush the fish at the creek mouths on the incoming and outgoing tides.

Southern Boat Launch. A boat ramp and parking area can be found on the western shore 200 yards south of the Schooner Cove turnoff. This is an area the guides and others use to access the southern section of the Marls. I have parked my car on the roadside and cast to bones cruising the shoreline. The creek system can be explored either on foot or by kayak.

Crossing Harbour. This area has numerous creeks and flats but can be difficult to access. Traveling 35 miles south of the airport roundabout you will come to a bend in the road just after passing the sign announcing the start of the Abaco National Park. At the Y take either the first or second road into the park toward Crossing Harbour. These are rough roads and not rental car company approved.

Sandy Point Runway. North of the Sandy Point Airport runway is a short dirt road heading west. Drive a half mile, park the car, then walk the 250 yards to the flats, bay, and creeks that lie north of Sandy Point. This is an area that is not often fished even though it is close to Sandy Point.

Sandy Point Shoreline. Where the main highway hits the Sandy Point shoreline you will see a small gazebo, table, and resting area. Park the car here and you will be surprised at the quality of fishing a scant 50 yards away. I prefer to walk the shoreline to the south, but either way you will see fish. If you are there during lobster season, the fishermen will be diving directly in front of you. Wave one of them over to buy some live lobster that has just been caught.

Sandy Point Town Flat. Drive through Sandy Point and just before reaching Rickmon's Bonefish Lodge is a short road to the right taking you to a parking area overlooking the Sandy Point Town Flat. Between your car and the flat is a deep boat channel that requires a kayak to cross. But once across, the walking is easy and well worth the effort.

Marsh Harbour to Treasure Cay

For the middle section of Abaco, set your mileage marker to 0 where the side road to Murphy Town (just north of Marsh Harbour) intersects the main highway. The S. C. Bootle Highway is the main paved road heading northwest from Marsh Harbour and ending in Crown Haven.

Boat Ramp. At mile marker 0 there is a dirt road heading west toward the Marls, ending at a boat launch and parking area. Guides and boaters use this ramp to reach the central section of the Marls. I have not had much success fishing either north or south along this shoreline, but it is close to Marsh Harbour if you only have a couple of hours.

Water Cay. There is a dirt road to the northeast found 4.9 miles north of mile marker 0 that ends at the shoreline and creek known as Water Cay. This shoreline and creek system has some decent fishing during the low tide but gets a little deep for a walk-and-wade angler during high tide.

Marls Road. There is a dirt road, 9.5 miles north from mile marker 0, that heads in a southerly direction into the Marls. Drive the three miles to the end of the road and then walk 250 yards to the water. Once you hit the shoreline, you can walk either left or right to fish a number of bays, flats, and creeks. Be sure to fish the shoreline as you make your way either north or south, especially on a low tide when the fish have left the mangroves.

Leisure Lee. Back on the highway and 11 miles north of mile marker 0 you will come to the Leisure Lee development. Exit the highway into the Leisure Lee development and follow the road heading left; there you will find access to a couple of smaller flats. You may need a kayak to cross the boat channel.

Hills Creek. Known locally as Turtle Cove, Hill Creek is located two miles northwest of Leisure Lee and has a boat ramp, dock, and canal. It has some excellent wading flats completely accessible at low tide, but once the tide rises a kayak is necessary. These fish see their share of flies and are not pushovers, but they are always there. It's an excellent place for a quick fish on the incoming tide if you are staying at Treasure Cay.

Treasure Cay to Little Abaco

Heading north from Treasure Cay, set your mileage marker to 0 at the junction of the S. C. Bootle Highway and the road to Treasure Cay. From Treasure Cay the road heads in a northwesterly direction through Coopers Town but then turns west to Fox Town after crossing the causeway to Little Abaco. At one time there was a small bridge connecting Abaco and Little Abaco, but it's now just a continuation of the main highway and you will barely know you have crossed it.

Gunpowder Road. Before heading toward Coopers Town there are a couple of spots within Treasure Cay to fish. At the very end of Gunpowder Road is an excellent small flat best fished during the incoming and outgoing tides. The fish don't hang around here but pass over the flat on their way in and out of Gunpowder Creek.

Gunpowder Creek. This is the creek system readily seen from the road within Treasure Cay. There are a few places, including Gunpowder Road, where you can access the creek. It's a beautiful creek system to kayak for an afternoon, but I have never done particularly well fishing it.

Coopers Town Boat Ramp. After driving northwest through Coopers Town you will see Coopers Drive on your left. This road is 19 miles north of Treasure Cay and has a large cell tower at its entrance. This short road heads to the Marls, ending at a nice boat ramp and parking area. The walk-and-wade angler can fish the shoreline here both right and left, but the best fishing is directly in front where you see the first series of cays. To get to the cays you need a kayak and then a paddle of just under a mile. You want to hit these cays as the tide is dropping and fish through the low tide and well into the incoming tide. The boat ramp is used by guides and other boaters for access to the northern Marls.

The Bluff. Continuing up the road, 2.4 miles past Coopers Drive, is a short road on the left that leads to what I call "the Bluff." Once you park the car, look over the Bluff to a beautiful bay with miles of flats and creeks surrounding it. It takes some "bush bashing" to get to the bay, but it's a great place for the DIY angler and buddies to spend a day.

Conch Rock Creek. Directly opposite the road to the Bluff is a short drivable path to the water. Park the car and take a short hike to the beach. In front of you is a great-looking series of small cays and bays, ideal habitat for large cruising "ocean" bones. Unfortunately, we also call it "Seaweed Bay," describing the long strands of seaweed rising from the bottom. You have an excellent chance of hooking the largest bonefish of the trip, but landing them is a different story. If you try it for an hour or two on a low tide, you're likely to produce one of the trip's "fish stories."

Little Abaco to Fox Town

In order to fish Little Abaco, reset your odometer to 0 once on the causeway separating Great Abaco from Little Abaco. You will know you are on the causeway when, heading west, the road becomes very narrow with water close to the road on both sides.

Mangrove Cay Bay. After passing the Wood Cay sign, 9 miles west of the Little Abaco causeway, you will see a short dirt road on your left (south). Park just over the hill and make the short walk to the bay. This is a beautiful flat that contains some nice fish, including a couple of large schools. I find the fish a little smaller here, more typical of Marls-sized fish. At low tide you can fish virtually to Mangrove Cay located directly south of you. This area gets pressured, so don't be surprised to have a few refusals.

Unnamed Bay. I'm sure this bay and creek have a name, but I have not been able to find it on any map. The bay is reached by driving 10 miles from the causeway, then taking the dirt road on the left heading directly south for 0.75 miles. Once you park your car, the walk is about 200 yards to the water's edge.

Green Turtle and Outer Cays

Green Turtle Cay is reached by catching a ferry north of Treasure Cay and landing in the quaint settlement of New Plymouth. Transportation on Green Turtle Cay is by golf cart, which just seems right for this small community. There is something perfect about loading your fly rod, lunch, and gear into your golf cart and heading to the flat. Golf-cart accessible flats include the Town Flats and Gilliam Bay south of New Plymouth and Coco Bay on the northern end of the cay. There are a couple of good guides on Green Turtle Cay, including Ricky Sawyer, who has been fishing the area for 40 years.

Looking on Google Earth you will find an untold number of small flats, bays, and creek systems throughout the outer cays bordering Abaco. The northerly cays offer an extensive array of fishing locations but are mostly out of reach to the self-guided angler. If you want to see the other cays of Abaco, my advice is to rent a boat from Donnie's on Green Turtle Cay, ask for suggestions, and spend the day playing "Columbus" and exploring some of the most beautiful waters I have ever seen.

Fishing Information

There is a surprising amount of self-guided fishing available on Abaco with enough variety to keep any fisherman happy. If you are looking for a chance at one of Abaco's larger fish, stick to the ocean side, for numbers of fish concentrate on the Marls.

Abaco is one of those places where a kayak comes in handy, so either bring an inflatable with you or book accommodations that include a kayak.

In the less-accessible areas the fish are eager to eat and aren't particularly leader shy or fussy about fly selection. There are also spots like Cherokee Sound where you have to be on your game to catch fish. For this trip take a normal supply of Charlies, Gotchas, Greg's Flats Flies,

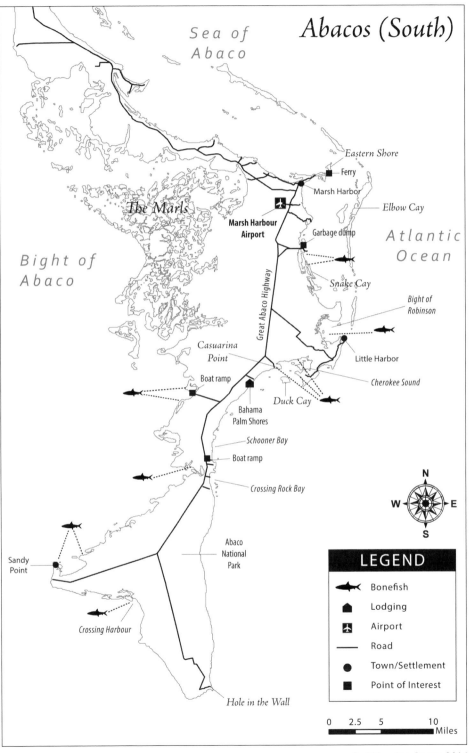

Abacos (South)

Sea of Abaco

The Marls

Bight of Abaco

Atlantic Ocean

Eastern Shore

Ferry

Marsh Harbor

Marsh Harbour Airport

Elbow Cay

Garbage dump

Snake Cay

Bight of Robinson

Great Abaco Highway

Casuarina Point

Little Harbor

Cherokee Sound

Boat ramp

Duck Cay

Bahama Palm Shores

Schooner Bay

Boat ramp

Crossing Rock Bay

Abaco National Park

Sandy Point

Crossing Harbour

Hole in the Wall

N
W E
S

LEGEND

- Bonefish
- Lodging
- Airport
- Road
- Town/Settlement
- Point of Interest

0 2.5 5 10 Miles

Rod Hamilton Design 2014

Dick Swan and his new portable flats boat the Bare Bones II

Sliders, Clousers, Pop's Bitters, and crab patterns. For the spookier fish include small weightless flies and a few with weed guards.

Standard nine-foot leaders with two feet of 12-pound fluorocarbon tippet are fine for all-around use. When fishing tight to the mangroves, bump up to 16-pound and down to 8-pound when face-to-face with the stony gaze of the PhDs cruising the Town Flats of Green Turtle Cay.

There are plenty of qualified guides on Abaco and the surrounding cays. I can recommend the following:

Junior Albury, Casuarina Point. www.jrsbonefishabaco.com

Justin Sands, Marsh Harbour. www.justfishjs.com

Ricky Sawyer, Green Turtle. www.abacoflyfish.com

Where to Stay

Variety is the name of the game on the Abacos. There are so many choices that the best plan of action is to search the two online vacation sites I use, VRBO (www.vrbo.com) and HomeAway (www.homeaway.com), plus send inquiries to a few of Abaco's many property managers.

To narrow the search, determine if you want to be on one of the outlying cays where you get around by golf cart, a smaller settlement in southern Abaco, or a little closer to the action in Treasure Cay or Marsh Harbour.

On Green Turtle Cay, there are a number of homes and small resorts suitable for fishing groups, couples, and families, and I can personally recommend the **Bluff House** (www.bluffhouse.com).

Treasure Cay offers a true tropical vacation experience where you can choose from resorts, homes, and condos while buzzing around in your golf cart. There are a number of local restaurants, a golf course, tennis courts, and beaches at your doorstep. If you want to fish the northern end of Abaco, Treasure Cay is an ideal location.

The largest town on Abaco, Marsh Harbour, serves as the hub for the island with all the services and amenities you would expect. There are a wide variety of rentals available from economy bungalows to the grandest of waterfront homes. We stayed at the **Wheelhouse** on Eastern Shores (866-599-6674; VRBO #410521), which is perfect for two couples.

Twenty miles south of Marsh Harbour are the settlements of Little Harbour and Cherokee Sound. Small and remote, both places offer a few homes and cottages to rent.

South of Cherokee Sound is the tiny enclave of Casuarina Point where you will find a cluster of charming homes to rent in the midst of seaside tranquility.

If Treasure Cay or Marsh Harbour will be home, arranging for groceries and meals will not be problem. Little Harbour, Cherokee Sound, and Casuarina Point will require more of a plan! Before heading south, do your shopping at the major grocery stores in Marsh Harbour.

Getting Around

The airports at Treasure Cay and Marsh Harbour are a little more than an hour's flight from South Florida and are serviced by several commercial airlines.

Subject to the carrier, flights can be found most days of the week between Fort Lauderdale (United, Sky Bahamas), Miami (American Eagle), West Palm Beach (Bahamasair), Orlando (American, United, US Airways, Bahamasair), and Nassau (Bahamasair, Sky Bahamas).

Bahamas Fast Ferry will get you from Nassau to Sandy Point in about three and a half hours (www.bahamasferries.com; 242-323-2166).

Car troubles. There's always something on a DIY trip.

Route and schedule information for the ferries from Abaco to the cays can be found at www.go-abacos.com/travel.

There are a number of car rental agencies to choose from; I can recommend **Sea Star Rentals** (www.go-abacos.com/seastar/), which has an office at the Marsh Harbour airport.

In the larger settlements like Treasure Cay and Marsh Harbour, bike and scooter rentals are also available.

Seven-Day Sample Trip

Quality fishing extends from Fox Town in the north to Sandy Point in the south and east to Green Turtle Cay, making it difficult to pick one place to call "home." For simplicity's sake I've picked Marsh Harbour, knowing full well that Little Harbour and Casuarina Point to the south, Treasure Cay to the north, and Green Turtle Cay to the east will suit others just as well.

Rent the two levels of Wheelhouse (VRBO #410521) in Marsh Harbour, putting you in the middle of the fishing with the added benefit that there are fish steps from the back door.

Pick up a car from Sea Star Rentals at the airport and make the five-minute drive to the Wheelhouse. Make sure to check for bones cruising out back before starting to unpack.

For the first day hire a local guide and fish the Marls. For the rest of the week fish the destinations listed in this section from Marsh Harbour to Sandy Point. First, concentrate on those locations closest to Marsh Harbour, like Snake Cay, and then move progressively south to the Bight of Robinson, Cherokee Sound, Casuarina Point, and the Boat Canal. Most of these locations are on the eastern shore so the tide table for Marsh Harbour will work fine with minor adjustments. The Boat Canal is located on the western shore, and, as mentioned previously, the tides are a couple of hours later in the Marls than on the eastern shore. The shoreline at Sandy Point always holds fish, and the large bay, flats, and creek north of Sandy Point are easy to access and worth a day's fishing.

Spousal Rating: 7

Abaco gets a high spousal rating and it is well deserved. There are lots of activities for the nonfishing spouse to keep busy and some of the nicest beaches in the world, such as those on Treasure Cay.

Nonfishing Activities

You can do it all in the Abacos! Golf, tennis, boat rentals, snorkeling, diving, and kayaking are just some of the activities to consider. Take a ferry to the different cays and spend a day exploring the town of New Plymouth on Green Turtle Cay, visiting the lighthouse on Elbow Cay, or buying a must-have canvas bag made by the sailmakers on Man-O-War Cay. Get lunch at Nippers on Great Guana Cay and spend the afternoon walking the cay's stunning beaches.

There is such an array of activities and sights while visiting the Abacos that it's difficult to narrow down the choices, but here are a few of my favorites:

- Lunch with Lincoln Jones
- Touring the lighthouse on Elbow Cay
- Renting a golf cart and touring Hope Town

Hopetown Lighthouse, Abaco

- Touring the foundry and lunching at Pete's Pub in Little Harbour
- Buying lobster directly from the fishermen in Sandy Point
- Visiting the Albert Lowe Museum on Green Turtle Cay
- Lying out on the beach at Casuarina Point and wondering, "Why don't we live here?"
- Visiting the Abaco National Park

Bits and Pieces

After fishing for 60 days straight, ranging from the Florida Keys, to the Yucatan, to three different Bahamian islands, I was starting to get a little complacent. One day, my fishing partner and I headed to a favorite flat at the very genteel hour of 10:00 a.m. and were back home resting comfortably on the deck by 3:00 p.m. Not exactly an exhausting day on the flats, but we were happy to be sitting on the back porch with Kaliks in hand, contemplating life.

Gazing out onto the pristine water in front of our rented home on Eastern Shores, the scene was idyllic and the four of us could not have been more comfortable, until those fateful words were spoken, "Bonefish!" The fire drill began. Spilling beer, pulling on boots, and grabbing the nearest strung-up rod, I tried to keep my eyes on the three six-pound bonefish happily feeding 70 feet from the deck in 18 inches of water. I stayed as spotter, and John eased into the water listening to my whispered instructions. One cast, a strong strip strike, and six pounds of silver magic screamed across the flat.

What is it about bonefish? After catching hundreds over the last couple of months the sight of a bonefish still turned two experienced fishermen and their adoring fans (wives) into complete babbling fools.

There it is. That's why we chase the silver ghost.

ACKLINS ISLAND

Lay of the Land

Are you interested in a rustic DIY island adventure that is more about fishing and less about a tropical vacation? Look no further than Acklins. With a total population of just under 500, the vibe here is quiet, unhurried, and peaceful.

Located at the southeastern end of the Bahamas chain, Acklins is one of four islands (Crooked, Acklins, Long Cay, and Castle) that form an atoll around the Bight of Acklins. This bight is one of the world's most spectacular bonefish fisheries. Acklins is long and narrow, sporting 120 square miles of hilly, desolate terrain along with beautiful coastlines, hidden caves, and seemingly endless white beaches.

American Loyalists settled these islands in the late 1780s, establishing cotton plantations that lost their economic viability following the abolition of slavery. Today, locals live primarily on commercial fishing, small-scale farming, minor tourism, and harvesting Cascarilla bark used to flavor the liquor Campari.

Dotted with small settlements from Lovely Bay in the north to Salina Point in the south, Acklins has one main paved road running the length of the island. Situated in the middle of the island is Spring Point, Acklins's largest settlement, home to the airport, government offices, a medical clinic, fuel, and minimal provisions.

Eric posing for an instant before releasing a fish

While some will enjoy the inherent challenges of "figuring things out" on the sparsely populated island, others may find the intermittent availability of goods and services frustrating. For example, the limited selection of groceries may or may not arrive by boat weekly, and the same goes for gasoline. Electricity tends to go on and off, and the land telephone lines are finicky. Cell phones generally work, and the Internet is available in some locations.

If staying in a self-contained rental property, bring plenty of supplies from Nassau. You won't find traditional restaurants but may come across a roadside kiosk selling Bahamian fare. Credit cards and traveler's checks won't do you much good as cash is king. And there are no banks or ATMs on Acklins! Bring your Google maps; even though the lodge says they have Internet, I wouldn't count on it. It's also advisable to make sure the group has one cell phone with a Bahamian SIM card. It may be the only way to talk to family back home.

The key to a successful trip on Acklins is to first decide where you are staying, figure out where your meals are coming from, determine who will rent you a car, and then, upon arrival, convert your internal clock to "island time." Nobody's in a hurry on Acklins.

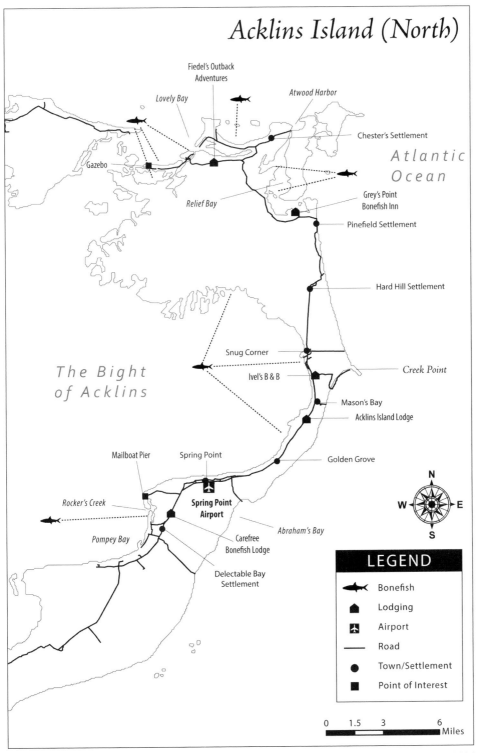

Acklins Island (North)

Fiedel's Outback Adventures

Atwood Harbor

Lovely Bay

Chester's Settlement

Atlantic Ocean

Gazebo

Relief Bay

Grey's Point
Bonefish Inn

Pinefield Settlement

Hard Hill Settlement

The Bight of Acklins

Snug Corner

Creek Point

Ivel's B & B

Mason's Bay

Acklins Island Lodge

Mailboat Pier

Spring Point

Golden Grove

Rocker's Creek

Spring Point Airport

Pompey Bay

Abraham's Bay

Carefree
Bonefish Lodge

Delectable Bay
Settlement

N
W   E
S

LEGEND

Bonefish	Bonefish
Lodging	Lodging
Airport	Airport
Road	Road
Town/Settlement	Town/Settlement
Point of Interest	Point of Interest

0   1.5   3   6
Miles

Rod Hamilton Design 2014

Where to Fish

In many ways Acklins offers the flats angler the best of all possible worlds. The choices range from a fully guided lodge to a simple DIY adventure with every option in between. Whatever you choose, the fishing pressure is light and the fish are aggressive, making Acklins an angler's dream.

For self-guided fishermen there are miles of wadeable flats easily reached by car. To expand the DIY fishable area, launch a kayak and paddle to those flats and creek systems that can't be reached on foot.

The road running north from Spring Point is in good shape and easy to navigate. The road running south from Spring Point is a combination of pavement and potholes. As you drive south along the main road, you will see dirt and sand side roads running to both coasts. As an inquisitive explorer I have been down most of them; some of the side roads to the west lead to flats and some lead to areas that are interesting but not "fishy." Before you go to Acklins, spend some time on Google Earth, identify the side roads, and take a printed Google Earth image with you. One of the side roads may lead you to your own "honey hole."

It's not necessary to fish south of Spring Point, but if you decide to do so, take the main road left when leaving the airport and drive south toward Salina Point. You will find a number of roads to the leeward side (right side) of the island taking you to flats on Delectable and Reserve Bays. The flats beside the road on Delectable Bay are good for wading, but I wouldn't spend much time there.

Reserve Bay. Some of the best flats in the south are found at Reserve Bay. Take the short road to the leeward side of the island approximately 11 miles south of the airport junction. There is good fishing walking both south and north on these flats. It's the ideal place for a couple of anglers to split up and fish the incoming tide.

Concrete Dock. Continuing south, turn right just before the Salina Point settlement and continue to the small dock. Walk the beach to the north where you will find some larger bones and big barracuda. This is where the fishermen clean their fish, conch, and lobster.

If you want to fish the southern portion of Acklins, my recommendation is to book with Felton Rolle of Salina Point Lodge and have him run you out by boat to the flats each morning and pick you up at the end of the day. As a bonus, there are some nice flats directly in front of the lodge.

Rockers Creek. My preferred fishing areas are located north of Spring Point. From the airport junction, head north for a quarter mile and take the dirt road to your left, heading toward the "mail boat" pier. Park at the old gas pump, and immediately to the south are a series of creeks and lagoons that fish very well on both the incoming and outgoing tides. This creek system is known among locals as Rockers Creek.

Spring Point Beach. The road north from Spring Point follows the coastline where you will be tempted to stop the car and walk the beach. One of the nicest bonefish (seven pounds) I have caught on Acklins was a single fish cruising this shoreline.

Mason's Bay. Farther north you will come to Mason's Bay. There are good fishable flats for the next several miles. In fact, you can stay at Ivel's Bed & Breakfast at Mason's Bay and fish either the flats directly in front of the B & B or the small creek systems to the south. I park at either the yellow schoolhouse or water treatment facility just north of Ivel's and access the flats from there. Though the fishing in front of the yellow schoolhouse is good, I prefer to hike the 1.5 miles north and start fishing the flats and mangroves from there. The fishing is excellent for the next two miles north (a total walk of 3.5 miles), and, because of the distance, the fish get very little pressure. In total there are six miles of walk-and-wade fishing starting from the flats south of Ivel's to the mangroves and creek systems to the north.

Couple of nice bones from a mangroves creek in Acklins

David with bonefish from a roadside flat

The road heading north and east from Snug Cove crosses the island to the ocean side. Here you will pass through Hardhill Settlement and then Pinefield Settlement.

Relief Bay. The first fishable area you will reach beyond the Pinefield Settlement is Relief Bay. This is a massive system that four people could fish for a week without setting foot anywhere else on Acklins. If you are staying at Grey's Point Bonefish Inn, the flats are immediately behind the lodge. Otherwise you will find access to the Relief Bay flats at two points: The first is approximately 2.3 miles north of Grey's Point Lodge where you park the car beside the road and make the short walk east to the flats; you reach the second by continuing north toward Chester's Settlement, taking the right-hand road at the Y, and then driving down the dirt road to the right 1.1 miles from the Y. Park your car where the dirt road ends at Outer Harbour and walk west up the creek system toward the open flats. The creeks and flats of Outer Harbour and Relief Bay are enormous, so it's important to have Google Earth maps with you in order to fully explore and understand the area.

Chester's Settlement. When you head back on the dirt road from Outer Harbour, bear to the right when you hit the pavement. The paved road will take you into Chester's Settlement, which accesses the north shore of Guana flats and the associated creeks. Once through Chester's Settlement the road veers to the right (north) and takes you to a bay where there can be good fishing along the beach and excellent fishing off of the point located at the road's end.

Guyana Creek. Once back at the Y, as you make your way to Lovely Bay there is a nice flat directly in front of you. This flat, locally known as Guyana Creek, is two miles long, easy to wade with a firm bottom, and contains good numbers of bonefish on the incoming tide. It's one of the easier flats to wade, and the fish remain accessible during high tide in the upper regions of the flat. If you stay at Fedel's Outback Fishing Adventures, the flats are behind his home down a short trail through the mangroves.

Lovely Bay. The road to Lovely Bay crosses a creek system 0.5 miles before entering the settlement. You will find good access and excellent fishing on a flat and creek system immediately to the southwest.

To reach an endless supply of flats and creeks, drive through Lovely Bay to the end of the road where a small gazebo has been constructed. Fishermen can walk and wade the shoreline here, but the ideal approach is to launch a kayak and cross either the south channel or the channel to the north. This begins an exploration of creeks and flats that go on and on. There are so many places to go with a kayak from the gazebo that it's difficult to know where to fish first.

Fishing Information

Even for the most diehard DIY angler, I recommend that you hire one of the local guides for a couple of days to fish the Bight of Acklins. It has the same cachet as the Marls of Abaco but with much larger fish. The bight is such a special fishery you need to do it once in your lifetime.

Acklins is a wonderful destination for those anglers new to bonefishing. When using a local guide, the "newbie" will see lots of fish and get a ton of shots; in addition, the fish are not fussed by the "blown" casts of

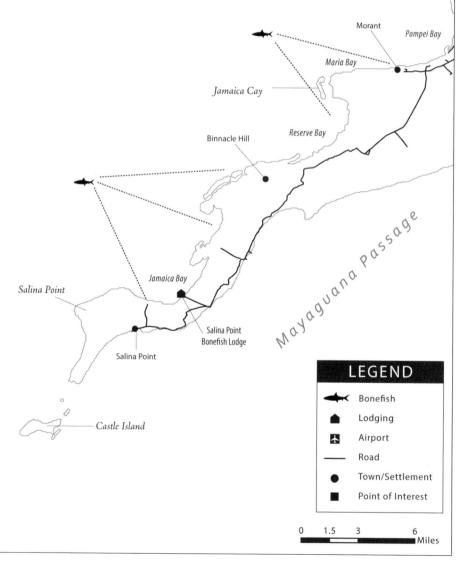

Acklins Island (South)

The Bight of Acklins

Morant
Pompei Bay
Maria Bay
Jamaica Cay
Reserve Bay
Binnacle Hill
Mayaguana Passage
Salina Point
Jamaica Bay
Salina Point
Bonefish Lodge
Salina Point
Castle Island

LEGEND

- Bonefish
- Lodging
- Airport
- Road
- Town/Settlement
- Point of Interest

0   1.5   3   6
Miles

Rod Hamilton Design 2014

a rookie. For the DIY angler, the variety of fishing locations will keep a group of six busy at new locations for a solid week.

As in most places, being on the flats at the right time is critical. The average bonefish is in the 3- to 5-pound range, but during the course of a week you will certainly cast to fish from 7 to 10 pounds. Acklins bonefish can hardly wait to get into the mangroves, so you need to be positioned to ambush them on their way in and out. I learned a very good lesson on Acklins from guide Reno Taylor: Fish the tide when it's perfect, no matter what time of day. Reno, who was taking us out in the local pastor's boat, was adamant that to hit the incoming tide we had to be on the water early. We picked him up on the side of the road in the dark, and he negotiated the boat through the channels out to the mangrove cays in the Bight of Acklins. We were wading the flats as the sun was coming up and we had hit the incoming tide just right. It's surprising how well you can see tails at sunrise.

The best times to fish Acklins are October through November and March through June. Because of Acklins's southerly location, the cold fronts that hit the northern Bahamian islands often miss Acklins. If you must fish between December and February, then Acklins can be a good choice.

Finding them in the mangroves is one thing, getting them out is the challenge.

The fish on Acklins see very few flies and are aggressive, so a standard selection of Bahamian bonefish flies will work well. Bring Gotchas and Charlies in size #2 to #6 in tan, cream, brown, and green; a few crab patterns like Pop's Bitters and Raghead; and a selection of Clousers. Here is also the place to break out Charley Cravin's Bonefish Junk. Since the fish are not leader shy, 16-pound fluorocarbon is fine.

Getting Around

Acklins is not an easy destination to reach and almost always involves overnight stays in Nassau.

Different airlines have flown into Spring Point from time to time, but the only regular flights that you can count on are Bahamasair's flights on Saturdays and Wednesdays. An alternative is to charter your own plane.

Bahamasair. www.bahamasair.com

There are relatively few vehicles to rent on Acklins, so it is best to have your lodge or accommodations organize a car. Both Salina Point Lodge and Ivel's B & B have cars to rent for their guests, and we have had good luck renting from **Big Brothers Car Rentals** (242-344-3297).

To the best of my knowledge there are no boats available for rent on Acklins. Since the Bight of Acklins is shallow and tricky to navigate, my recommendation is you leave the boating to an experienced guide. For the self-guided days, bring your own inflatable kayak or use a hard-shelled kayak provided by a lodge or local.

Where to Stay

It's not easy to find independent accommodations to rent on Acklins, and since there are no restaurants or fully stocked grocery stores on the island, it is best to stay at a location that offers both food and lodging.

Fedel's Acklins Outback Fishing Adventures. Fedel and Erika Johnson have opened up their home, located in Lovely Bay, to give anglers a unique home-away-from-home experience (www.acklins.com). Three guest rooms, each with two single beds, easily accommodate six anglers.

Erika has hot coffee and breakfast ready before you open your eyes and will clean your room and have your laundry washed at the end of the day. Her packed lunches hold you for the afternoon, and dinner is cooking when you get back and start swapping fish stories.

Fedel offers fully guided days or you can DIY from his excellent northern location. He has kayaks available and productive flats 250 yards from his back door.

Grey's Point Bonefish Inn. Owner Newton Williamson and his family run Grey's Point Bonefish Inn (www.greyspointbonefishinn.com), located 20 miles north of the Spring Point Airport, with the objective to provide a relaxing and memorable stay.

Six rooms accommodate up to 12 anglers, guaranteeing the personal service Grey's Point Inn prides itself upon.

Grey's offers both guided and self-guided days with two canoes and one kayak available for clients.

Oh yeah, and some of the best flats are just 100 feet from the lodge.

Ivel's Bed & Breakfast. Iral and Velma, both born and raised on Acklins, built their dream bed and breakfast in 2004 (www.ivelsbedand breakfast.com). This modern B & B is located on the water in north-central Acklins at Mason's Bay. Ivel's has four guestrooms, six suites, and a family-size cottage, easily housing 10 anglers.

Car rentals are available for guests, making this an ideal spot for those fishermen who want to hire an independent guide for a few days and then explore the island on their own the rest of the time.

All meals are available at Ivel's.

Carefree Bonefish Lodge. Felton Rolle had the self-sufficient, budget-conscious angler in mind with this newly built modest duplex cottage, located a mile and a half south of the Spring Point Airport (www.vrbo .com/261406). The cottage is best for two couples or four anglers.

Units have full kitchens, linens, towels, and utensils—but you will have to figure out where the food is coming from! A good option is to bring it with you when you come from Nassau. Talk with Felton about arranging a vehicle.

Salina Point Bonefish Lodge. This seven-room lodge was built by owner Felton Rolle in 2009 (www.vrbo.com/206778). It is at the southern end of the island set on 800 feet of white sand and comfortably accommodates 10 anglers in the five rooms.

Felton has built a do it yourself fishing lodge that can be combined with guides if requested. His unique DIY excursion includes shuttling anglers by boat to the most productive flats and then picking them up at the end of the day. For those who can't get enough fishing during the day, the flats immediately out front of the lodge can be good. There is also a rental car available to guests who want to explore other fishing locations along the southern end of Acklins.

The lodge has a full-service kitchen that provides three meals a day, including a packed lunch. If you let him know in advance, Felton will have your favorite beverages on hand.

Seven-Day Sample Trip

On a seven-day trip, I would combine guided trips to the Bight of Acklins with self-guided days to the various northern flats.

Book with Fedel Johnson, have him rent you a car, and bring five buddies. Each day two fishermen are guided by Fedel to fish the Bight of Acklins and the other four fish the DIY locations from Spring Point north.

On the DIY days, fish Relief Bay and Guana Creek, which is right behind Fedel's home, then kayak from the gazebo west of Lovely Bay to the flats and creeks both south and north. Spend one day hiking the 1.5 miles north of the yellow schoolhouse at Snug Cove and fishing the mangroves and creeks to the north. Spend another day fishing Rockers Creek south of the mail boat pier.

Each day rotate the fishermen with Fedel, giving everyone two days of guided fishing in the Bight of Acklins.

Nonfishing Activities

People go to Acklins to fish! There is virtually no tourism on Acklins other than fishing.

Spousal Rating: 2

A spousal rating of two is one of the lowest I have given as there is very little for a nonfishing spouse to do. There is no infrastructure or tourist-type activities developed, and if the fisherman has the car, the nonfisherman is stuck reading a book. Kayaking together, some snorkeling, or exploring the island by car are the few available nonfishing activities.

Among other issues, this car had no brakes, but it got us to the flats and back.

Bits and Pieces

I have rented enough cars on the Out Islands to not set the bar too high. All I ask for from my rental vehicle is that it starts, stops, and goes forward and backward. Working lights, windows, and air conditioning are just unexpected luxuries.

One of our rentals on Acklins met three of my four requirements: it started and went forward and backward, but without warning the brakes ceased to work. As the four of us contemplated one of life's mysteries (are brakes necessary?) we began the drive home. Surprisingly, we made it without incident, and when we informed the vehicle's owner of the problem, he wasn't worried in the least, "No problem, happens all the time." That is Acklins in a nutshell.

CAT ISLAND

Lay of the Land

This fishhook-shaped island, centrally located in the Bahamas chain, is 48 miles long and between 1 and 4 miles wide. It is home to Mount Alvernia,

The Hermitage on Cat Island located on Como Hill, the Bahamas' highest elevation at 206 feet

the nation's highest point at 206 feet above sea level and well worth the short hike to see a panoramic view. The mountaintop is the site of the Hermitage, built by Monsignor John C. Hawes (also known as Father Jerome) as a scaled replica of a 12th-century monastery.

The island, lying 130 miles southeast of Nassau, is home to 1,650 residents who work hard for what they have as farmers, fishermen, and tourism service providers. They live by the philosophy "What nature and the Lord will provide," making this a peaceful, gentle place.

There continues to be speculation around the name of the island, which was known as San Salvador for almost 400 years. Arthur Catt, famous British sea captain or notorious pirate (depending on whose side you are on!), may be the island's namesake. Some say the island was named for the hordes of wild cats the English found on their arrival in the 1600s. Loyalists arrived after escaping the American Revolution in 1783, developing one of the more prosperous Out Islands by building cotton plantations as the mainstay of their early economy. Abandoned homes and structures litter the landscape, left untouched to provide homes for departed spirits. These properties are never sold, sitting as testaments to past generations.

With miles of idyllic deserted beaches, rolling hills, dense green forest, and rocky cliffs, the lush island sanctuary provides an oasis for those looking to get away from modern-day living. On paper, driving the length of this laid-back island shouldn't take that long as there is a good main highway running its length from Orange Creek in the north to Hawk's Nest in the south. However, with the many small villages, friendly people, and beaches to visit, it is worth taking some time to see it all!

Five minutes south of Orange Creek is Arthur's Town, the government headquarters in the north. With a population of about 400, there is a police station, airport, clinic, and some small grocery stores. Stop in at Pat Rolle's Cookie House Bakery, an institution on the island, for something yummy or to learn about the area. Driving 15 miles south you enter Bennett's Harbour, one of the area's oldest settlements. Centrally located Fernandez Bay leads on to the New Bight Airport and New Bight settlement, which has a grocery store, liquor store, service station, and car rentals. This is also where you catch the trail to Mount Alvernia and the Hermitage.

Old Bight is four miles south, and from here you can drive to Port Howe on the east or travel west along the stunning coastline to Devil's Point. Nurse-staffed clinics are in Arthur's Town, Smith Bay, and Old Bight. There is one commercial bank just north of Fernandez Bay, and though the larger settlements have grocery stores, fresh supplies can get low if the mail boat hasn't made its regular trip to the island. Credit cards are not widely accepted except at lodges and hotels. Confirm that your accommodations have wi-fi or you may be checking emails in the Bahamas Tel parking lot—like I did!

Where to Fish

Cat Island is one of those locations where there are more places to fish than you might have heard. With the exception of two creek systems, all the fishing hot spots can be reached by car.

It takes a couple of hours to drive the length of the island, so it is best to pick your accommodations close to where you want to fish.

Northern Cat Island

Orange Creek. This is one of the better-known areas on Cat Island to fish. Access is simple and there are always fish there. Famed local

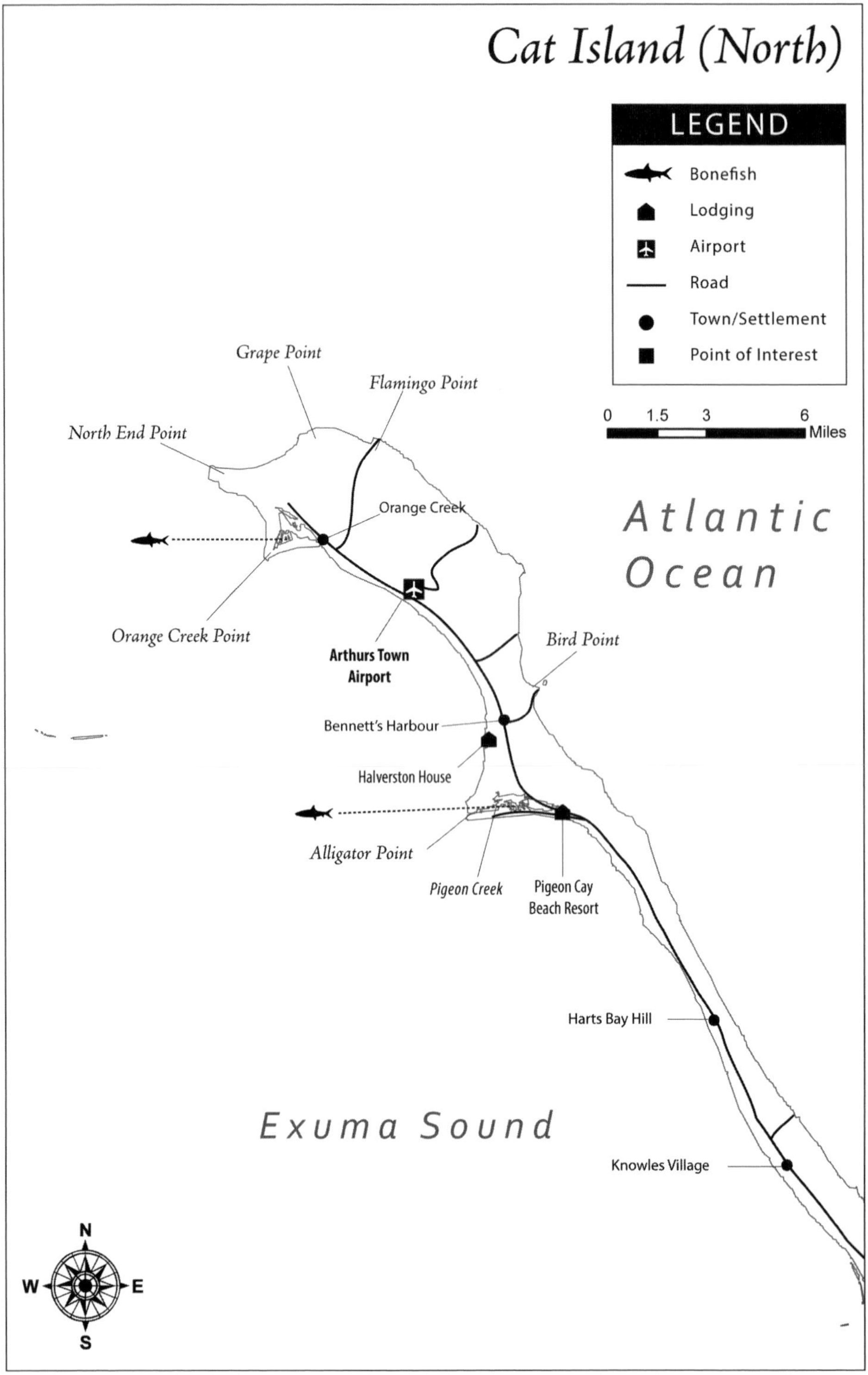

Cat Island (North)

LEGEND

Bonefish
Lodging
Airport
Road
Town/Settlement
Point of Interest

0   1.5   3   6
                 Miles

Grape Point

Flamingo Point

North End Point

Orange Creek

Atlantic Ocean

Orange Creek Point

Bird Point

Arthurs Town Airport

Bennett's Harbour

Halverston House

Alligator Point

Pigeon Creek

Pigeon Cay Beach Resort

Exuma Sound

Harts Bay Hill

Knowles Village

N
W   E
S

Rod Hamilton Design 2014

School of fish waiting for my Greg's Flats Fly (Photo courtesy of Pat Ford)

guide Willard Cleare told me he favored fishing an incoming tide right through to the high. At high tide the fish seem to roam the flats instead of moving into the mangroves. Follow the main highway to Orange Creek Settlement, and after passing the Orange Creek Inn you will see the creek entrance on your left. Park the car anywhere along the road and step onto the flats. This isn't a large system, but it's big enough for three fishermen to comfortably spread out.

Bennett's Creek. This beautiful creek takes a bit of work to get to, but is worth the effort. The best way to reach it is to take the short road to the main cement dock in Bennett's Harbour. Launch a kayak on the incoming tide and paddle 15 minutes up the creek to the point where it widens out. From here you can walk and wade for the rest of the day, exiting on the low tide. The creek entrance is big and a large volume of water enters and leaves on each tide, along with a bunch of bonefish that don't see many flies. If you know what you are doing, there is a channel that connects Bennett's Creek and Pigeon Creek.

Pigeon Creek. This creek lies south of Bennett's Creek with its entrance to the ocean at Alligator Point. It's a perfect creek and flat for the walk-and-wade angler—easy to get to with a nice firm bottom, and the fish have a regular routine that is easy to figure out. There are two ways to access the creek; the first is to take a left off the main highway on the road to Pigeon Cay. Drive past the Pigeon Cay Beach Club, which is an excellent place to stay, and continue to the end of the road. Park here and take the short trail to the creek with the widest part of the flat in front of you. The second access point is along the main highway before reaching Thurston Hill. The creek is on the left (when heading north), and there are a couple of points to walk from the road to the water. At high tide the fish scatter throughout the flat and into the mangroves. On the incoming and outgoing tides they use the deeper channel on the far northern shore against the limestone rock as their highway.

North Shore. There are several places to fish on the north shore that are mainly unexplored and receive virtually no attention. I will leave this area up to the more adventuresome, but it can be reached from several roads including the road at Arthur's Town Airport.

Central Cat Island

Smith Bay. Located slightly north of Fernandez Bay, this is a popular spot and easy to get to. If you are staying at Island HoppInn, it's just a matter of walking out your back door to the south end of the bay. Otherwise, park beside the highway south of the government dock and walk in from there. Most people prefer the southern end of Smith Bay, but there are nice flats on the north end as well. These fish see a little more pressure, so long leaders and lighter flies are necessary. At high tide the fish make it into the mangroves, so I would advise fishing on the low and incoming tides.

Fernandez Bay Creek. On the southern end of Fernandez Bay is a large, complex creek system with two ocean entrances. The first opening is immediately south of the beach and can be reached by walking down the beach and then into the creek. The bottom is soft, so I prefer to stay on the rocks and walk the perimeter until I'm well into the creek. The flats dry completely at low tide, making it necessary to time the tide correctly. My preferred way to fish this system, which is admittedly more difficult, is to kayak from the Fernandez Bay beach around the point to the southern opening. Paddle as far up the creek as you can go and start fishing from there. This is a much harder fishing day as the paddle is about 1.5 miles, but it's worth it.

Musgrove Creek. I'm not sure if this is really the name of the creek; like many places in the Bahamas it has two or three names. To get there use the New Bight Airport road as a marker and take the side road to the water 1.8 miles south of the airport. Once on the access road, turn right before crossing the small bridge and follow it to the creek mouth. This small, intimate creek always has fish on the low and incoming tides but is only large enough for one or two fishermen. The best approach is to fish the mouth at low tide and walk up the creek from the mouth toward the little bridge on the creek's top end. The creek empties into a small bay that also has cruising bones on low tide and as the tide turns. On the northern end of the bay is another small creek system. I have only fished the mouth at low tide and not explored farther up.

Armbrister Creek, Bottom End. This is one of my favorite places to fish, as it's a long creek with a wonderful mangrove ecosystem along both shores and the top end. There are plenty of places for the fish to hide, so it's best to intercept them on the way in and out. Access to the creek is at two different locations. First, continuing south on the main highway, you'll reach the turn to Pilot Harbor approximately six miles south of the airport, before reaching Moss Town. Follow the road around to the mouth of Armbrister Creek to fish the beautiful ocean flat out front. This is the perfect spot to intercept fish on the outgoing tide. Continue to drive along the side of the creek, cross the culvert, and look for the short road on the right. Park where you can and step into the creek here. There is excellent fishing from this point up to the old dilapidated rock road.

The second access point is back on the main highway continuing south to Old Bight.

Armbrister Creek, Upper End. The road to this area is across the street from the Old Bight Primary School, approximately 8.2 miles from the airport. Driving down the road you cross the creek and if you keep going straight can park at one of Cat Island's most beautiful beaches. If you are there to fish, take the dirt road right (just before the beach) and follow the creek system until you find the abandoned stone road on your right. Park here and walk out the road to where it has collapsed. Enter the creek and fish either north or south depending on the tide.

Joe's Sound. This sound is on the same road as Armbrister Creek, but instead of turning right at the beach turn left. Once you park the car,

A pair of "happy" bonefish (Photo courtesy of Pat Ford)

walk as far as possible then cut across the mangroves to the creek. It's not easy walking at first and I have sunk up to my knees, but the bottom gets firmer once you reach the open water.

Southern Cat Island

Frankfort Creek. Located on the southern end of the island, inside Springfield Bay, Frankfort Creek is one of the more popular systems on Cat Island. It's reached by driving south on the main highway toward Devil's Point. When you reach the roundabout, find the short road with a dilapidated building on the southern portion of the roundabout. Park at the building and follow the well-used trail onto the flat. It's a large area and best fished on the lower and incoming tides. Once the tide reaches midway or higher, the fish spread out and head into the mangroves. The entrance to Springfield Bay is to the left, which is the direction to head on the low tide. The fish congregate toward the opening and then feed back into the creek on the incoming tide.

Cutlass Bay. As you head toward Port Howe, Cutlass Bay, a nice oceanside sandy beach with cruising fish on a low tide, is on the right.

Flamingo Bay. A little farther east of Cutlass Bay lies Flamingo Bay. This small beach has some good fishing at low tide.

Port Howe. Where the road takes a hard left in Port Howe, park beside the old Deveaux Plantation building and walk to the oceanside flats. These are very good flats and always produce fish. It is best to walk to the left and fish the north corner.

Winding Bay and Little Winding Bay. I have it on good authority that both of these bays are excellent, but I have never fished them. Access is problematic unless you have a boat. Little Winding Bay can be reached at low tide by walking the beach south from the Greenwood Beach Resort; according to the *Cat Island Visitors Guide*, there are "two natural hiking trails" to the bays. I suspect they are part of the trails to the plantation ruins in the area but I've never been on them.

Greenwood Beach Resort Beach. If you are staying at this resort, there is some limited bonefishing along the beach.

French's Bay. Located at Devil's Point, this stunning white-sand beach has some excellent fishing in the eastern corner.

Hawks Nest Beach. Before reaching Devil's Point take the road north toward Hawks Nest Resort and Marina. Once you have crossed the island, a sign will point to the left down a potholed dirt road toward Hawks Nest Resort. Continue to drive straight instead of taking the road to the resort. This is a beautiful long beach with plenty of bonefish on the incoming tide.

Hawks Nest Creek. Just before reaching Hawks Nest Resort you will begin seeing the creek system on your left. This is a large system that holds lots of fish. I prefer to fish more toward the ocean entrance, but there are a number of spots to wade throughout the entire system.

Fishing Information

The fishing on Cat Island is a little different than on some of the more famous Bahamian islands. There are no large oceanside flats to speak of, and most of the fishing is concentrated in the creeks. There are plenty of places to choose from and lots of variation to keep anglers happy for a solid couple of weeks. Even though the fishing is very good, there doesn't seem to be much pressure. The fish readily take a fly and, other than Pigeon Creek and Smith Bay, I have not sensed that the fish have seen many anglers. Virtually every fishing location can be reached by car, making for an easy holiday. The usual box of flies will work, so there is no need to get too specialized. Overall, I lean toward a size #4 tan Gotcha or Orange Butt Bunny fly with rubber legs. One thing about fishing the creeks, you can almost always get out of the severe ocean winds by getting back into the creeks. That's a nice break, especially if you're new to bonefishing.

There are several local guides on the island:

Willard Cleare. orangecreekinn@yahoo.com

Nathaniel Gilbert. tangobeachcottages@yahoo.com

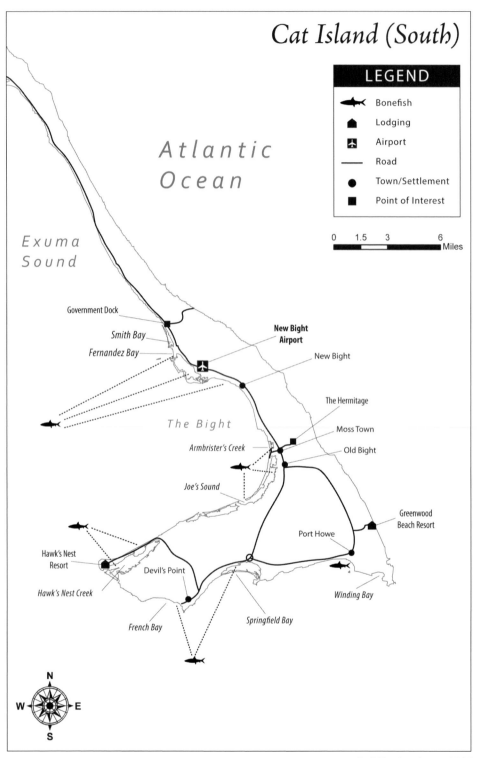

Cat Island (South)

LEGEND

Bonefish
Lodging
Airport
Road
Town/Settlement
Point of Interest

0   1.5   3   6
                  Miles

Atlantic
Ocean

Exuma
Sound

Government Dock
Smith Bay
Fernandez Bay

New Bight
Airport

New Bight

The Hermitage

Moss Town

Armbrister's Creek

Old Bight

The Bight

Joe's Sound

Greenwood
Beach Resort

Port Howe

Hawk's Nest
Resort

Devil's Point

Hawk's Nest Creek

French Bay

Springfield Bay

Winding Bay

N
W   E
S

Rod Hamilton Design 2014

Where to Stay

There are a number of quality resorts to choose from along with a variety of houses and cottages. Some of the homes come with cars and kayaks, so be sure to ask. Check out websites like VRBO and HomeAway for available private rentals.

Orange Creek Inn has 16 motel style rooms, all with kitchenettes and air conditioning (www.orangecreekbahamas.com). It is clean, comfortable, affordable, and adjacent to a spectacular five-mile deserted beach. It's also within 10 minutes of two restaurants and next door to a grocery store. Some units have a small kitchen.

Pigeon Cay Beach Club is on northern Cat Island (www.pigeoncay bahamas.com). This club has seven deluxe cottages steps away from the beach. Located one mile off the main road below Arthur's Town Airport, they will stock your fridge if you want to cook for yourself, or they are happy to cook all meals! Bikes, kayaks, and canoes are available for guests to use.

Halvorson House Villa Resort, located in Bennett's Harbour, offers five comfortable, clean bungalows steps from a pristine white sandy beach (www.halvorsonhouse.com). Matt and Sooner Halvorson have built a beautiful family-friendly property complete with a Kid's Club for the young (and old!) that is also great for couples. The open kitchen serves meals made to order from a variety of local and international dishes, or you may choose to eat out. All villas have window screens, A/C, Egyptian cotton sheets, and plush bath towels. Kayaks, paddleboards, bikes, and snorkeling equipment are complimentary for your enjoyment.

Island HoppInn is situated on beautiful Fernandez Bay (www. islandhoppinn.com). Owner Cathleen Perdok has one mission, to spoil her guests! Offering one- or two-bedroom suites equipped with A/C, a queen bed, hide-a-bed couch, microwave, and fridge, this intimate resort is perfect for families or couples. Enjoy a delicious meal or beverage served at their new tiki bar overlooking the crystal blue ocean. Kayaks, inflatable boats, and many other "water toys" are included.

Greenwood Beach Resort, an oasis on the water, has been owned and operated by the Illing family for over 20 years (www.grenwood-beachresort.com). Most of the 16 rooms at this resort have ocean views only 150 feet from the beach, and it offers a freshwater pool, cozy dining room, and an honor system bar.

Hawks Nest Resort and Marina offers recently remodeled beachfront rooms on the remote southwest side of the island (www.hawks-nest.com). Three-bedroom homes are available for weekly rental. The property also has the Dining Room for meals and the Club Bar.

Getting Around

The two airports on Cat Island are Arthur's Town Airport (ATC) in the north and New Bight Airport (TBI) located centrally.

Sky Bahamas has scheduled flights most days from Nassau to Arthur's Town and New Bight Airport and Bahamasair flies daily except for Wednesdays.

United Airlines offers scheduled flights from Fort Lauderdale and Miami to both airports on Cat Island.

Sky Bahamas. www.skybahamas.net

Bahamasair. www.bahamasair.com

United. www.united.com

When arranging your accommodations, ask about transportation to and from the hotel, rental property, and airport.

Car rentals range from $80 to $100 per day. Try one of the following:

Gilbert's. (242) 342-3011

New Bight Car Rentals. (242) 342-3014

Taxis are available in most major settlements and routinely stationed at the airports to meet incoming flights.

Seven-Day Sample Trip

Book the week at the centrally located Island HoppInn on spectacular Fernandez Bay. Before going to bed on your arrival day, walk out the back door for a couple hours of fishing on Smith Bay. Hire Willard Cleare for the first full day of fishing on Orange Creek on the north end of the island; this is his home turf and nobody knows the creek like he does. On the second day, drive north past the Pigeon Cay Beach Resort and spend the day fishing Pigeon Creek. On the third day, fish Armbrister Creek on the outgoing tide from Pilot Harbour up the creek to the old stone causeway. The fourth day, park at the roundabout and fish the creek on the incoming tide as the bones filter onto the large flat. Day five, head over to the Greenwood Beach Resort and fish Cutlass Bay, Flamingo Bay, and the ocean flats of Port Howe. Last day, head south to Hawks Nest Creek and fish during the low and incoming tide. At high tide head to the beach at Hawks Nest for the cruising bones. If you have time before your flight leaves, walk back to Smith Bay for a couple of hours to catch the fish you missed on day one.

Spousal Rating: 7

Cat Island is a quiet place with beautiful beaches and if the nonfishermen in the group just want to chill, this island is perfect.

Nonfishing Activities

You can find many things to do on Cat Island, but it won't be in the form of nightlife! This island is perfect for travelers content to create their own sightseeing map, choosing from diving or snorkeling around blue holes, kayaking, hiking, and biking, all in a relaxed atmosphere! The beaches are breathtaking. Some have white sand, others are pink—but whatever the color, crowds are not an issue. The best beaches are found on the leeward side. Get a history lesson at the Columbus World Museum in Knowles or simply strike up a conversation with any longtime resident, many of whom love sharing stories that probably include their ancestors!

Visit the Hermitage at the top of Mount Alvernia, located three and a half miles south of the New Bight Airport. The monastery was built by Father Jerome, a world-famous architect and priest who came to Cat Island in 1939 seeking solitude. He built at least four churches, a school, a convent, and a clinic on Cat Island but is perhaps best known for his tribute to St. Francis of Assisi built on Comer Hill, renamed Mount Alvernia.

Bits and Pieces

Driving with me when I'm exploring is at best boring and at worst torture. I drive down every dirt road and goat path in hopes of finding the next fishing hole. My "go to" formula is nine roads to nowhere for every road to somewhere. My wife and I were on one of those journeys when I turned onto a sand road with my usual refrain, "Let's see where this goes." At the end of the road, we were looking at a beautiful compound of buildings nestled on the kind of beach you only see in magazines. Thinking it might be rental accommodations, I went up to the door and was greeted by a big "hello" and "come on in." Turned out we were at somebody's home, and they could not have been more welcoming or gracious. That is how the people are on Cat Island. In no time, a couple of retirees from Connecticut were showing us around their beautiful new home. We spent an hour with them, and it flew by like minutes. They weren't fishermen but did happen to mention a spot where they had seen another person fishing. I stopped by the location, took a quick look, and saw two large bonefish cruising the mangroves. Went back to the car, tied on a Bonefish Junk, made one cast, and a beautiful seven-pound Cat Island bonefish was smiling for the camera. You never know what's down an old dirt road!

ELEUTHERA

Lay of the Land

Eleuthera is a long, slender 110-mile track ending in the shape of a Y, which is also known as the "whale's tail"! Referred to as the birthplace of the Bahamas, it is called Citagoo by the locals. The terrain is a mixture of white-faced cliffs, coral sand beaches, rolling green hills, and valleys dotted with lakes. The average width of the island is no more than two miles at any point, ensuring you will always be near the water. At its closest point in the northeast, Eleuthera is just 30 miles from Nassau. The 11,000 residents are largely farmers, fishermen, and shopkeepers, servicing an economy based on fishing, boating, and tourism. It's not a flashy place, and visitors will feel the remoteness of the island yet know they are welcomed here by the friendly locals. It takes about three and a half hours to drive the good interconnected highway end to end, with most points along the way accessible.

Eleuthera, pronounced "e-loo-ther-uh" and taken from the Greek word meaning freedom, was founded in 1648 and became the first permanent settlement in the Bahamas. Captain William Sayle, a former governor of Bermuda, led a group seeking religious freedom here, landing in Governor's Harbour. Bringing their slaves, these loyalists built an early economy based on agriculture, shipbuilding, and salvaging shipwrecks off

Haynes Library in Governor's Harbour, Eleuthera

the reefs. Pineapples have been grown in the rocky soil since the early 1800s and the crop remains an important export along with tomatoes, citrus fruits, and corn.

Spanish Wells, located on St. George's Cay, is off the northern tip of Eleuthera and is the perfect place to stay if you are exploring the north. A short ferry ride gets you to this vibrant fishing village, where harvesting the Bahamian lobster, or crawfish, and servicing the many boaters passing through help the settlement thrive.

From the North Eleuthera Airport (one of three on the island) take a five-minute taxi ride to the ferry dock and another five-minute boat ride to get to historic Dunmore Town on Harbour Island. This is one of the oldest settlements in the Bahamas and it's easy to see brightly colored homes, activity at the government dock, and the Loyalist Cottage, all on a 20-minute walk!

Looking for a place to get pampered in the Bahamas? Harbour Island can deliver. Rated as having one of the best beaches in the Bahamas, the island is known for its three and a half miles of hard-packed, picture-perfect pink sand. Called "Briland" by the residents, this three-mile-long cay offers a wide variety of accommodations, restaurants, galleries, and quaint shopping. This is the place to be if the trip is all about the family and a little DIY fishing. Continuing south you will pass Upper Bogue and Lower Bogue just before reaching the stunning Glass Window Bridge, one of Eleuthera's more popular attractions. Given the name by sailors because they could see under the naturally formed bridge of rock, it connects North Eleuthera to the southern part of the island. Violent seas washed this natural wonder away in the early 1900s, and it has now been replaced by a manmade structure where you can see the incredible contrast where the churning dark blue Atlantic Ocean meets the calm turquoise waters of the Caribbean Sea. Often referred to as "the narrowest place on earth," it is located north of Gregory Town, a quiet settlement just two miles away from Surfer's Beach.

Governor's Harbour, the commercial hub of Eleuthera found in the north-central region of the island, is the perfect place to stock up on groceries and other supplies. You will find a post office, the telephone office, a government medical clinic, banks, and car rentals. Taking the Queen's Highway south, pass through the settlements of South Palmetto Point, Savannah Sound, and Tarpum Bay to reach Rock Sound, which offers the best grocery and hardware store on the island. It also has good gas supplies but lacks accommodations and restaurant options.

The top of the "whale's tail" at the southern end of Eleuthera is Deep Creek, where most people are fishermen or employed by the Cape Eleuthera Institute, also known as the Island School. The creek is actually a shallow tidal creek that empties at low tide, with the term "Deep" used as it is in the Deep South. Take the time to tour the Cape Eleuthera Institute, a facility that promotes connecting people and the environment. Also nearby by is the Cape Eleuthera Resort and Yacht Club.

Where to Fish

Eleuthera is a long island, and if your trip is not properly planned you can spend a good portion of it in the car. I prefer to stay centrally in places like North Palmetto or Governor's Harbour, keeping the drives either north or south to an hour at most.

Eleuthera Island (North)

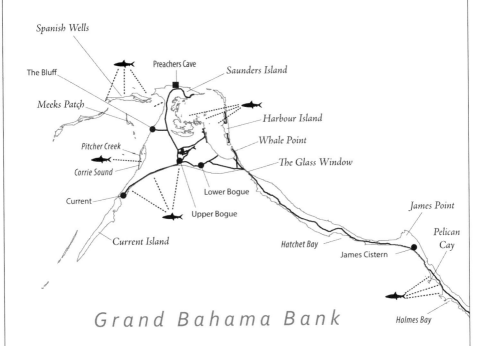

Spanish Wells

Preachers Cave

Saunders Island

The Bluff

Meeks Patch

Harbour Island

Pitcher Creek

Whale Point

Corrie Sound

The Glass Window

Current

Lower Bogue

Upper Bogue

James Point

Current Island

Pelican Cay

Hatchet Bay

James Cistern

Holmes Bay

Grand Bahama Bank

LEGEND

- 🐟 Bonefish
- ⌂ Lodging
- ✈ Airport
- — Road
- ● Town/Settlement
- ■ Point of Interest

0   2.5   5   10
Miles

N
W   E
S

Rod Hamilton Design 2014

Governor's Harbour, North

Governor's Harbour. As they say, this location "is a fun place to visit but wouldn't want to fish there." There's always a nice school of fish in the harbor, but they get harassed regularly and are tough to catch. The fishing can be very frustrating and it's an unusual setting. Boats and local fishermen are always around, the sound of cars driving past is constant, and curious tourists watch to see how you're doing. These fish have seen every fly known to man, but rumor has it the Gummy Minnow is the way to go.

Levi Island and Balara Bay. On your way north from Governor's Harbour, look for the Worker's House on the right and then turn left at Nixon's Auto Repair. This is a nice rocky flat with a mixture of grass and sand, best fished at low tide. Once a quality fishing area, it has received a lot of pressure over the last 10 years.

Alabaster Bay. Just south of the airport, the Queen's Highway touches Alabaster Bay. The crescent-shaped beach has some bones cruising the shore at low tide. The fishing is not good enough to make an entire day of it but should be fished along with the Airport Flats at Pelican Cay.

Pelican Cay, Airport Flat. This used to be an excellent flat but seems to be on most anglers' rotations, making the fish wary and difficult to catch. There are two accesses to the flat; the first is from Alabaster Bay to the south and the second is along the northern airport fence line.

Gregory Town Cove. This settlement is on the way north past Hatchet Bay. The small town has a beautiful little harbor that often holds a school of bones at low tide. It's a nice place to visit and well worth pulling over and scanning the bottom before moving on.

Twin Sisters Beach. Before reaching the Glass Bridge, pass Goulding Cay Point and you will then see Twin Sisters Beach. If the wind is not coming in from the west, there are a couple of nice flats to fish for a few hours.

Bottom Harbour. North of the Glass Bridge take the road right to Whale Point and Bottom Harbour. There is a good flat on the south end of Bottom Harbor.

Ferry Dock, North. Approaching the ferry dock to Harbour Island, take the road to the north and follow it to the end. From here, there is a nice series of flats that you can reach by walking along the beach. Another option is to put your kayak in and make the 0.6-mile paddle to the large flat and creek systems around the point. Once around the point, the flats and creek lie out in front of you to the west and north. The total paddle to get into good flats is about one mile.

Harbour Island. There are a couple of good flats here. The first is slightly north of town on the leeward side and it almost always has fish on it. As you might expect, these fish receive a significant amount of pressure, but they are catchable. The next flat is located at the northern tip of Harbour Island on the northwest side. This is a good flat but really only wadeable at low tide.

James Bay. The road to the Spanish Wells ferry hugs gorgeous James Bay. Fishing is decent along the entire shore, but the best fishing is north toward the Spanish Wells ferry dock.

Bluff Settlement. South of the settlement is one of the better creek systems on Eleuthera, but it is difficult to get to. As a self-guided angler you need to launch a kayak and paddle south along the shore for just over a mile. If the wind is down it's a nice paddle and well worth the effort.

Current Settlement. The road follows the water from Lower Bogue to the settlement. Along the way are numerous places to pull off and fish, but the best is closer to Current at Upper Cove Beach. This is a spectacular beach that provides good fishing at low tide.

Governor's Harbour, South

Cupids Cay. This is located on the other side of the peninsula from Governor's Harbour and can be reached by parking right beside the ocean flat off Bay Street or walking over from Governor's Harbour.

Pau Pau Bay. South of Governor's Harbour and across the Queen's Highway from North Palmetto is Pau Pau Road. Follow it to the end where it meets Pau Pau Bay and you will usually find a school of bones.

South Palmetto Bay. Five miles south of Governor's Harbour is North Palmetto on your left (or the Atlantic side), and the road to South Palmetto is on your right (the Exuma Sound side). Follow the road to the South Palmetto Bay pier where you can find bones on either side.

Ten Bay. To get to Ten Bay drive 3.7 miles south of the Palmetto Point crossroads and turn right at the small Beach Access sign. This beach has something for every member of the family, and you can combine lounging, snorkeling, swimming, and fishing in one place. Bones tend to be at either end of the bay, with some large barracudas patrolling the middle.

Savannah Sound, North. This flat is one of the more popular DIY flats in the Bahamas. Most people know about it, many have fished it, and all have cursed it. These fish graduated from Harvard and have brought more than one angler to tears. I still give it a try once each trip because it is such a great test, but even when you think you have it figured out, the catch rate is closer to two fish than ten. The nice thing is there are always fish present and you will always get a cast; it's just difficult to hook up. They don't like stripped flies, so it's very long leaders and superlight flies made with materials that move on their own in the current. Good luck!

Savannah Sound, South. The flats of Savannah Sound are large, extending south from the settlement for three miles. I have kayaked it all and find there are sections of Savannah Sound that fish significantly better than the well-known flat directly in front of the park. To get to the southern flats, drive through the settlement and look for a dirt road heading to the left 1.85 miles south of the road to Windermere Island. Follow this road to the water and launch a kayak. It's a short paddle over to Windermere Island where you will find some great flats against the shore. The fish move in and out of the mangroves on each tide.

Tarpum Bay. Continuing south, you come to the small fishing village of Tarpum Bay. There are two fishing locations here where you can find shoreline cruisers. Find the first by walking north along the beach, and the second is between the two docks right in town.

Winding Bay. Heading out of Tarpum Bay, turn left at the gas station and you're on the road to Winding Bay. There are several access points, but since the fish are located at both the north and south ends, access in the middle is as good as any.

Half Sound. Since you found Winding Bay, continue south along the same road past the primitive boat launch until you reach the road's end. To the left is a nice opening to the ocean with a good flat and creek in front, and to the right (west) are the mangroves and indents where the fish like to dig out food. Half Sound is well worth fishing on the low and incoming tides.

Starved Creek and Poison Point. On the way through Rock Sound remember to get gas, then measure three miles from where the road leaves the bay and heads inland. At this point there is a gravel road going north that runs out to the end of Poison Point. The road is gated after one mile, so park here. The water on the north side is Starved Creek, which can be very good at times on the incoming tide. Directly ahead is Poison Point and to the left (south) of the point is a very good bay with a flat. The bay is a little difficult to get to because you're walking over treacherous "death rock" and through the mangroves; still, it's an excellent flat to fish.

Jack Bay. Less than two miles from the Starved Creek Road is a road to the left that leads to Cotton and Jack Bays. Jack Bay can be quite good, with a nice sand beach and a clear delineation where the mottled bottom of turtle grass meets the white-sand bottom. You will often see fish weaving in and out from the grass onto the sand.

Cotton Bay. South of the deserted marina and golf course, another defunct Bahamian dream, is Cotton Bay. I've never been particularly successful here but have heard it can be good at times.

Davis Harbour. Pass through Green Castle and at the T in the road you will find Waterford Settlement. Park on the left at Davis Harbour Marina where there always seems to be a school of small bones in the deep channel.

Waterford Creek. Back in the car, continue north to the end of the spit on the road from the marina, but don't get on the main highway. This is the entrance to Waterford Creek.

Rocky Creek. South of the T and Davis Harbour is Rocky Creek, another good system that deserves attention.

Princess Cay Creek. At Bannerman Town you will begin to see glimpses of cruise ships. The Princess Cruise Line has bought some property here where they anchor and ferry passengers back and forth to the beach. The general public is not allowed inside their gates but the juxtaposition of the real Eleuthera on one side of the fence and "Disneyland" on the other side is something to behold. At the entrance to the Princess Cay beach is a bridge with a small flat to the south that fishes well but is difficult walking. I prefer the much larger creek system to the north that can be excellent. The northern flats can be accessed farther up the road by parking at the abandoned church.

Lighthouse Beach. A truly spectacular beach waits for you at the end of this very long four-wheel-drive road. Though it holds bonefish, it's quite a distance and is more of a place to explore, swim, and experience the beauty of Eleuthera than to fish.

Plum Creek. Back at the T, head north toward Deep Creek and Cape Eleuthera. Two miles from the T is a dirt road to the left running beside a church. Follow this road across the stone causeway and you will see a good access point at the southern portion of Deep Creek on your right. Continue on until the road reaches the ocean and you are at the mouth of Plum Creek. The wading can be tough inside the creek, but the fish enter and leave the creek on each tide. The mouth and beach flat are easy to wade and that's where you find the fish at dead low tide.

Deep Creek. You can enter Deep Creek either from the south (see Plum Creek) or from the settlement of Deep Creek. There is a rock jetty to drive and walk out onto, or you can see from the road quite a number of other places to access the flats. Ask in town and someone will direct you to a path leading to the flats. Deep Creek gets some attention, but it's so far away from the tourist areas of Eleuthera that it gets fished less often than Savannah Sound. The fish move in and out of this very large creek on each tide, but it takes a while to figure it out.

Broad Creek. At Deep Creek the road cuts across the island and emerges on the opposite side at Broad Creek. Take the first right to the beach and walk south to Broad Creek. There is a nice flat out front, and the fish enter and leave the creek on each tide.

Pear Bay. Heading north toward Cape Eleuthera, the road touches the water at Pear Bay, a beautiful oceanside flat that fishes well at low tide.

Fishing Information

The tides on Eleuthera can be either your greatest allies or biggest enemies. The tide on the ocean side is two hours earlier than the tide on the leeward side, and the tides north and south can vary just as much. What that means is that once you understand them, you can fish a quality low tide and incoming tide on the ocean side, then jump over to the leeward side and fish the same tide. Of course, if you haven't figured out the tides, you may fish a crappy high tide on one side and repeat the same mistake on the other. My advice is to download a tide chart from the Internet in advance and before arriving use it to plot your week's fishing.

Ten years ago the self-guided fishing on Eleuthera was terrific. The great fishing, combined with the beautiful beaches, quality rentals, and ease of getting around, made it an ideal location for fishermen and nonfishing partners alike. Today it is still a beautiful place to go, but the fishing has become significantly more difficult. The trick is to get off the

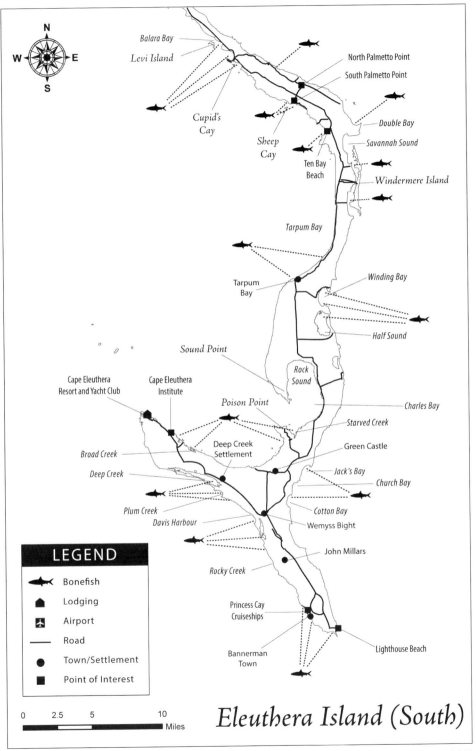

Eleuthera Island (South)

Rod Hamilton Design 2014

beaten path, put in the extra effort, and don't fish where everyone else does. There are still great places on Eleuthera to fish and honey holes ready to be found.

Places like Governor's Harbour, Airport Flats, Ten Bay, and Savannah Sound are all beautiful and hold fish. The trick to having success is to lengthen the leader, make sure the last four feet are fluorocarbon, downsize the tippet to eight-pound, and use smaller and lighter flies that don't "plop." Try to think outside the box and use flies the fish may not have seen and materials that move by themselves with the current. These fish don't like stripped Charlies.

I prefer the southern section of Eleuthera ranging from Tarpum Creek to both ends of the "whale tail."

Fly selection on Eleuthera is a little different than the conventional Bahamian destination. For the smart fish make sure you downsize to #8 to #10. Have some nonweighted and deer-hair patterns that land softly, as well as an array of flies tied with material that moves on its own, including rabbit, rubber legs, fin coon, and marabou. Don't forget the Gummy Fly for Governor's Harbour. For other areas conventional choices work, mostly in size #6, like Greg's Flats Fly, Orange Butt Bunny, and Pop's Bitters.

Though Eleuthera is primarily a DIY destination, there are some quality guides available.

Stuart Cleare, Harbour Island. (242) 333-2072
Paul Petty, Governor's Harbour. (242)-332-2963
Alfred McKinney Jr., Deep Creek. (242)-334-8184

There are a couple of places in the north where a kayak is necessary, but I haven't needed one either centrally or in the south. If you want to rent a kayak, Rodney Pinder of Palmetto Point has them available.

Rodney Pinder's Kayak Rentals. (242) 332-1891

Where to Stay

There are options available including beautiful beachfront homes, smaller hotels offering comfortable and clean accommodations, resorts that can deliver a spa experience, and modest cottages. Honor your budget and then determine where you want to be. Eleuthera is a long island and it might get a little old to be in the north and discover you are mostly fishing in the south! If transportation is an issue, something central might be better. HomeAway and VRBO are loaded with places to rent throughout the island. This is one place you won't have any trouble finding what you want.

The Pink Sands, situated on the north end, will give you the ultimate pampered hotel experience (www.pinksandsresort.com).

The Rainbow Inn is a small oceanfront resort in Central Eleuthera suitable for families, couples, or hardcore anglers (www.rainbowinn.com).

Coco de Mama is just minutes from Governor's Harbour Airport on the lee side of the island (www.cocodimama.com).

The Duck Inn is another great bet in this area (www.duckinncottages .com).

Getting Around

With three airports servicing the island, which one you should fly into is a good question! Land at North Eleuthera Airport (ELH) if your final destination is Harbour Island or Gregory Town. Governor's Harbour (GHB) is the choice if you are going to Palmetto Bay, Savannah Sound, or Tarpum Bay. And use the Rock Sound Airport (RSD) for destinations in the south, such as Rock Sound and Deep Creek.

Eleuthera is one of the easiest Bahamian islands to reach, so many commercial carriers including US Airways, American Airlines, Continental, and Silver Airways service the island. Direct flights are available from Fort Lauderdale and Miami, Florida, or get there via Nassau.

Bahamasair. www.bahamasair.com

Pineapple Air. www.pineappleair.com

To really see the island, renting a car is a must. The two-lane Queen's Highway is in pretty good shape, with the occasional rough spot. It will take you from one end of Eleuthera to the other. Side roads are a different matter and can range from fully paved to four-wheel-drive only. It is best to arrange your car rental in advance from a company located at one of the airports. Vehicles are typically over 10 years old with varying rates.

Golf carts rented by the hour or for the day are a good way to get around in places like Spanish Wells or Harbour Island. Locate Harbourside Golf Cart Rentals in Spanish Wells and choose from a number of rentals in Harbour Island. Find kayak or bike rentals in larger settlements or inquire when booking accommodations about what is available.

Seven-Day Sample Trip

Staying in North Palmetto, fish Pau Pau, South Palmetto, and Ten Bay on the first day, catching the outgoing tide through low tide and halfway through the incoming. Then at the end of the day head over to Savannah Sound where the fish will humble and humiliate you, providing the reason you need to open the scotch. The next morning head to Tarpum Bay, checking to see if the fish are around the two piers. If so, spend an hour fishing, then move on to Winding Bay. Fish both ends of the bay, then head over to Half Sound for the low and incoming tides. On day three, drive to Starved Creek to fish the creek from well into the mangroves to the ocean and back. Then fish the bay on the west side of Poison Point. On day four, fish the Princess Cay creek systems, focusing primarily on the northern section, and then move slightly north to fish Rocky Creek and Waterford Creek. Day five is back down to the whale's tail to fish Plum and Deep creeks, then cross the island to Broad Creek. Day six is a drive north to see the countryside and shake it up a little. Hit Twin Sisters Beach where you can check out the Glass Bridge, then go to Bottom Harbour and finish at Upper Cove Beach in Current Settlement. If you have time on the last day, make a quick run back down to Savannah Sound. You've been thinking about those fish since they schooled you on the first night, so give it one more try before jumping on the plane.

Spousal Rating: 7

The spousal rating changes considerably on Eleuthera as you head south. Harbour Island on the north end of the island is fantastic and you can't get a much better tropical paradise with luxury accommodations. The area around Governor's Harbour has some beautiful beaches, offers some nice single-family homes to rent, and is an ideal location from which to explore the island with the family and do some fishing. Rock Sound's spousal rating plunges and I would stay here only with a group of fishermen.

Nonfishing Activities

Bike, hike, kayak, or walk—there are endless ways to explore and enjoy Eleuthera! Starting with the beautiful beaches, walk, swim, snorkel, or read a book—it's up to you. Feeling energetic? Try surfing near Gregory Town in the north-central location of Surfer's Beach or dive the tidal current at

Current Cut. Explore the caves of Eleuthera starting in the north with Preacher's Cave, then head to South Palmetto Point and just above Ten Bay Beach where the underground systems are home to a huge colony of bats—be sure to bring a flashlight! Finish with another nice cave system found in Rock Sound. Visit the Glass Window Bridge, then travel 0.6 miles south to find the Queen's Bath, gorgeous natural pools on the Atlantic side. Enjoy a dip if the sea is calm and it is a low tide, otherwise do not go down to sea level. Start your weekend by tracking down a Friday night fish fry in Governor's Harbour for BBQ, music, and the beverage of your choice. No matter what your activity of the day might be, you can always count on beautiful surroundings and friendly, helpful residents extending a wave of greeting.

Bits and Pieces

I'm not going to tell you where this happened because the effort to get there was so great I feel like I deserve to keep its location a secret. I'm telling you about it because there are lots of bonefish on Eleuthera; it just takes a little effort to find them. Three of us had parked the car because to the right was a nice flat that was easy to walk and we knew it held fish. To the left was a mucky, nasty creek bed, filled with tangled mangrove bushes and those god-awful mounds and craters the size of garbage cans. It was obviously going to be a bitch to walk. I went left, the other two went right. The muck was everything I had imagined—a couple of good steps then I would sink right up to my thigh; I'd crawl out and go forward a few more feet, then sink up to my knees, holding onto mangroves to pull myself out; one more step then down a mound and into a crater. The tide was out and it took me 45 minutes to get to any meaningful water, but meaningful it was. Out of sheer exhaustion I flicked my fly into a pool and was instantly onto a fish. I had my camera with me and over the course of the next 90 minutes I landed 20 fish, all on film. How did I get out? As luck would have it, I found a nice easy exit. A great ending to a spectacular day.

GRAND BAHAMA

Lay of the Land

Grand Bahama is the northernmost island of the Bahamas and just 55 miles east of Florida. It is the fourth-largest island in the Bahamian chain at 90 miles long and 12 miles across at its widest point. Tourism, the mainstay of the economy, is boosted by activity generated through the Grand Bahama Port Authority and the quarry. A majority of the 52,000 Grand Bahama residents live in Freeport, the second-most-populous city in the Bahamas. Settled for centuries (and definitely upscale), it feels more casual than Nassau.

The sparsely populated outlying areas provide rustic stays with peaceful, deserted beaches on the eastern edges of the island and Old World charm in the West End settlement, formerly a hideout for rumrunners during Prohibition. The Spanish named the island Gran Bajamar, meaning "Great Shallows," for the treacherous coral reefs surrounding it, but the Lucayans called it Bahama. Pirates took advantage of Spain's lack of attention, setting up shop to lure passing ships onto the reefs only to run aground and be plundered. Although the island was claimed by the British in 1670, piracy continued to thrive for another 50 years.

Freeport is the "downtown" of Grand Bahama, attracting visitors with its commerce, industry, and resorts. Lucaya, called the Garden City, is a tourist destination centered around beaches and hotels. West End is the oldest, westernmost settlement and the capital, but has little economic importance to Grand Bahama. McLean's Town is the easternmost settlement and a 30-minute ferry ride from Abaco. Freeport is home to the international airport, in addition to modern grocery stores, hospitals, clinics, and all the services one would hope to find. Cell phone coverage and Internet are found all over the island.

A great school off the southern shore of Grand Bahama (Photo courtesy of Pat Ford)

Grand Bahama (East)

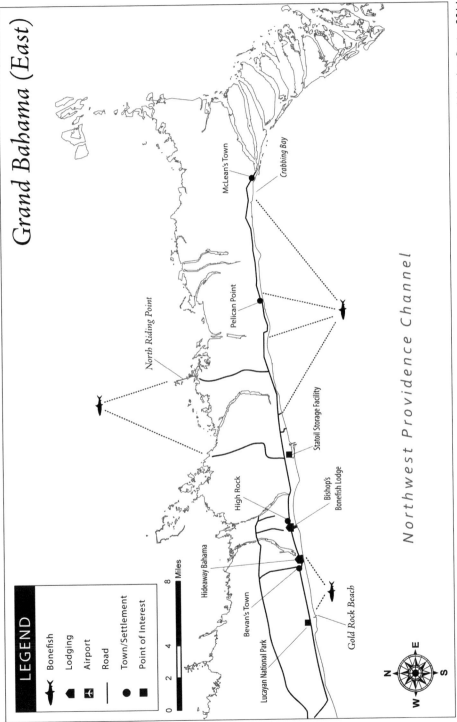

Rod Hamilton Design 2014

Where to Fish

Grand Bahama is not my top choice for a DIY trip but is an excellent destination if you want a quick tropical getaway with your family and to get in a few days of fishing. Without a boat, you won't find those classic white flats the Bahamas are known for, but there are enough beaches to walk and creeks to investigate to keep anyone happy for a week.

Freeport and Port Lucaya are considered the central section of the island and either is a good place to stay, but the fishing opportunities are poor. If you want to be closer to the fishing, pick a location either east or west of Freeport.

Freeport and Port Lucaya

This is the tourist section of Grand Bahama with the usual resorts and beach activities engaged in by the sun seekers. The fishing is spotty in this area but can be OK in the mornings and evenings when the swimmers and sunbathers are not around.

Fortune Beach. Located on Fortune Bay Drive east of Freeport, this beautiful beach almost always holds bonefish at low tide. It's a perfect place to take your spouse for the afternoon, fish for a couple of hours, and end the day with lunch at the Banana Bay Restaurant and Bar. When sitting on the restaurant's deck, make sure your rod is strung up and leaning against the railing. Take it from me, you wouldn't be the first person to be digging into your burger when a tail pops up out on the flat.

Xanadu Beach. This beach is close to Freeport and easy to reach off Mall South Road and Dundee Bay Drive. It holds bones but is actively used by swimmers and sunbathers. Early morning and late afternoon are the times to fish Xanadu Beach.

Taino Beach. Taino, Lucayan, and Silver Point Beaches all have fish from time to time but get very busy during the day. If you are staying at one of the resorts in Port Lucaya, get up early when you'll have the place to yourself.

Grand Lucayan Waterway Jetty. East of Fortune Bay is the entrance to the Grand Lucayan Waterway. There is a long jetty protruding from shore where you will always find locals fishing for snapper and bucket fish, a term that comes from the phrase "whatever's in the bucket is dinner." In the western corner of the jetty next to the beach is a small cove that holds bonefish.

Airport Flat. This is a nice flat and creek system that can be reached just west of the airport by following the Grand Bahama Highway west from the airport, then traveling north on Queen's Cove Road.

East of Freeport, South Shore

The south shore is made up of magnificent beaches and the occasional flat. The beaches are easy to get to, with lots of access points and good fishing during the low and incoming tides. The flats are few and far between, but there are miles of shoreline to walk to look for cruising bones.

Barbary Beach. There is a wonderful beach east of the Grand Lucayan Waterway, as well as a series of bays that all contain bonefish from time to time. This area is generally deserted and a beautiful spot to spend the day. I prefer the bays closer to the Grand Lucayan Waterway, but there are miles of beach to explore. As you approach the beach, you will see a series of small rock outcroppings protecting of the bays. Concentrate your fishing around those areas. Fortune Bay Drive stops at the waterway, so you have to circle north and find your way over the canal using Casuarina Road and then back down to Barbary Beach.

Lucayan National Park. From the beaches of Lucayan National Park east to High Rock there are approximately four miles of shoreline to walk and wade. This 40-acre national park is worth seeing and includes a spring creek, a massive cave system (Ben's Cave), and one of Grand Bahama's most spectacular beaches, Gold Rock Beach.

Searching the flats of Barbary Beach, Grand Bahama

145

Bevan Town. This small community is located 55 minutes east of Freeport and three miles east of the Lucayan National Park entrance. It consists of not much more than a gas station (Smitty's) but is home to Hideaway Bahamas where we stayed for a week and which I can highly recommend. Staying here puts you right on the beach and halfway between the Lucayan National Park and High Rock. There are a couple of access roads to the beach in Bevan Town. This section of the beach fishes well both east and west on all tides except the very highest. Don't be afraid to blind cast into those sections where the sand meets the turtle grass; for a change of pace, hit the blue holes with a heavily weighted Clouser to catch dinner.

High Rock. Once you enter High Rock, take the first road to the beach. When the road hits the sand, follow it to the right and park near Bishops Bonefish Lodge. Fish from here west, toward Hideaway Bahama, a total of two miles.

Statoil Storage Facility. East of the Statoil storage facility is a nice beach that can be walked for almost five miles. There are several deserted access roads; pick one to drive down and park your car. You are likely to be the only one on the beach looking for the bonefish that frequently cruise the shoreline.

West of Pelican Point. Where the road meets the water and the creek empties into the bay is a wonderful small flat that fishes well at low tide.

Pelican Point. Just past the settlement is access to the beach. From the parking spot there are flats and coastline that can be fished in either direction. The area around Pelican Point is a good bet when the winds make the north shore impossible to fish.

Crabbing Bay. Well before reaching McLean's Town you will see a clearly marked road heading south to the cemetery at Crabbing Bay. This is one of the better bonefishing flats on the southern shore. There are plenty of fish here and it's a nice spot to target tails in the evening. This area receives some pressure, so the fish tend to be a little more difficult to catch here than other places on Grand Bahama.

East of Freeport, North Shore

The north shore of Grand Bahama east of Freeport is famous for bonefishing. All you have to do is look on Google Earth to see the miles and miles of perfect habitat. Numerous guides trailer their boats to one of the launching areas that service the north shore. Depending on the wind direction, the north shore can be either protected or buffeted, a major factor in deciding if this is where you want to fish for the day. The north shore is best fished using a skiff, but there are a few spots the self-guided angler can fish. If you have a kayak, it opens up many more miles of shoreline and creeks. Bring along your Google Earth printouts, since the roads can be a little tricky to navigate.

Dover Sound Boat Ramp. Used frequently as a put-in by the guides, this road is located just east of the airport. On Google Earth it can be identified as the area crisscrossed with a massive manmade canal system, waiting for homes that have never been built. The fishing here is very good and a kayak allows access to the creeks and shoreline within the first couple of miles in either direction. To fish the shoreline and creeks to the east, put in at the boat ramp; to fish the shoreline and creeks to the west (toward the airport), drive down the little dirt road from the boat ramp to the closest canal and put your boat in there. When I last fished Dover Sound (October 2012), the Grand Bahama Highway stopped at the Grand Lucayan Waterway due to construction. To get to Dover Sound from Freeport, use East Sunrise Highway to Casuarina Drive, go over the Grand Lucayan Waterway, and then turn left on the Grand Bahama Highway. Take the last road to the north on Grand Bahama Highway (east side of the waterway) to reach Dover Sound.

Water Cay Boat Ramp. Another area used extensively by the guides is Water Cay. To reach this boat ramp, take the dirt road north when you reach the highway curve approximately seven miles west of the Lucayan National Park parking area. Once you park your car at the boat ramp there are some areas to walk, but the bottom gets soft. The best bet is to launch a kayak and paddle for a mile in either direction.

Boat Launch Opposite Statoil. The entrance to the Statoil storage facility is 3.8 miles east of High Rock. Across the street from the entrance heading north is a dirt road taking you to a boat launch. The road heads north for two miles then takes a short right and then left and continues for another three miles to the water. To the west of the boat launch is good water that can be reached by kayak. The paddle to the east is a little less than a mile but opens up some nice flats and creek systems. There is plenty of good water, so the trick is to find those places where the bottom is firm enough to wade.

North Riding Point Pier. Heading east on the Grand Bahama Highway for five miles past the Statoil entrance is a dirt road heading to the North Riding Point Pier. The dirt road is a little more than five miles long but leads to nice wadeable flats on both the west and east sides of the road. There is a good creek system close to the road that can be reached by a short kayak trip and another farther east that requires a paddle of over one mile.

East of Freeport, North Shore

As you take the Queen's Highway to the West End, you will note that the road heads in a northwesterly direction, but the coasts are still referred to as the south and north shores. There are only a couple of smaller flats to fish, but there are some nice beaches on the south shore.

Paradise Cove. Approximately 20 minutes west from the airport and past the settlement of Homes Rock is Paradise Cove. This is a nice beach and flat with an unusual bottom, pockmarked with indents providing places for fish to eat and hide. The bottom is firm and easy to walk and well worth fishing on a low and incoming tide. There is a good dirt road to the beach just beyond the Paradise Cove sign.

Bahama Beach. Located northwest of Paradise Cove, on the south shore, this scenic beach is normally deserted and at times has some good fishing. Several roads provide access to Bahama Beach.

Bootle Bay. Northwest of Bahama Beach and prior to the highway crossing to the north side is Bootle Bay. Take one of the roads south to the water and park your car beach side. There are miles of coast to the north to fish.

Old Bahama Beach Club. This upscale, boutique hotel and marina is located on an ideal beach and bay in the West End. This beautiful bay holds bonefish along the shore and can be waded at low tide.

Fishing Information

Grand Bahama is well-known for its bonefish and this reputation is well deserved. There are hundreds of miles of flats and bonefish habitat surrounding Grand Bahama, but you need a boat to reach most of it. There are numerous independent guides scattered throughout the island and an

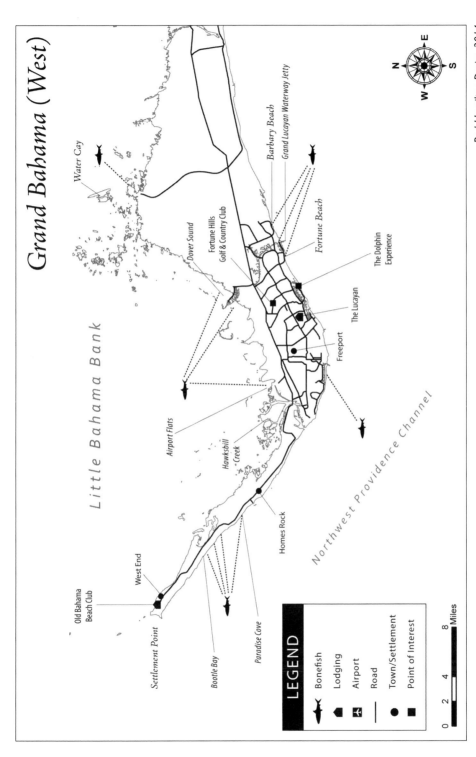

Grand Bahama (West)

Little Bahama Bank

Northwest Providence Channel

Water Cay

Old Bahama Beach Club

West End

Settlement Point

Bootle Bay

Paradise Cove

Homes Rock

Hawksbill Creek

Airport Flats

Dover Sound

Fortune Hills Golf & Country Club

Barbary Beach

Grand Lucayan Waterway Jetty

Fortune Beach

The Dolphin Experience

The Lucayan

Freeport

LEGEND

- Bonefish
- Lodging
- Airport
- Road
- Town/Settlement
- Point of Interest

0 2 4 8 Miles

N W E S

Rod Hamilton Design 2014

endless array of places to rent. When looking at maps of Grand Bahama, you will note the island lies west to east, different than the typical north to south axis of Bahamian islands. As a result, much of the fishing information refers to the "south" or "north" shore.

The tides vary substantially from end to end and between the north and south shores. There are tide tables available for Freeport and Settlement Point but nothing for the north shore, which has at least a two-hour difference from the south shore.

The northern location of Grand Bahama means that it is susceptible to cold fronts from December through February, but on the plus side the water is ideal for bonefish from May through September when water temperatures in the southern islands may be too warm.

There are some big fish on Grand Bahama, so don't be afraid to have flies that are size #2 or larger. I like the spawning shrimp–style flies in size #4 like Peterson's Spawning Shrimp or Bonefish Junk along with some large tan Clousers, Pop's Bitters, and Greg's Flats Flies. If you fish Crabbing Bay, I'd suggest dumbing down the fly by reducing flash, weight, and size. For these spookier fish I like a size #8 to #10 unweighted Pop's Hill Special, Pink Puff, or Lefty Kreh's Shallow H_2O Fly. Tie a few with weed guards.

I don't know of any kayak rental stores on Grand Bahama, so bring your own or rent a home that has kayaks on the property. To fish the north shore properly you need a kayak.

Grand Bahama has a number of good-quality independent guides located throughout the island. Most of them can be found on the Internet, but here are three I can recommend:

Captain Perry Scuderi. www.captainperry.com
The Pinder Brothers. www.angleradventures.com/GRANDBA
Greg Vincent. h20bonefishing.com

Where to Stay

Want to be where the action is? Looking for an exclusive resort experience? Maybe you prefer a cottage on the beach or an intimate bed and breakfast? Grand Bahama has something for everyone and every budget. Freeport and Port Lucaya have all of the above from high-end resorts and private villas to one- and two-bedroom condos on the water. The

Internet is your best friend in this hunt; I'd suggest going to the usual suspects, VRBO.com and HomeAway.com, for private rentals and to GrandBahamasvacations.com for a list of hotels and resorts.

Below are a couple of alternatives we can recommend outside the resort areas of Freeport and Port Lucaya.

Old Bahama Bay, located in the West End, combines Bahamian resort charm and island luxury (www.oldbahamabay.com; 242-350-6500 for calls outside the United States and 888-800-8959 for U.S. reservations; sales@oldbahamabay.com). This is an all-suite beachfront resort with 67 junior suites and 6 spacious two-bedroom suites.

Hideaway Bahamas is located in Bevan Town, east of Freeport (www.hideawaybahamas.com; 242-374-4483; sales@hideawaybahamas.com). It offers a spacious two-bedroom, two-bathroom cottage situated just 50 feet from the water with a fully stocked kitchen, eating area, and dining room. There are also six condos of different configurations and a luxury home for rent.

Getting Around

There are two airports on the island: Grand Bahamas International Airport located in Freeport, which services the majority of travelers, and a small cargo airport in the West End. Depending on your starting point, there are a number of scheduled commercial airlines providing service to Freeport.

American Airlines, from Miami. www.aa.com

Silver Airways, from Fort Lauderdale. www.gosilver.com

Delta Airlines, service from Atlanta, Georgia. www.delta.com

US Airways, from Charlotte, North Carolina. www.usairways.com

West Jet, nonstop from Toronto, Canada. www.westjet.com

Bahamasair, from Nassau. www.bahamasair.com

Cars are the way to go on this spread-out island. Rental cars are available at the Freeport International Airport with rates ranging from $50 to $100 per day. Motor scooters can be rented for about $35 per day and are found in Port Lucaya and Freeport. Public buses, or jitneys as the locals call them, operate from the Port Lucaya Marketplace to the downtown area, and from downtown to the outlying areas of the West End and East End.

A free government-owned ferry travels daily between Sweeting's Cay and McLean's Town or you can take Pinder's Ferry Service for travel daily between Crown Haven, the Abacos, and McLean's Town.

Seven-Day Sample Trip

On Grand Bahama you have to pick the type of holiday you want. If you want to be where the action is, then stay at one of the resorts in Port Lucaya. I have chosen a more laid-back approach, renting the beach cottage at Hideaway Bahamas in Bevan Town. Hire one of the local guides in McLean's Town for the first day to get a feel for the place, understand what the tides are doing, and observe what flies and strategies the locals employ. Stay on the south shore for the next couple of days to fish the four miles of beach in front of your cottage, two miles north one day and two miles south to Bishops the next. Day four, hit the beaches west of Pelican Point on the outgoing tide, finishing up at Crabbing Bay on the low tide. The next day throw your kayak in the car and head to North Riding Point. Fish both sides of the peninsula heading out to the old pier, then jump in your kayak and paddle east to the extensive creek systems that are within a mile. Reserve day six for a little island exploring and head west of Freeport toward Old Bahama Bay. Time it so that you hit Paradise Cove on a dropping tide for a few hours of fishing. On the last day, choose between hitting Dover Sound with your kayak, which makes for a strenuous day, or going back to the beach in front of the cottage to catch the fish you missed on day two.

Spousal Rating: 7

Grand Bahama gets a spousal rating of 7 because it offers everything a spouse or family could want on a tropical vacation. However, the DIY fishing is a little limited and you shouldn't expect to have "killer" days.

Nonfishing Activities

Grand Bahama is one part natural beauty and one part resort, providing the potential to create the Caribbean holiday you desire. Get out and shop at the Port Lucaya Marketplace, take a tour to see the blue holes, coral reefs and turtle grass, stingrays, nurse sharks, and more! Swim with dolphins or simply visit them at the UNEXSO dolphin center. Spend the day at the Lucayan National Park, home to one of the oldest underwater cave systems in the world. Want some indoor activity? Take advantage of duty-free shopping, visit the casino, and finish the day with a relaxing meal, choosing from a wide variety of restaurants.

Bits and Pieces

When you fish in the Bahamas you have to be prepared to cast into some strong winds, but October 25, 2012, was the toughest. That's when Hurricane Sandy paid Grand Bahama a visit. Five of us had rented a home in Bevan Town, hoping to fish and explore the island for 10 days, but Mother Nature had a different plan. The fierceness of the storm is now a faint memory, but the attitude, kindness, and generosity of the locals has endured.

Once we made up our mind to ride out the storm, preparations began. The grocery stores were packed, but everyone was happy, helpful, and

Hurricane Sandy from the front porch, surrounded on all sides by rising water

relaxed. There were long lines at the gas stations, but not a harsh word was said or impolite action taken. There was no sense of panic or worry, just a determined attitude to get on with the business at hand. Neighbor helped neighbor and everyone banded together as one big family.

When Hurricane Sandy hit, the wind and rain was intense, but it was the water surge that created havoc. The rising waters stopped just short of our front door, but the roads were flooded and we were marooned on our little patch of grass. There was no power for five days, no chance of driving the roads, and only bottled water for cooking, bathing, and drinking. This is when you find out what a "family" really is, and that is what we experienced on Grand Bahama. Everyone helped out everyone else and provided what goods and services they could spare, and those unfortunate souls whose homes were flooded were moved by foot into other homes that had survived.

It was a heart-warming experience and is my fondest memory of Grand Bahama.

GREAT HARBOUR CAY

Lay of the Land

The district known as the Berry Islands, often referred to as "the fish bowl of the Bahamas," is composed of 30 islands and 100 cays. They start on the eastern edge of the Great Bahama Bank 35 miles northwest of Nassau and 150 miles east of Miami. Sailors, boaters, fishermen, and more than a few millionaires know all about the pristine white-sand beaches and tree-lined shores of the Berry Islands. The mostly uninhabited islands are home to wildlife like terns and pelicans, while the 700 residents earn their living harvesting lobster and conch, along with some fishing and tourism. At the top is Great Stirrup Cay, with the main islands of Great Harbour Cay, Bond's Cay, and Chub Cay to the south.

Great Harbour Cay (GHC) is the largest of the chain; most of its eight-mile-long coast features beaches, and it's a mile and a half wide. A causeway takes you over the ocean inlet and into Bullock's Harbour, or the Village, which is the main settlement where most residents live. GHC experienced a development boom in the late 1960s when celebrities vacationed here, but activity slowed and it has been quiet for the past 40 years.

A double out of a huge school (Photo courtesy of Pat Ford)

Key infrastructure elements like roads, runways, electrical power, and telephone service are in good condition and well maintained. There are no ATMs, however, and credit cards are accepted only for marina services, slips, and fuel, as well as some lodging. GHC has a medical clinic, airport, a couple of small grocery stores, and liquor outlets in the Village. Being heavily dependent on supplies arriving by the mail boat means you should think about buying a cooler, loading it with the food you really want, and bringing it over from Nassau. A couple of restaurants and a few roadside stands are the options for eating out. Internet is sketchy, so confirm in advance if your accommodations have it.

Where to Fish

Shark Beach. Immediately east of the airport, this is a classically beautiful Bahamian beach and an ideal location for your rental accommodations. The beach itself is worth a stroll with your fishing rod in hand when you have a couple of free hours. Bonefish can be found along its length, typically during the incoming tide.

Sugar Beach. Located north of Shark Beach, this 3.5-mile stretch of white sand has some fish but offers little defined structure, so it's not

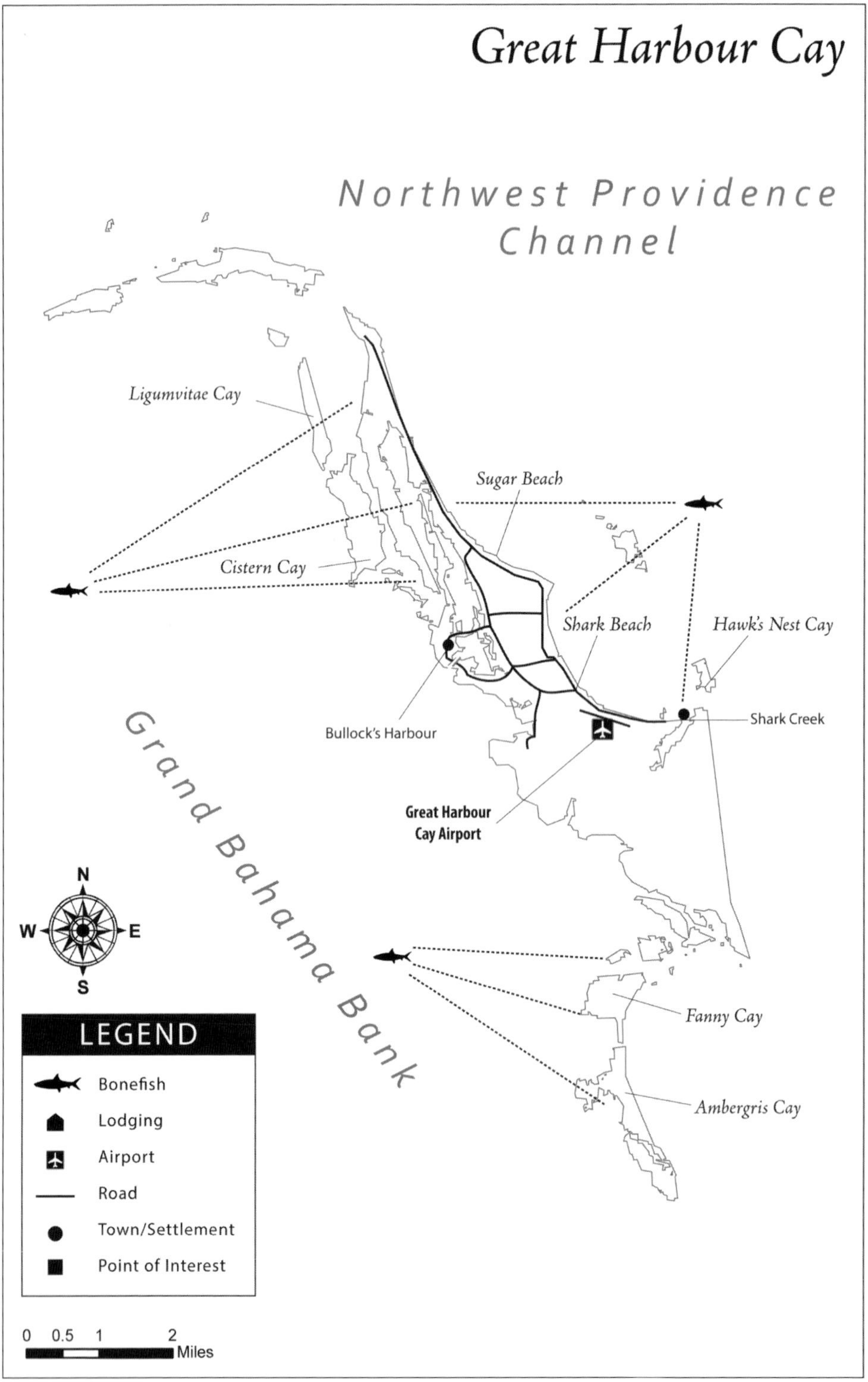

Great Harbour Cay
Northwest Providence Channel
Ligumvitae Cay
Sugar Beach
Cistern Cay
Shark Beach
Hawk's Nest Cay
Shark Creek
Bullock's Harbour
Great Harbour Cay Airport
Grand Bahama Bank
N
W
E
S
LEGEND
Bonefish
Lodging
Airport
Road
Town/Settlement
Point of Interest
Fanny Cay
Ambergris Cay
0 0.5 1 2
Miles

Rod Hamilton Design 2014

easy to know where they hang out. If your spouse decides to sit out on the beach with a good book, take your rod along.

Back Creek, South. The main creek and flat system within the interior of GHC is referred to locally as Back Creek. It is a long system running north and south for over two miles. The southern portion can be accessed by either entering the creek off the causeway or driving north and finding the overgrown road located 300 yards from the turn. Once in the creek and heading north, you'll find the bottom is firm, visibility is good, and the fish seem to be evenly distributed. A deep channel runs along the western edge where the fish hang out at low tide. Once the creek begins to fill, the fish leave the safety of the channel and begin spreading out over the flats. This regular routine makes it simple to determine where the fish are at each stage of the tide. Interestingly, since the causeway was constructed, the creek does not fully empty, providing plenty of water for the fish. Note that the tide table is two hours later inside the creek than in the outside waters.

Back Creek, Northern Section. Travel 2.2 miles past the Carriearl Hotel to where the hill begins to flatten and the creek appears on the left. At the bottom of the hill you will find a well-hidden trail through the mangroves to the water. The flats are a mixture of turtle grass and sand

The beauty of the flats—you never know what you might see

157

with good wading except in close to the mangroves. The fishing here is excellent but is accessible to the guides by boat, so the fish are pressured here more than in the southern section. The deep channel that runs the length of Back Creek is too deep to wade but makes for some interesting "mini" flats around the mangrove island.

Bullock's Flat. This is a large flat on the south end of Cistern Cay, reached by launching a kayak at the mail boat dock. It's an excellent spot with plenty of fish, but the turtle grass bottom provides perfect camouflage for your quarry and makes sight fishing difficult. The bottom is soft and wading can be exhausting. It's a perfect place for a boat or stand-up paddleboard. Guides fish this area as well.

North End. These flats are reached by driving up the coastal road and either parking where the road ends or stopping at the gates located a half mile to the south. This is a large expansive flat, a half mile wide and 1.5 miles long. The bottom is turtle grass broken up by sand patches. The fish are tough to see on the turtle grass, so it's best to stake out and watch the sand-covered "holes." The wading on the northern end is firm but starts to get soft and lumpy as you head south.

Lignumvitae Cay. This cay is visible directly in the west when fishing the North End flat. There is some good fishing here, and the cay can be reached with a 0.75-mile paddle by kayak from the end of the road.

Goat Cay. Located just north of Lignumvitae Cay, this small island has a nice beach on the western shore that holds bonefish. After fishing Lignumvitae Cay, make the short paddle to Goat Cay, then make a one-mile paddle back to the car; it's well worth the effort. Both Lignumvitae and Goat cays fish best on the low and incoming tide.

Shark Creek. This picturesque flat and creek system is found at the southern end of the road, past the airport and runway. It's an impressive creek making its way though the entire width of the island. The eastern creek mouth and flats of Shark Creek can be good, but for whatever reason, what appears to be the perfect habitat for bonefish holds fewer fish than expected. The channel out of the creek is deep and crossing it requires a kayak.

Hawks Nest Cay. These flats are located off the south end of GHC and less than a half mile east of Shark Creek. They are beautiful ocean flats to walk and wade, but on the several occasions I have fished here, I have only caught a few fish each time. You can walk to Hawks Nest Cay across the Shark Creek channel at mid to low tide.

Water, Caesar, Fanny, and Ambergris Cays. This is the group of cays located to the southeast of GHC and reached by boat from Bullock's Harbour. They provide the best fishing on GHC and some of the finest bonefishing in the Bahamas. After a day here, you will wonder why you bothered to fish anywhere else. It's not uncommon to see thousands of fish coming at you in waves as they work the tides over miles of pristine flats. It's a five-mile run from Bullock's Harbour, and the flats stretch for another five miles after that. This is obviously too far for a kayak, making it imperative that you arrange for a boat rental before arriving on GHC.

Fishing Information

For me, the key to a successful trip on GHC is to arrange a boat rental for four of the seven days. Without a boat, the DIY fishing is OK, but with a boat you're very likely to have the best bonefishing of your life.

Setting up for a perfect presentation (Photo courtesy of Pat Ford)

Interestingly, some of the fish in the creeks are harder to catch then you might expect, considering the lack of pressure. To prepare for the creeks, downsize the flies and go light on the flash. In many places the bottom is a mixture of turtle grass and sand, so have an ample supply of flies with weed guards. The creeks' bottom color ranges from tan to green to brown, so bring the appropriate colors to match. On the large, white-sand flats of the south, go with creams and light tan, but there is no need for weed guards. The schools can be seen 100 yards away, so the strategy is different than in the close confines of the creeks. No need to be subtle here, so use larger flies, more in the #2 to #4 range, with lots of flash and some rubber legs so they can see the fly from a long distance. Bonefish Junk, big Clousers, and tricked-out Gotchas work well.

There are only a handful of guides on the island and the best known are Percy Darville and his two brothers:

Percy Darville. fivehearts2@hotmail.com

Where to Stay

Accommodations on Great Harbour Cay are limited but range from magnificent beachfront homes to townhouses at the marina to small one-bedroom bungalows. The best way to find out what is available is through the websites VRBO.com and HomeAway.com. Try to find a place that comes with a car, bikes, kayaks, and possibly a boat. My recommendation is to stay on either of the two beaches on the east side.

The Carriearl Boutique Hotel is an option and offers four-bedroom ensuite rooms with satellite TV, wi-fi, a pool, restaurant, kayaks, and bikes on site (www.carriearl.com).

Getting Around

GHC is a short 15-minute hop from Nassau and about an hour from southern Florida.

Berry Island Air. berryislandair@gmail.com

United Airlines, from Fort Lauderdale. www.united.com

LeAir charters. www.leaircharters.com

Most things are within a mile or two, so bikes come in handy, but renting a car is the way to go. There are very few options for renting a car other than from homeowners.

Happy People Car Rental. 242-367-8117

To insure a successful fishing trip, arrange for a boat to access the southern flats. There are a couple of options and make sure your rental is confirmed prior to leaving home. The boats range from 17-foot whalers with 90 horsepower to larger boats up to 20 feet.

Happy People. 242-367-8117

Dino Hanna. dino.hanna@ami.com

Seven-Day Sample Trip

Head out the first day with Percy Darville and get to know the area. He has lived on GHC all of his life—nobody knows where the fish are and how to catch them like Percy does. On day two, fish the southern portion of Back Creek, paying special attention to the pattern of the fish as they head to the deep channel on the dropping tide and back onto the flats once the tide begins to rise. On day three, fish the flats at the mouth of Shark Creek and out to Hawks Nest Cay on the low tide. For the rest of the time in this area, rent a boat from Dino Hanna and make the five-to-eight-mile trip to the cays and flats south of Bullock's Harbour.

The "gang" celebrating the end of a terrific week

Spousal Rating: 5

If you are staying on Shark Beach or Sugar Beach in a nicely appointed home and just want some piece and quiet, GHC will be fine. There is very little else going on but reading, swimming, walking, and beachcombing.

Nonfishing Activities

Great Harbour Cay is a quiet, lovely island suited more for R & R than for shopping. Ride a bike to Sugar Beach Caves near the northern end of the island for exploring or snorkeling, make the drive north to see the island's highest point, or visit the Bajito, a shallow area in the south that is a treasure trove of sand dollars and shells at low tide. Shark Creek, the southernmost point of the island, is a popular shark fishing spot. And, the island has a nine-hole golf course if you really want to get off the beach!

Bits and Pieces

In the 1960s and 1970s there was a development boom going on in GHC. Grandiose plans were designed to satisfy the needs of movie stars, titans of business, and the hordes of American tourists who were expected to find the beauty of GHC irresistible. Those dreams can now be seen as unfinished structures and deserted real estate developments on Cistern Cay and GHC, including what once was a magnificent 18-hole golf course. Now you can play the remaining nine holes using whatever golf clubs are around and your car as the golf cart. This is the only place I have seen where you get out of your car and hit the ball, then get back in your car and drive to the ball and hit again. Fore!

GREAT INAGUA

Lay of the Land

Great Inagua is the third-largest island in the Bahamian Archipelago. It is 45 miles long, 25 miles wide, and positioned 370 miles southeast of Nassau. Fifty miles east of Cuba, this southern island offers some of the most unique fishing opportunities in the Bahamas.

Scraping salt off the pond in Great Inagua

Salt is the business of Inagua with a large Morton salt plant providing virtually all of the employment for the island's 1,000 residents. Normally hot and dry, the weather on Great Inagua is ideal for salt production, and the island has more cacti than anywhere else in the Bahamas.

This is not a typical tourist destination. Super friendly people here make for an easy lifestyle, but one that the traveler must adjust to and not the other way around! One of the main attractions on Great Inagua is the Bahamas National Trust Park and Wildlife Sanctuary, a bird watcher's paradise.

Matthew Town is the capital and home to the only harbor found on the island. Here you will find the Great Inagua Airport, a medical clinic, the Bank of the Bahamas, and a lighthouse built in 1870 that provides a good view of Cuba on a clear day. A few miles of paved road can be found from the airport to Matthew Town, but expect dirt roads to compete with potholes everywhere else!

Great Inagua has virtually no infrastructure for tourists and only a few places to stay for a visiting fisherman. There is one grocery store that is totally dependent on the supply boat. If the boat arrives you may have fresh fruit, vegetables, and meat; if not, you might be eating peanut butter

Rod Hamilton waiting for a donkey shish kabob from roadside vendor in Great Inagua

out of the jar. Consider bringing from Nassau a cooler of foods you would like. Both Internet and phone service are usually available, but don't count on it. I always bring a satellite phone to Great Inagua. There are a couple of small restaurants and on Friday and Saturday nights there may be one or two roadside shacks cooking ribs, chicken, or donkey.

Where to Fish

As you may have guessed, Great Inagua does not receive much fishing pressure, and most of the island remains unexplored by self-guided anglers. The limited infrastructure and lack of roads to areas that look great on satellite maps but are difficult to access make fishing difficult. The entire southern shore is prime habitat and holds fish, with some areas more productive then others. Every creek, flat, and bay visible on Google Earth that is reachable by car or kayak is worth fishing.

Lighthouse Beach. Drive south out of town on the coast road toward the lighthouse. The beach is 1.5 miles long, so park the car at the end of

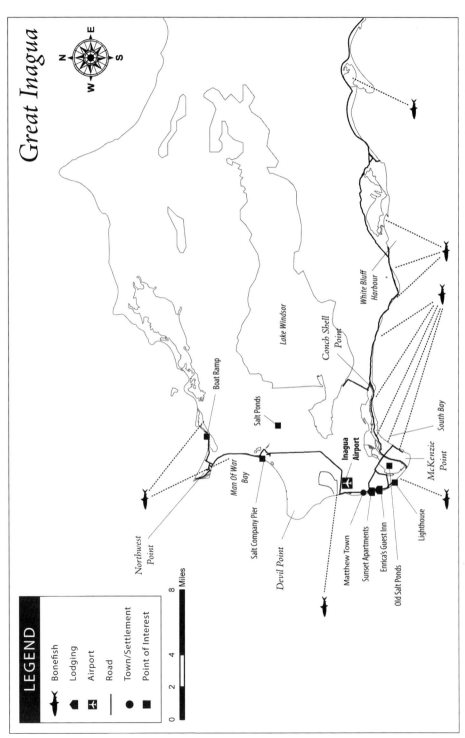

Great Inagua

Rod Hamilton Design 2014

LEGEND

Bonefish
Lodging
Airport
Road
Town/Settlement
Point of Interest

Miles

0   2   4   8

Northwest
Point

Boat Ramp

Man Of War
Bay

Salt Company Pier

Devil Point

Matthew Town

Sunset Apartments

Enrica's Guest Inn

Old Salt Ponds

Lighthouse

McKenzie
Point

South Bay

Inagua
Airport

Salt Ponds

Lake Windsor

Conch Shell
Point

White Bluff
Harbour

the road or stop earlier, wherever looks good. This is an excellent beach, and bones are always cruising the shoreline on the incoming tide. At high tide you can walk the shore and at low tide walk out on the flats fishing the turtle grass and potholes.

Abandoned Salt Ponds. When you first arrive in Matthew Town, ask a local which road leads out of town to the abandoned salt ponds. Similar to Long Island, this vast expanse of ponds has been diked, then crisscrossed with roads. Unlike Long Island, these ponds are easier to figure out and fish. You can walk the roads and dikes looking for fish or simply enter the water and wade. The key is to look for ponds that you know rise and fall with the tide as a result of breaches in the dikes or canals. The ponds are easy to access; drive out of town until the road and the ponds meet and fish to the right or left, or drive straight across and fish the south bank.

South Bay, South. I know the location's name is confusing, but after you cross over the salt ponds south of town and continue straight ahead,

Heading to the next flat (Photo courtesy of Vince Tobia)

the road ends at South Bay. From here you can fish both north and south. Immediately before the end of the road a "goat trail" heads to the right (southwest); follow this either in the car if it will make it or on foot. At the end of the road, follow the trail to the water where you will encounter a beautiful flat and beach. On the shore to your right are mangroves where it is too soft to wade, preventing you from reaching the southern flat. The locals have built a path in behind the mangroves that takes you through the bush for 300 yards and comes out on the southern flat. This is a spectacular area to fish and is good from the shoreline out to the protective reef. At low tide the fish move out to the reef and back into the turtle grass and sand flat as the tide rises. This is a large area with enough room for four fishermen to spread out.

South Bay, North. The section of South Bay to the north is fishable but not as good as the water south of the road. There is another small access road to the upper end of this beach approximately 1.3 miles up the road if you don't want to walk the beach. On the far north end of the bay is a nice cove that often holds schools of bones.

Double from one of our "secret" spots

South Shore Road. Once you pass over the salt ponds, take the road to the left. This is the main road for the south shore and provides access to the eastern section of the salt ponds, beaches, and a couple of very good creeks. Plan to explore the numerous branches and pull-outs, fishing every section of beach that looks good. Some places are better than others, but the entire south shore holds fish. The two-track sand road parallels the shore for 11 miles until coming to a well-defined point of land. Here the offshore reef meets the land and forms a protected flat, holding bones and other species.

White Bluff Harbour. Continuing on for another three miles, you reach a spectacular creek and flat system with a large ocean entrance and good tidal flow. It can be fished either by kayak or by making the one-mile walk from the car. Take the small spur to the right off the main road at the point it begins leaving the coast. Alternatively, you can drive completely around the system and park on the eastern end. This is an easy place to spend the entire day. It's about 15 miles by road once you take the road left over the salt pond, but it takes an hour to reach. You just can't go much faster than 10 to 15 miles per hour on what really are two tracks in the sand. Those hoof prints you see are the wild donkeys that roam Great Inagua.

Eastern Creek. This creek may have a name locally, but I have not heard it. Once past White Bluff, continue on the road for another two miles to a small creek and then another three miles to a large opening and bay. These areas seldom get fished because of the drive.

Airport Flat. North of the airport is a creek with direct access to the ocean and flat in behind. It's reached from the main road north of the airport by continuing straight instead of making the hard right-hand turn that would take you to the Morton salt plant and northern sections of the island.

Man of War Bay. After passing the Morton salt plant, continue north and the road rejoins the ocean at Man of War Bay. The bottom is a mixture of sand, limestone, and turtle grass, making it ideal for bones. There are a couple of good spots to focus on. One is the section of beach north of the large cement dock. The other is the northwest corner where the road leaves the water and crosses to the north shore.

North Shore Creek. This is the last system on the north shore that can be reached by road. Follow the road north from Man of War Bay until you arrive at the ocean, then turn east. Carry on for two miles and park where the locals launch their boats. The creeks are still to the north and contain good populations of bones. The road used to continue past this point but was blown out by a hurricane.

Fishing Information

As large as the island is, the number of areas for the self-guided angler is limited. It's the perfect place to go with one or two buddies, but a group of six would hit most places each day. There are no boats available for rent, so the only way to fish the north shore creeks and flats is with the only guide on the island, Ezzard Cartwright. If you have the opportunity, hire Ezzard for at least one day to fish Lake Windsor for the tarpon and snook. The bonefish here are larger than typical Bahamian fish, averaging close to five pounds. I go with large flies, size #2 to #4 and on the white flats use lots of flash. On the limestone and turtle grass flats inside the reef I downsize and carry a couple of flies with weed guards. There are good numbers of permit swimming the waters of Great Inagua, so make sure you have a selection of crab patterns with you. I like the Raghead and EP crabs that also work well for bonefish. Even if you don't book a tarpon trip with Ezzard, put a couple of streamers in the box. On our last trip my buddy hooked and fought a 30-pound tarpon on a Crazy Charlie while stalking bones.

There is only one guide on the island and occasionally he has a helper that can take two other fishermen. If you go with four or more fishermen, hire Ezzard Cartwright every day and rotate through the fishermen and locations. Schedule some days for bones and permit on the north end of the island and some days in Lake Windsor for tarpon and snook.

Ezzard Cartwright. (242)-339-1362

Where to Stay

The options on Great Inagua are limited. There are a few private residences listed on VRBO and HomeAway that would work if they can arrange for a rental car as well.

Sunset Apartments has two duplex-style units and is owned by Ezzard Cartwright (242-339-1362). If you are fishing with Ezzard for a few days this will work well.

Enrica's Inn Guest House is relatively new and nicely appointed with kitchens and air conditioning (www.enricasinn.com).

Getting Around

Bahamasair makes the 90-minute flight between Nassau and Matthew Town on Monday, Wednesday, and Friday. Flights are not guaranteed and often late, so check the most current schedule and leave plenty of time to make outbound connections.

Bahamasair. www.bahamasair.com

Car rentals can be difficult to arrange and are best done through the provider of your accommodations. Here are a couple we have used:

Sam & Renee Car Rental. (242) 339-2149

Ingraham-Rent-a-Car. (242) 339-1677

Seven-Day Sample Trip

On the first day, hire Ezzard Cartwright to fish his regular haunt on the north end of the island. Next day, fish the Lighthouse Beach and end up at the salt ponds in the evening. For the third day cross the salt ponds and fish the south shore flats. On the fourth day make the long drive along the south shore to the eastern flats and creeks. On day five, head the other direction to the north shore, park where the locals launch their boats, and fish the two lagoons. On day six, hire Ezzard to fish Lake Windsor for tarpon and snook. On the last day before the plane leaves, fish the creek just north of the airport runway.

Spousal Rating: I

There are very few amenities on Great Inagua and I don't recommend this trip for a nonfishing partner.

Nonfishing Activities

The 183,740-acre Inagua National Park was established in 1965 and is home to the world's largest population of West Indian Flamingos. Once close to extinction, this bird made a comeback 40 years ago and its numbers

The flamingos of Great Inagua (Photo courtesy of Melissa Maura)

now stand at 60,000. Other birds of interest include the endangered Bahamian parrot and white-crowned pigeon, plus thousands of egrets, herons, cormorants, owls, and pelicans. Take the informative ranger-led tour of the park, which can be arranged by contacting their main office in Nassau (242-393-1317; bnt@bnt.bc). Look out for wild boar and donkeys too!

Bits and Pieces

When I'm on a fishing trip, I could care less about what I eat. I can and have survived happily on peanut butter sandwiches, three meals a day for seven days. Naturally, this is not the case for most people and certainly not for my band of traveling companions. They like to eat well, which means I'm the beneficiary of a bunch of great meals. Just after arriving in Matthew Town, I was looking after the rental car when my friend emerged from the grocery store with a look of panic on his face saying, "Buddy, we are in trouble!" Now, on a fishing trip that usually means there's a hole in the boat, the rods are broken, or the luggage didn't arrive. In this case it meant the supply boat hadn't been in port for three weeks and there was no food on the shelves. Fine for me, but it was like the end of the civilized world for him. Since there was no fresh or frozen meat, chicken, bread, vegetables, or fruit, we lived on canned whatever for five days until the supply boat landed. Food issues aside, it was a wonderful trip, the fishing was good, and I ate a donkey shish kebab for the first time.

LONG ISLAND

Lay of the Land

Divided by the Tropic of Cancer, this 80-mile-long and 4-mile-wide island lies 160 miles southeast of Nassau and is known for scenery that is incredible and diverse. The southwest coast has beautiful white beaches with calm blue bays, while the northeast side has steep rocky headlands overlooking dark stormy waters. Add rolling hillsides, swampland, cave systems, and white flat expanses where salt was extracted and you have Long Island!

Don Causey with a nice bonefish from Long Island while dealing with howling winds

Approximately 5,000 people live in the place originally named Yuma by the Arawaks and renamed Fernandina by Christopher Columbus in 1492. This is believed to be his third stop of that voyage, following San Salvador and Rum Cay. Lucayans lived in the cave systems here first, until they were taken away to Cuba and Hispaniola as slaves. The first Loyalists arrived after fleeing the American Revolution, establishing working farms and raising cattle and sheep. By the 1790s, settlers from the Carolinas built successful cotton plantations that collapsed with the abolition of slavery.

Today the economy is based on fishing, farming, and tourism. Pothole farming dating back to the Arawaks compensated for poor soil conditions and made use of the limestone found on the island. Still the preferred method today, pothole farming involves farmers placing top-soil in large holes of limestone rock (naturally occurring or manmade) where they plant anything from peas, squash, and corn to bananas and mango trees.

Long Island is a quiet place, home to friendly people who value their history and celebrate life and community as it exists here. The Queen's Highway provides a good road from Columbus Cove in the north to Gordon's Settlement in the south, with side roads that are often nothing more than cleared dirt. The northernmost settlement is Seymour's, home to about 200 people. Going south is Burnt Ground and then Stella Maris, which has an airstrip, marina, and plantation-style resort complex. Fifteen minutes farther south is the settlement of Simms, one of the oldest on the island, which has a nurse-staffed medical clinic, telephone and gas station, a couple of restaurants, and small stores.

Ten miles farther south is Salt Pond, home to the annual Long Island Regatta usually held in May. The mail boat comes in here, so it is gener-ally well stocked with groceries, over-the-counter medication, hardware, and household goods. Next is Deadman's Cay, the largest settlement, outfitted with a medical clinic and the main airport for the island. Several settlements run together here and you will find restaurants, a number of small hotels, and a couple of gas stations.

The island's capital is Clarence Town, which has most services includ-ing a medical clinic, gas station, several restaurants, and a good supply of groceries. Continuing south you will see more small villages that dot the length of the island, the occasional restaurant and tavern, and ruins dating

Mail boat docking at Salt Pond, Long Island

from the days of the plantations until you arrive all the way to Gordon's at the bottom of the island, where you might just feel like you are at the end of the world! Banks can be found in Stella Maris and Deadman's Cay, gas stations and grocery stores are usually closed on Sundays, and don't forget to confirm Internet and cell phone service in advance.

Where to Fish

As the name suggests, Long Island is long, so it's best to pick a place to stay where you can reach the flats in a reasonable period of time. If you stay in the north, concentrate on the northern fishing areas and if you stay in the south, concentrate in the southern section. From a purely geographic point of view, a central location like Salt Pond or Deadman's Cay makes the most sense and you won't be spending two hours each day driving.

I have used the odometer where I can, as many of the side roads don't have names and may not be easily found.

Starting at the Deadman's Cay Airport road where it intersects with the highway, set your odometer to 0 and head north.

Public Dump Road. This utilitarian name refers to the area two miles north of the airport road where there is public access to the island's dump. This is the only entry point for a walk-and-wade angler to enter a large flat and mangrove system. Park the car at the dump, making sure it is out of the way of other vehicles, and then walk east behind the dump to

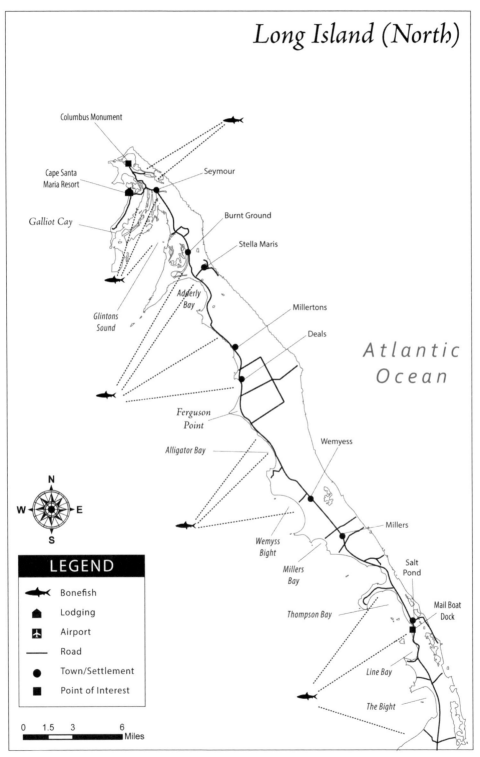

Long Island (North)

Columbus Monument
Cape Santa Maria Resort
Seymour
Galliot Cay
Burnt Ground
Stella Maris
Glintons Sound
Adderly Bay
Millertons
Deals
Atlantic Ocean
Ferguson Point
Wemyess
Alligator Bay
Millers
Wemyss Bight
Salt Pond
Millers Bay
Mail Boat Dock
Thompson Bay
Line Bay
The Bight

N
W E
S

LEGEND
Bonefish
Lodging
Airport
Road
Town/Settlement
Point of Interest

0   1.5   3   6
                  Miles

Rod Hamilton Design 2014

Getting ready under the shade of a casuarina tree (Photo courtesy of Sam Root)

a large expansive flat. It's a long walk at low tide but a great place to fish, and it opens up a huge area both north and south.

Gray's Landing Drive. This is found 6.8 miles north and located across the highway from a cell tower. It's a long drive to the end of road, but there are good rocky flats both north and south of the old concrete dock.

Minnis Street. At 9.7 miles on the odometer turn left on Minnis Street and drive to the end of the road. It's easy to get to and one of my favorite places to hit on the incoming tide. The bottom is rocky with potholes, so wading isn't particularly easy, but fishing can be very good as the tide rises and the bones are looking to get back into the mangroves. You can fish both the north and south sides of the mangrove island depending on the direction and strength of the wind.

Pinder and Salt Pond. This is an unmarked road 10.5 miles north of the airport and just before the road sign marking the border between Pinder and Salt Pond. Drive to the end of the road to fish this nice flat. I prefer to fish the southern section.

Roadside. At mile 12.6 the road runs beside the water and there's a good place to park the car. This is a low tide flat and can be fished from here south to Line Bay.

Thompson Bay Peninsula Road. You will see beautiful Thompson Bay prior to getting to the road, but at mile 15.6 you will find the dirt road that runs the length of the peninsula. At low tide there are plenty of areas to fish from the point back to the bay's beach. Find an access point to fish the peninsula's south shore.

Wemyss. Once you reach the settlement of Wemyss, mark the Anglican Church and carry on north another half mile where there is access to fish the beach of Wemyss Bight. At times there is good fishing for cruising bonefish along the shoreline, and it's a great spot to bring the kids to play while you keep your eyes open for tails.

Alligator Bay. This nice stretch of water is north of Wemyss where the road curves back to the water at Alligator Bay. You can park the car at the side of the road, grab your rod, and fish. I prefer to fish the southern end of the bay, which can be reached by driving down the road south of the settlement and heading to the marina. Park at the marina and begin fishing the southern corner of the bay while wading north.

Doctor's Creek Cove. This is a tiny little cove beside the road in the settlement of Doctor's Creek. Just pull the car over and spend five minutes looking for tails. It's surprising how many times fish will be rooting around in this spot completely oblivious to the road traffic.

Deal Beach. This settlement is north of Simms where a nice beach parallels the road and provides an excellent place to both cast a line and relax. The entire length of the beach is fishable, but I prefer the rockier section located at the south end during low tide.

Harvey's Bay. This bay is situated north of Deal Beach. I can't say I have had lots of luck at Harvey's Bay, but if you want to stop for a little rest, there are bones cruising the shoreline.

Millertons. Upon reaching Millertons the road meets back with the water and follows it for just under a mile. There are plenty of places to pull over and fish.

Adderley Bay. This large bay is one of my favorite spots to fish on Long Island and always seems to be productive on the incoming tide. It is directly across from the Stella Maris sign. At low tide, the water completely leaves the mangroves and the fish are somewhere out in the bay. If the tide is low in the morning or evening, this is an ideal area to look for tails. On the incoming tide the fish are eager to get back into the mangroves, and it's possible to set perfect interception points while walking the mangrove edge. It is a large bay so the fish can be spread out and a little difficult to find at times, but they are there. You can park on a short dirt road on the north end of the bay that gets close to the water or just park beside the highway and make the short walk through the mangroves to the water.

Burnt Ground. Burnt Ground Settlement is the beginning of some nice creek systems located on the northern end of the island. Immediately before the Burnt Ground Settlement sign is a small pullout on the left-hand side of the road. Park here and you can see a narrow creek that winds its way down to the bay. This is a great spot; there is little pressure and the fishing extends south for a distance of approximately one mile. Depending on the tide, you can catch the fish either moving up the creek during an incoming tide or exiting the creek on the outgoing tide.

Glinton Dock. As you enter Glinton, turn left at the Eagle Eyes Bonefishing Guides sign and drive to the end of the cement dock. Walk south along the shore for 400 yards to reach the mouth of the creek system. Catch fish leaving the creek on the outgoing tide. Fish the shoreline on the low tide.

Glinton Sound. Once you reach Glinton, locate the Anglican Church. Approximately 0.43 miles from the church is the ball field on the left side of the road. Off in the distance you can see Glinton Sound. To get to Glinton Sound park the car and enter the mangroves behind the ball field's washroom structure. It is a bit of a walk, but there are literally miles of flats in front of you.

Seymours. As you enter Seymours you will cross a small causeway with a large creek and flat on your left and a smaller section of the same creek system on your right. Park on the left side as you head north and fish this large creek down to the bay. The fishing here can be very good and well worth a day. The top end of the creek next to the road always seems to have fish at high tide.

Newton Cay. As you drive north from Seymours, continue on the paved road until you reach the end at Newton Cay. On your left is the outlet to a creek system that begins at the Columbus Monument Flat and flows south to this spot. The creek has another entrance with good tidal flow on the north end as well as an entrance at Newton Cay. Fish enter the creek on each tide, and the fishing is good throughout the creek's entire length.

Columbus Monument Flat. This used to be one of those secret spots, seldom fished and a favorite on the north end of Long Island. To get there, backtrack on the pavement from Newton Cay toward the Cape Santa Maria turnoff but, before reaching the corner, take the dirt road heading north. For reference, the dirt road to the Columbus Monument is 0.37 miles north of the Cape Santa Maria turnoff. The road has deteriorated over the years but is still passable for most vehicles. There is a nice parking area at the monument, but to reach the flat you should park your car about a half mile before the main parking area. At this spot you will find a nice path to a picture-perfect flat and creek. I did say it's not a secret anymore! There are lots of fish here, so it's just a matter of getting the tide right.

For fishing the south end of the island, reset the odometer to 0 at the junction of the Deadman's Cay Airport road and the highway, then head south.

Library and Museum Flat. This very productive flat is located across the street from the Long Island Library and Museum. The road to the flat is 1.6 miles south of the airport, directly opposite the N. G. M. Major High School. Drive to the end of the short road to fish the flats to the south. There are a couple of small creek openings 100 yards south, and the mangrove flats fill up quickly when the tide turns. This is a quality location and just the right size to fish during one tide.

Cartwright. Drive 2.8 miles south to an unmarked short dirt road opening up to excellent flats and lagoons. This area deserves some special attention.

Mangrove Bush. You can find Mangrove Bush at mile 4.5 where the road follows the water again for one mile. You can park your car anywhere along here and walk to the shoreline.

Hamilton. Past the sign that welcomes you to Hamilton at mile 5.3 there is a short gravel road to your right. This is an important spot, as it allows the only access to a large area to the south. You can walk out to the little cays at low tide and fish the small lagoons to the south, although the bottom is soft in places.

"Pinky" Knowles with a nice bone from Deadman's Cay, Long Island

Funeral Home. This landmark is located at mile 7.4 on a long dirt road before a small funeral home. This is a rough road, particularly at the end where you need to cross over a small wooden bridge. Once you reach the ocean, head north until you can't drive anymore and hike the remaining distance to the creek.

Dean's Blue Hole. The road intersection to Dean's Blue Hole is at mile 7.5; rather than taking the road left to the hole, go right. Follow this long road and when you first see the water, take the short left and cross the culvert. This is the very top end of a long creek and flat that holds some good fish. The outlet to the ocean is on your left, a distance of approximately 2.8 miles. Park at the ruins of an old building and walk south down either the beach or the creek toward the ocean entrance.

Clarence Town. Here is a nice series of well-known flats with direct access to the ocean about three miles from the center of Clarence Town. Because there is a series of roads to follow, it is best to get a good look on Google Earth to understand the road system before heading there.

Dean's Blue Hole on Long Island (Photo courtesy of Sam Root)

The flats are located southeast of Clarence Town between Clem Cay and Long Island.

Galloway. As you exit Clarence Town there is a paved road between the two inland lakes heading south on your right to Galloway Landing. Follow this road all the way to the ocean. At the ocean, head north to the right; this gets you close to the ocean outlet of a creek heading to the north. From here, there are approximately three miles of water to fish. Now backtrack and head south, following the road along the ocean toward the Diamond Salt Works ponds. The road used to go the entire length of the salt ponds and a driver could make it to Morrisville, but it has been washed out. Still, this is an excellent way to fish the northern section of the salt ponds.

Diamond Salt Works. Once you enter Morrisville, south of Clarence Town, you will pass the Morrisville Elementary School. One kilometer south of the school is a road into the heart of the Diamond Salt Works salt ponds. This is a huge, complex series of ponds that can get confusing. Bonefishing can be good in the ponds, but it is important to find those locations where the dikes and gates have been compromised and there is direct tidal flow in and out of the pond. The best way to find the "good"

Wading a Long Island flat (Photo courtesy of Sam Root)

ponds is to drive to the road bordering the beach and head north past the Diamond Works infrastructure ruins.

Gordon's. The last place to fish in the south is the creek system at the end of the road in Gordon's. There is a short dirt road that provides access to the creek where boats are tied up. At the end of the road there's a parking area next to a beautiful sand beach. It's best to walk up the beach toward the creek mouth and access it from there.

Fishing Information

There are countless locations on Long Island to DIY as can be seen by the list above. Central Long Island has the largest concentration of wade-able flats and creeks, but the northern areas are awfully inviting. Southern Long Island's flats and creeks are spread out and there are fewer of them, but a few of the creeks are enormous and almost never get fished.

Other than for fishing the salt ponds at Deadman's Cay, there isn't a real need for a kayak on Long Island; a rental car will get you to lots of fish.

There are a number of local guides on the island and listed below are three respected guides that have fished these waters all their lives. If

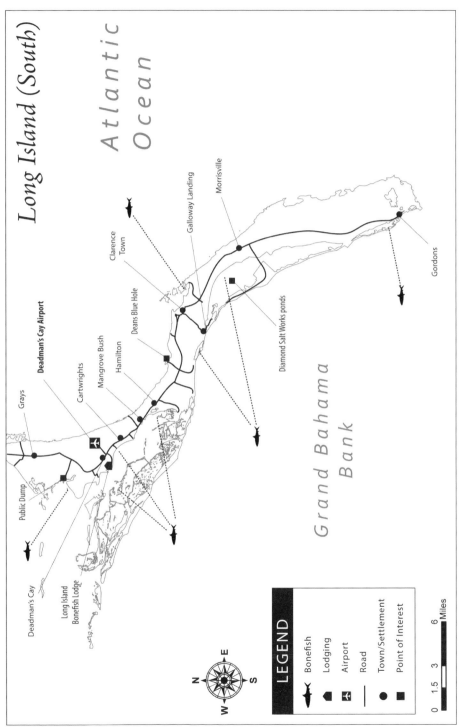

Long Island (South)

Atlantic Ocean

Grand Bahama Bank

Galloway Landing

Morrisville

Clarence Town

Deans Blue Hole

Deadman's Cay Airport

Mangrove Bush

Hamilton

Cartwrights

Grays

Public Dump

Deadman's Cay

Long Island Bonefish Lodge

Diamond Salt Works ponds

Gordons

LEGEND

Bonefish
Lodging
Airport
Road
Town/Settlement
Point of Interest

0   1.5   3   6
                    Miles

N
E
W
S

Rod Hamilton Design 2014

you are staying in the north call Docky, and if staying centrally fish with Loxley or Markk.

Docky Smith. www.bonafidebonefishing.com

Loxley Cartwright. icbones@gmail.com

Markk Cartwright. www.longislandbonefishinglodge.com

The usual flies and equipment work fine on Long Island. There is no need to get fancy since the fish don't receive much pressure. On my last trip I only saw two other self-guided fishermen on this very large island. I suggest going with a typical Bahamian box, size #4 to #6 tan, cream, and brown Crazy Charlies and Gotchas, some Clousers including green, and a good selection of crab patterns. Because some of the oceanside flats are rocky with holes and crevices, you should take along a few flies with weed guards.

Long Island does offer a rather unique opportunity to fish the maze of salt ponds left by the now-defunct Diamond Salt Works. It's unlike any other bonefishing experience and certainly worth trying. Once you learn the patterns of the fish entering the ponds through breaks in the dikes or canal system, you can count on the fish doing the same thing on every tide.

Where to Stay

Cape Santa Maria Beach Resort is located on the west coast, known for mile after mile of calm blue water and white sandy beaches (www.capesantamaria.com). With 20 beachfront bungalows and a handful of beautiful new villas, the resort will help your time on Long Island feel special yet relaxed.

Stella Maris Resort Club is set on a gorgeous green bluff overlooking the Atlantic (www.stellamarisresort.com). The plantation resort offers a wide range of vacation rentals, including comfortable one-bedroom and two-bedroom bungalows and luxurious waterfront homes. They offer a casual dining room, bar and lounge, satellite TV, pools, bikes, and complimentary island excursions.

Chez Pierre's is built on a beautiful and virtually deserted beach in Millers Bay (www.chezpierrebahamas.com). Its six comfortable cottages with screened porches reflect the simple and pure lifestyle of the Bahamas. Kayaks and snorkeling equipment are available for guests, excellent breakfasts and dinners come out of the restaurant, and Pierre may be able to help with a car rental.

Long Island Bonefish Lodge's owner, Nevin "Pinky" Knowles, provides an all-inclusive, assisted DIY bonefishing experience only five minutes by boat from the hard-bottomed walk-and-wade flats of Deadman's Cay (www.longislandbonefishinglodge.com). The accommodations are suitable for eight anglers in two duplex-style cottages, each side furnished with two queen-sized beds and a bathroom. The dining area, bar, and lounge are found in the main building where the coffee is on at 6:30 each morning with breakfast following! Lunch is made-to-order sandwiches, snacks and drinks are available to eat on the flats, and dinner back at the lodge varies each night with a Bahamian flair.

Long Island Breeze Resort is located in Salt Pond where Michael McKnought's waterfront location offers island-style atmosphere and delivers all the comforts we hope for when on vacation (www.longisland breezeresort.com). Choose budget-conscious private bungalows, select well-priced ocean-view cottages, or go top-of-the-line and reserve their deluxe ocean-view apartment, offering a full kitchen, living room, office, and dining area. Meal plan options are available; you may also choose to pick up something at the grocery store across the street or eat out. Watch the weekly mail boat arrive at the dock next door from the beautiful deck surrounding the pool, or get out of the sun and relax in their large, open dining room and bar.

Getting Around

Bahamasair will get you from Nassau to Stella Maris on Monday, Thursday, and Friday and has daily flights between Nassau and Deadman's Cay. Pineapple Air flies from Nassau to both airports most days of the week, though flights to Deadman's Cay are only Monday and Friday. Southern Air flies to both Deadman's Cay and Stella Maris most days of the week.

Check their current schedules at the following websites:

Bahamasair. www.bahamasair.com
Pineapple Air. www.pineappleair.com
Southern Air. www.southernaircharter.com

Even if you just feel like hanging out at one of the resorts, consider renting a car for at least a couple days of exploration.

Mr. T's. (242) 337-1054
Seaside Car Rental. (242) 338-0041
Unique Wheels Rental. (242) 225-7720

Inquire about airport transportation and car or scooter rentals when booking accommodations. Kayaks, boats, and bikes are often available as well.

Seven-Day Sample Trip

There are so many places to fish, choosing where to go for the week is tough. I'd stay at Nevin Knowles's Long Island Bonefishing Lodge in Deadman's Cay since it is central to most of the prime fishing areas and has the added advantage of easy access to the Deadman's Cay salt ponds. On the first day take advantage of the assisted DIY plan offered by the lodge and go out with Markk Cartwright to fish the salt ponds. On day two drive to Hamilton (see instructions above) and fish the cays just offshore, turn next to the lagoons, and then keep walking south. Day three, fish the Library and Museum flat on the outgoing, low, and incoming tides. Day four, head to Clarence Town and fish the flats immediately to the south and then cross the island and fish the creek north of Galloway Landing. Day five, head north and fish the Columbus Monument flat, and for day six make the walk out to Glinton Sound for a full day of fishing. If you are fishing on day seven, take the assisted DIY trip back out to the salt ponds.

Spousal Rating: 7

My wife and I enjoy Long Island and it ranks as one of our favorite destinations. There are some nice deserted beaches and places to lie back and enjoy the tropical sun, but the charm of Long Island is more about its history, culture, and activities not easily found on other Bahamian islands.

Nonfishing Activities

Experience history at the top of the island and take the short hike up to the Christopher Columbus monument at the top of the north end cliffs,

Getting the conch ready for lunch at the Long Island Bonefishing Lodge (Photo courtesy of Sam Root)

which overlook stunning bright green seas. The Adderley's Plantation ruins are on the lands of Stella Maris and can be dated back to the 1790s. Hamilton's Caves are one of the Bahama's largest systems, with 50-foot-wide passages and 10-foot ceilings. Contact Leonard Cartwright at 242-337-0235 for cave tour information.

The Long Island Museum and Library is in Buckleys, and St. Mary's Anglican Church, thought to be the oldest Spanish church in the Bahamas, is south of Salt Pond. Drive into Clarence Town and see the famous twin churches built by Father Jerome. On the left side of the road is St. Paul's Anglican Church with a red roof, built when Father Jerome was an Anglican, and on the right side of the road is St. Paul's Catholic Church with a blue roof, built after he converted to Catholicism!

Crystal clear waters, unspoiled reefs, and amazing marine life make water activity of all kinds a natural. Long Island has numerous dive sites but is best known for Dean's Blue Hole, the deepest recorded blue hole at 600 feet, found just south of Clarence Town. Located in a protected calm bay, you can scuba dive the steep walls of the blue hole or snorkel on top!

Bits and Pieces

I first went to Long Island 12 years ago when my son was nine years old and my wife was . . . (apparently I'm not allowed to say). My experience as a self-guided angler was growing, but there was a lot I didn't know. The catch rate was low but the memories are clear, and to this day it still ranks as one of my all-time favorite trips. There weren't many DIY anglers at the time and there certainly wasn't any information available on where to fish. It was the blind leading the blind and it couldn't have been more fun. We stayed at Stella Maris and rode our "fat tired" rental bikes down the hill to Adderley Bay every morning to pick off one, two, or three bones before riding back up the hill for breakfast. My son and I stalked side-by-side as we crept up on feeding fish and it was a joyous time. I remember those mornings together like it was yesterday.

NORTH ANDROS

Lay of the Land

Andros, considered a single island geopolitically, is composed of hundreds of small islets and cays connected by mangrove estuaries and tidal swamp-lands. Bights, or bays, separate its three major islands: North Andros, Mangrove Cay, and South Andros. Nicknamed "the Sleeping Giant," the entire land mass, which is 100 miles long and 45 miles wide, is located 30 miles west of Nassau and 138 miles from Fort Lauderdale.

Our attention will focus on the "big island" of the Bahamas, North Andros, which is the sixth-largest island in the Caribbean yet one of the least explored. The Spanish named it La Isla del Espíritu Santo (the Island of the Holy Spirit) when they arrived in the mid-1500s looking for slave labor. Pine and hardwoods are found in the north, and most residents concentrate in the east, while the west coast remains largely undeveloped.

The legends of Andros are as rich and important to the residents as any fact one can look up in a book. Many of the locals still believe in the chickcharnies—a mythical creature half-man and half-bird with red eyes, three fingers, and three toes. It is said to cause mischief to those that look at one and grimace but to cast lifelong good luck to those showing respect. Buried treasure at Lusca and Morgan's Bluff and the half-shark half-octopus guardian of the inland blue holes are just two more myths for you to ponder.

As the most important farming region and supplier of fresh water in the Bahamas, Andros is a great provider. The area also has a long tradition of boat builders, straw work, and woodcarving.

The world-famous Joulter Cays are eight miles north as the crow flies from the tip of Andros. Back on the mainland is Morgan's Bluff, Lowe's Sound, and Nicholls Town, three northern villages supplying fresh food and water, with some restaurants, a bank, a government medical clinic, and various lodging options among them. Gas stations can be found in each town. Continuing southwest is San Andros, home to one of two airports in the north.

Traveling south 15 miles on the Queen's Highway you will find Stafford Creek, then Andros Town (also known as Fresh Creek), where the second of the airports in the north is located. Centrally located Fresh Creek is the commercial hub of North Andros where you will find a small grocery store, a few restaurants, and the Atlantic Undersea Testing and Evaluation Center (AUTEC), operated by the U.S. Navy. The United States and the United Kingdom conduct special operations training and sonar and submarine research in the Tongue of the Ocean. A 30-minute drive will get you to the bottom of North Andros at Cargill Creek and Behring Point. Cell phones and Internet are found everywhere in a mostly cash economy.

Where to Fish

North Andros is known for its many fishing lodges, famous guides, and large fish. But what isn't well publicized is the number of world-class flats and creeks that are easy to reach and can be waded by the self-guided angler.

Many of the roads are difficult to find so I've used the odometer where possible to pinpoint locations.

When leaving the Andros Town Airport, set the odometer to 0 and drive south toward Behring Point.

Somerset Beach. Two miles south of the airport is a short sand road leading to a beautiful beach. Fish cruise the shoreline, but the best opportunities are south toward the mouth of Somerset Bight.

North Andros (North)

LEGEND

- Bonefish
- Lodging
- Airport
- Road
- Town/Settlement
- Point of Interest

Northwest Providence Channel

0 2 4 8 Miles

Joulter Cays

Morgan's Bluff

Nicholls Town

Red Bay

Lowe Sound

Conch Sound Settlement

San Andros Airport

Mastic Point

Mastic Bay

Main Lumber Road

Queen's Highway

Cemetary

Blanket Sound

Stafford Creek

Staniard Creek

Eva's Bonefish Lodge

Rod Hamilton Design 2014

Somerset Bight. This is one of the better spots to ambush fish as they move in and out with the tide. Located two miles from the airport, take the short road to the left and then turn right at the T. Follow the right spur for approximately one kilometer and park at the widened area. Walk through the mangroves to the water where the mouth of the creek is to the left and extends to the right for about a mile. A well-defined channel down the middle of the creek into the bight serves as the bonefish highway on changing tides.

Davis Bight Creek. At the four-mile mark turn left toward the water and follow the road to a pull-off, located where the chain blocks the road. Immediately to the north is the bottom end of the creek formed by Somerset Bight. Walk north, staying as dry as possible for a quarter mile, and then cut through the mangroves to the open water in front of you. The mouth is farther north, so on the falling tide the fish will head out to sea and then reverse on the incoming tide. The creek is surrounded by mangroves and at high tide the fish are out of reach. The bottom is soft and can be difficult to wade but improves as you reach the opening.

Davis Bight. Leaving your car parked at the same spot as above, don't walk north; instead, head east toward the large body of water off in the distance. This is a beautiful series of flats and creeks that three or four folks can fish for a week. It has everything you could ask for: oceanside flats to the north, large channels carrying fish in and out on each tide, mangrove edges to work, and a good solid bottom for wading. The entire area holds fish, but I prefer crossing to the far eastern side to fish the channel and flats to the south.

Bowen Sound. At mile 8.4 you enter the small settlement of Bowen Sound. Take the road to the left and wind your way down to the boat ramp. Then walk south along the rock bank for one kilometer until you come to an opening into a creek and a couple of small cays surrounded by flats. This is a neat place to fish, but not easy to reach.

White Bight. At the Man-O-War sign turn toward the water at mile 12.5. This overgrown road ends at an old manmade stone dike. It's a bit treacherous, but walk the stone dike through the mangroves until you hit open water. From the end of the dike, you can walk either north or south. The north section is a good oceanside flat that holds some big bones. If you go one more mile, you will find a small creek and opening to the ocean with a small flat out front. Walking south from the stone dike you'll see a mixture of ocean flats for the first mile and then will reach the sand flats of White Bight. The end of the bight is just under two miles south of the dike, so it makes for a good day's fishing.

Mount Pleasant. At mile marker 16 you will arrive at the road to the Mount Pleasant Lodge. This is a great place for the self-guided angler to stay and provides direct access from the cottages to the coves, beaches, cays, and bays of White Bight.

Behring Point. This small settlement is situated at the very southern end of North Andros. Once you cross over the bridge from Cargill Creek there is a small flat on the left and then a number of spots to pull over and wade between the bridge and end of the road. The bottom can be very soft and difficult to wade.

Back at the Andros Town Airport let's head north. The destinations north are not all delineated by mileage markers, but the distances are shown where required.

Fresh Creek, South Shore. Fresh Creek itself is a massive system with a large outlet to the ocean north of the airport. For the self-guided angler there are a couple of areas that can be reached by car, and more of the creek opens up if you have a kayak. One and a half miles north of the airport is a dirt road heading inland that follows the south shore of Fresh Creek for a short distance. Drive to the end of the road and park in the widened area. From here walk the 100 meters to the creek to find a nice hard-bottomed flat both west and south. As you continue west up the creek the water becomes deeper, forcing you close to the mangroves. There is a large blue hole approximately three-quarters of a mile from the car. This is a surprisingly good flat that the fish use as they move in and out with the tide.

Small Hope Bay. There is a dirt road leading to the water 1.2 miles north of the Small Hope Bay Resort's driveway. This resort is a nice place to stay and is situated on the beach, close to the fish! Once you park the car at the water's edge, walk the 100 meters to the right until you reach a small creek opening. There is a small flat at the creek mouth that can be good on low tide.

Fresh Creek, North Shore. You will reach the settlement of Love Hill and Rev. Leroy Hanna Drive 1.9 miles from Small Hope Bay's driveway. Follow Rev. Leroy Hanna Drive inland for another two miles until you come to the Central Andros National Park sign. Turn right and continue to follow the signs to the Blue Hole tourist attraction, or continue straight to reach the north shore of Fresh Creek. This road cuts off miles of paddling to reach the most westerly flats of Fresh Creek.

Staniard Creek Beach. The beach is located 14 miles north of the airport on the Queen's Highway. There are a few places to stay in Staniard and it serves as a good "home base" for fishing the north. Once you have entered Staniard Creek, cross the bridge and take the right road paralleling the beach. If you stop your car and look over both sides, you will be able to see the bonefish that hang around the bridge. Both the north and south ends of the beach hold bonefish, but the north end flat is much larger and holds more fish. To reach the southern corner of the beach, follow the road south to the parking lot where guests take the shuttle boat over to Kamalame Cay Resort. This is a small flat but always holds fish on the low tide. From this point you can also cross the road and try the flats at low tide on the south shore of the Staniard Creek outlet.

Staniard Creek. When entering the settlement of Staniard Creek, take the left at the T and drive to the end of the road. This puts you on the west side flats 200 yards from the mouth of Staniard Creek. It's not a large flat, but the fish travel across the white, hard-bottomed sand as they leave and enter the creek. It's easy to get to and makes an excellent ambush spot if you only have an hour or two. This is an ideal place to launch a kayak to fish the creek and mangrove islands behind Kamalame Cay.

Queen's Highway. There are several places to pull the car off the highway between Staniard Creek and South Blanket Sound for walking access to the waters behind Kamalame Cay. It's about a 300-yard trek, but once there it opens up for miles of fishable area.

South Blanket Sound Entrance. Follow the road off the highway into the settlement of South Blanket Sound and turn left at the ball field. Park your car on the water's edge; from here you can see the mouth of South Blanket Sound on your right and the flats, channels, and islands that appear at low tide in front. At low tide the channels can be waded, opening up a large series of sandy oceanside flats. Fish for cruising bones in the shallow water and blind cast with Clousers into the channels where the fish are holding. The channels get deep as the water floods, forcing wading fishermen back to the beach. It's best fished with a kayak so you don't have to worry about wading back across the channels.

South Blanket Sound Creek. Drive past the ball field and continue to the end of the overgrown road. Park the car and walk 200 feet through the bush to the creek. The ocean opening is on the left and in front of you, and to the right is a vast walk-and-wade area tucked in behind Kamalame Cay. Many of the areas can be reached on foot, but it is best to use a kayak to get across the channels. In a boat it's possible to cover more ground between the small cays and inlets scattered throughout the area. This is a great fishing destination with ample room for a number of anglers and enough nooks and crannies to spend an entire week exploring.

Stafford Creek Sand Flat. Continue 0.8 miles north of the South Blanket Sound turnoff to the road to the Stafford Creek Sand Flat. This is a beautiful firm sand flat to fish on the incoming and high tide. At low tide it's dry, which is the time to shift to the ocean flats and follow the fish in with the tide. At low tide the south corner of the bay often holds fish as they wait for the tide to turn.

Stafford Creek Cemetery. After crossing the bridge over Stafford Creek, take the first right when you see the Love at First Sight Hotel, take a right at the main access road, and then turn left at the water. This is the road to the Stafford Creek Cemetery and parallels the ocean heading north. Park at the end of the road, string up your rod, and get ready to fish for the rest of the day. You are looking at a huge area including multiple ocean entrances into the creek, an enormous oceanside flat, mangrove islands, and cays, in addition to an intricate creek system that travels for miles. There is so much to fish it is hard to know where to start, but you can walk north on the ocean flat for two kilometers to get into some very interesting places.

Conch Sound. This settlement is south of Nicholls Town, located on a beautiful white sandy beach where a series of flats can be waded at low tide.

Fishing Information

North Andros is one of my favorite places to fish with a group. The variety of habitats, ranging from massive creeks to miles of ocean flats, will keep anglers wishing they could extend their stay. Certain locations, such as the waters off the Stafford Creek Cemetery and Blanket Sound, are so large that a group can concentrate on them for a week. A kayak comes in handy, and it's worth the effort to bring your own.

By and large the fish don't receive much pressure and readily take properly presented flies. All the local guides like larger patterns in size #2 to #4, and that is what I use on the oceanside flats. For the creeks I tend to

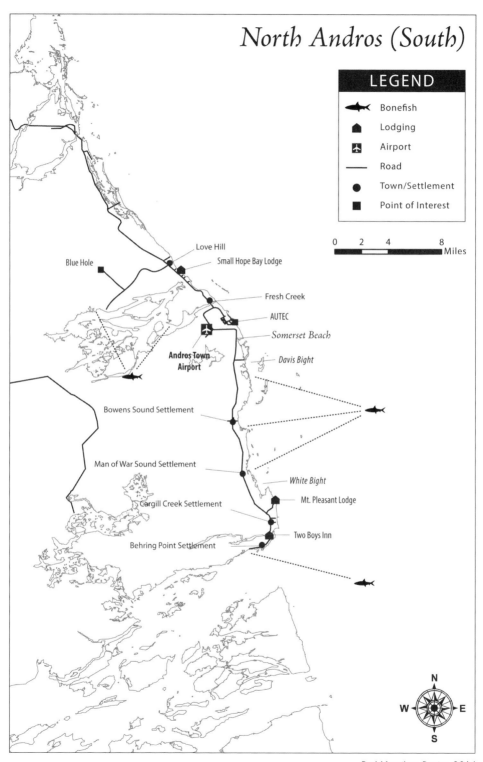

North Andros (South)

LEGEND

- ⊰— Bonefish
- 🏠 Lodging
- ✈ Airport
- — Road
- ● Town/Settlement
- ■ Point of Interest

0 2 4 8 Miles

Love Hill
Blue Hole
Small Hope Bay Lodge
Fresh Creek
AUTEC
Somerset Beach
Andros Town Airport
Davis Bight
Bowens Sound Settlement
Man of War Sound Settlement
White Bight
Cargill Creek Settlement
Mt. Pleasant Lodge
Two Boys Inn
Behring Point Settlement

N
W E
S

Rod Hamilton Design 2014

go a little smaller. Since you are not generally fishing water as deep as the guides do, I use slightly lighter weights than they recommend but stick to the bigger flies for those large ocean fish.

There are so many guides on Andros it is hard to pick out a couple, but below are some of the tried and true.

Frankie Neymour. www.twoboysinn.com

Benry Smith. www.evasbonefishinglodge.com

Where to Stay

Love at First Sight Hotel in Stafford Creek is good for a couple, family, or large group (www.loveatfirstsights.com). They have nine affordable double rooms with private baths, provide wi-fi, and serve authentic Bahamian meals.

Small Hope Bay in Fresh Creek is an all-inclusive hotel that provides 21 rooms in beachfront cottages, meals, beverages, bar drinks, and more (www.smallhope.com)! Ask about the wind surfer, four ocean kayaks, and other watercraft available for guests to use.

Two Boys Inn in Behring Point can take up to eight anglers in four rooms with A/C, two queen beds, and private bath (www.twoboysinn.com). Meals are served family style, starting with made-to-order breakfasts and ending with happy hour appies and authentic Bahamian home cooking.

Mount Pleasant Fishing Lodge, built in 2001, is framed by six miles of uninhabited coastline (www.mtpleasantfish.com). Family owned and operated, this property has been in the Farrington family for 100 years. If you haven't satisfied your desire to fish after a whole day on the water, simply walk the 50 feet from one of the four private cottages to hard-bottomed flats and fish until dark.

Getting Around

Airline schedules are in constant flux in the Bahamas, so speak with your accommodations provider for their suggestions. There are two airports that service North Andros: San Andros Airport near Nicholls Town and Andros International Airport located in Andros Town.

Sun Air offers a direct flight from Fort Lauderdale, Florida, to Andros Town several days a week.

LeAir. www.flyleair.com
Western Air. www.westernairbahamas.com
Sun Air. www.sunairexpress.com
Taxi service can be found at both airports.

As on many of the Out Islands, car rentals are an informal arrangement. It is advisable to check on price and availability before you arrive.

Tropical Car Rentals, Nicholls Town. (242) 329-2515
Executive Car Rentals, Conch Sound. (242) 329-2081
Jerome Scott, Andros Town. (242) 368-2255
Shores Car Rental, Blanket Sound. (242) 368-6140

Seven-Day Sample Trip

The most central location is Fresh Creek with several homes, cottages, and lodges in the area. Rent a car at the Andros Town Airport and from Fresh Creek you'll seldom drive more than 30 minutes to fish. On day one, hire a local guide and fish either the Middle Bight with a run over to the west side or head north and fish the world-famous Joulter Cays.

On day two, head north and launch your inflatable kayak in Staniard Creek and fish behind Kamalame Cay. Change it up on day three and hit the extensive ocean flats off Man-O-War Settlement and wade south, fishing all of White Bight.

The next day, get up early and make the 25-minute drive to the Stafford Creek Cemetery and catch the early morning tails, fishing the rest of the day on the 2.5 kilometers of ocean flats and creek. Day five, hit Davis Bight Creek three kilometers south of the airport on the incoming tide, then the large flats and mangrove edges of Davis Bight on the high tide.

On the last day of fishing drive to South Blanket Sound and launch your kayak at the sound's mouth and fish the channels, small cays, and inlets behind Kamalame Cay. If you catch a later plane on the last day, fish the small flat on the south shore of French Creek on the way to the airport.

Spousal Rating: 3

Andros is not known for its beaches although there are some beautiful ones. There aren't many tourist activities other than bonefishing and exploring the remarkable natural environment, so I would make it an anglers-only trip.

Nonfishing Activities

North Andros is a remarkable natural environment with the soft tropical sandy beaches of the north sweeping back to surprising, sweet-smelling pine forests. Divers come here to experience the Tongue of the Ocean, a 6,000-foot abyss, just past the world's third-largest barrier reef. It's enticing to explore the caves of Morgan's Bluff, a wide system of subterranean limestone caves, take a look at Uncle Charlie's Blue Hole, or see how many of the 200 species of birds you can spot.

Red Bay, located off the northwestern coast of North Andros, is a remote village originally settled by Seminole Indians from Florida fleeing a life restricted to a reservation. The people stayed hidden until approximately 50 years ago and remain a small, self-sufficient tribe where basket-weaving crafts continue and are considered masterful. Visit Androsia, a batik fabric and garment manufacturer producing a complete line of clothing, accessories, and fabric sold by the yard (www.androsia.com).

Androsia bonefish fabric drying. Andros, Bahamas

Bits and Pieces

Andros is a special fishing destination, offering the self-guided angler more variety then almost anywhere else, but the one environment that keeps drawing me back are the oceanside flats. I can't think of another place I've fished where a rental car is the only transportation needed to access miles and miles of hard-bottomed ocean flats. The draw to this type of habitat is the opportunity for shots at those large, dark-colored behemoths that travel as a single or in pairs. Spotting can be challenging since the bottom is a mixture of vegetation, coral, and dark rocks, but the adrenaline rush from seeing the tail of a 10-pound fish lasts for days.

THE EXUMAS

Lay of the Land

The Exuma archipelago comprises more than 360 cays 130 miles long, beginning a mere 30 miles southeast of Nassau. Great Exuma is the largest of the Exuma Islands at 37 miles in length, and it connects to Little Exuma in the south by a causeway. Small villages dot Great Exuma with the largest settlement being George Town, found in the center. Contagious feelings of peace and serenity flow from the friendly 4,000 residents, most of whom are employed in some kind of marine activity related to fishing, diving, or boating. Tourism and farming make up the other primary economic contributors.

In the 1700s Loyalists from North America fled to the islands, seeking refuge for themselves and their slaves to reconstruct their former way of life. The famous Hermitage Estate found in William's Town on Little Exuma was one of the many cotton plantations the expats built. Lord John Rolle, who imported the first cottonseeds to the island, ultimately freed his 300 slaves in 1835, passing down over 2,000 acres of crown land along with his name. Today the family name Rolle accounts for 60 percent of the native population in the Exuma Islands. The ruins of his original 970-acre property are a reminder of the significant role cotton plantations and slavery played in the island's culture.

Well-known as a boater's paradise, Exuma is building a reputation as an excellent DIY bonefishing destination. The main highway is in good

A monster Bahamian bonefish (Photo courtesy of Pat Ford)

shape, making exploration of the area easy. The airport is 15 minutes northwest of Exuma's capital George Town, where you will find a medical clinic staffed with a doctor, dentist, and nurse working somewhat regular hours. Banks, ATMs, and reasonably stocked (by Out Island standards!) grocery and hardware stores are here as well.

But it isn't all business! There are picturesque anchorages to visit along the waterfront, a number of small restaurants and roadside eateries to choose from, books to trade at the lending library, and George Town's terrific straw market showcasing locally made baskets, handbags, and hats. Landlines, cell phones, and Internet are everywhere but confirm "what works, where?" in advance.

Where to Fish

The Exumas provide great fishing for the self-guided angler and should be near the top of your bucket list. There is some fishing on the windward side, south of George Town, but most of the quality flats and creeks are

Exuma Island (North)

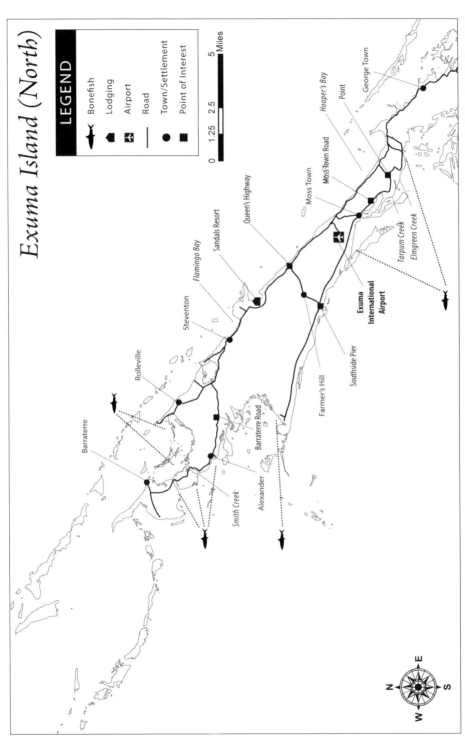

LEGEND

- Bonefish
- Lodging
- Airport
- Road
- Town/Settlement
- Point of Interest

0   1.25   2.5   5
Miles

Barraterre
Rolleville
Smith Creek
Alexander
Barraterre Road
Farmer's Hill
Southside Pier
Steventon
Sandals Resort
Flamingo Bay
Queen's Highway
Moss Town
Moss Town Road
Hooper's Bay
Point
George Town
Tarpum Creek
Elmgreen Creek
Exuma
International
Airport

N
W   E
S

Rod Hamilton Design 2014

located on the leeward side from Barretarre south to Little Exuma. Of all the places I've fished, the Exumas are one of the destinations where having a kayak makes the difference between an average trip and a great trip. Ensure the place you stay has a kayak and will let you transport it throughout the island, or else arrange your own. Many of the areas, streets, and creeks identified do not have formal names, so the references used are my own. Don't be afraid to ask the locals for directions.

Airport Flats. These are some of the most beautiful flats in the Bahamas and easily reached by self-guided anglers. To be clear, these are the flats located south and east of the abandoned airport runway, next to the U.S. military installation, south of George Town. For years the guides of Great Exuma would fish these flats with their clients, but I see them less and less as kayakers and wading fishermen have discovered the area for themselves. The flats are so extensive that I've broken them up into three sections with separate access points to each. As long as you have a kayak to cross the shoreline channel, you can fish it all. The fish here get pressured and see enough flies to make them skittish, but I have found them more

Kim with a five pounder from Exuma, Bahamas

catchable than some other difficult places like Cherokee Sound on Abaco or Savannah Sound on Eleuthera.

Airport Flats, West. This section comprises the flats and cays extending west from the abandoned runway, including Mary, Bonefish, and Gutter cays. They start due south of the kayak put-in and are reached with a paddle of just more than a half mile. Once across the channel you can walk and wade the flats all the way to Bonefish Cay at low tide and then fish completely around the mangrove edge. There are too many cays and flats to name in the immediate area, but a kayak makes many of them accessible for DIY fishing. To reach the put-in, drive to the old airport then down the runway to the garbage/recycling area and take the dirt road to the left, following it to the boat ramp used by locals. Launch your kayak here and paddle due south across the channel to the cay in the distance. This is not the place to fish at high tide; the fish are out of reach deep into the mangroves.

Airport Flats, Middle. There are numerous places to access the middle flats; the easiest is to stay at one of the homes located on the shore. Take either of the entry roads into the Master Harbour residential area, a grand unfulfilled dream of the 1960s, and head to the leeward side of the island. Once you reach the shore, there are several places to put in. My preference is the one at the northern end of the residential development where the road ends close to a nice cove. I launch the kayak here, paddle the 100 yards across the channel, anchor the kayak, and fish to the west. From here you can walk two miles to the west and three miles to the east.

Airport Flats, East. This is the one section of the flats where you don't need a kayak. At high tide the water reaches your waist and it's calf deep at low tide. As you enter Rolletown from the north, take the dirt road heading south. The road stops at the water about one kilometer from the Queen's Highway. At the water's edge you will see a vast flat in front, enticing you to wade from there. Though it is good in every direction, I prefer to walk the rocky shoreline east (left) for a half mile before entering the water. Walk the 200 yards across the channel and begin fishing. There are schools of bones that follow the tide and seem to be less spooky than those in the middle section. Once standing on the flat, it is a beautiful sight to behold. You can literally see five miles west, with nothing in front of you but white Bahamian bonefish flats.

Man-O-War Cay. This area is reached by driving south from George Town to Rolletown and reaching the water by taking the first road to the left on the ocean side. The turn is found on the north edge of Rolletown once you have passed the two bends in the road. The road leads to a boat launch and is a good place to put in the kayak. From here it is a half-mile paddle to the shore of Man-O-War Cay where you can walk or kayak the bays and flats to the north. In addition, there are other spots along the coast to launch where the paddle to the south end of Man-O-War Cay is as short as 300 yards. Good fishing can be found along the leeward shore of the cay on the incoming tide.

Moriah Harbour Cay. Both the west and eastern ends of Moriah Harbour Cay have excellent flats. You can reach the western end by kayaking across the channel south from Man-O-War Cay or putting in south of Rolletown. If staying at Exuma Vacation Cottages, launch off their dock and make the half-mile paddle to the western flats. To reach the eastern flats, drive south toward the old Peace and Plenty Lodge and put in from the road. The eastern flats and creeks are a longer paddle around Goat Cay, but there are some wonderful areas to fish.

Sand Point. You may have to ask a local about this site. After crossing the bridge to Little Exuma, take a left and drive to the ocean opening at Sand Point. You can put in on the ocean side and paddle around the point or put in on the bay side. Either way you need a kayak to fish the interior flats.

Little Exuma Mangrove Flats. Cross the bridge to Little Exuma and take the first right to a series of extensive mangroves and creek systems. One mile from the highway there are two different short dirt roads to pull off. You need a kayak in here, but it's a great place to explore. Continue on the same road for another 1.2 miles to a path leading through the mangroves and to the water. This is a good place to put in the kayak as it opens up an endless array of flats, creeks, and mangrove cays.

Turtle Cove. Halfway between Moore Hill and William's Town is a zigzag road to the ocean side. Drive to the bottom to find a small creek opening and creek system.

Scott's Creek. Driving to William's Town on Little Exuma, go past the Santana Fish Fry Shack then take the road to the right. This takes you to a concrete pier, boat ramp, and Scott's Creek. Launch the kayak and paddle down the creek to the ocean. There are two nice flats that are easy to wade, and there always seem to be fish on the incoming tide.

Hartswell Flat. In Hartswell, look for the old residential development large enough to hold hundreds of homes but in fact holding very few. Once in the development, follow the roads to the southeast corner where you will find the bonefish flats of Hartswell. This is an excellent group of flats with substantial flow to bring the fish in and out with the tide. These can be waded, but a kayak comes in handy.

Almgreen Creek. North of George Town and directly across the island from Hooper's Bay is Almgreen Creek at Bullard's Landing. Leaving the Queen's Highway at Tar Bay, head toward the Hermitage. At the Hermitage, take the left turn to Bullard's Landing. Launch your kayak here at the opening of Almgreen Creek and you can paddle to the southeast up the creek to the flats and mangroves.

Tarpum Creek. Instead of turning off the road to Almgreen Creek at the Hermitage, continue straight to a small settlement and at the right-hand turn take the dirt track to the water. This is Tarpum Creek with excellent fishing on the flats and in the creek. A kayak is necessary here.

Exuma Airport Creek. Located south of the Exuma International Airport in Moss Town is a large creek system that can be fished by kayak. The simplest way to reach it is from the Queen's Highway 0.4 miles south of the airport on the road to Moss Town. Follow this road for 1.3 miles to the boat dock that is directly on the creek providing access to the flats. This is Pindling Drive, which follows the shoreline and provides access to a number of fishable creeks and flats both north and south.

Southside Pier. North of the airport, drive through Farmer's Hill to the leeward side of the island to reach the Southside Pier. Put the kayak in here and paddle to the south about 0.5 miles where you will find a little creek and mangrove system that is home to a good population of fish.

Alexander Flat. This is a large creek and flat located on the leeward side of the northwest end of the island. It can be accessed from a couple of places. The first is down a rough path from Richmond Hill Settlement and the second is farther north from the small settlement of Alexander. Once in Alexander, there is a short road leading to a parking area where the locals tie up boats. The creek and flats are massive, and a kayak is necessary to reach the fish.

Bone from a creek on the north end of Great Exuma

Smith Creek. This is the first creek crossed on the way to Barretarre. Use this creek to access the flats north or south of the bridge. Both directions are excellent, so make the decision based on the direction of the tide.

Odi Creek. The second bridge to Barretarre crosses Odi Creek one mile north of Smith Creek. The two creeks are part of the same system so you can put in at either place, but Odi Creek is a little closer to the northern sections of the flat.

North End. There are two nice beaches and flats on the north end of the island. The first is just north of Rolleville where the Queen's Highway takes a hard right-hand turn at the water. You can fish the shore here or paddle a kayak out to the small cays 250 yards offshore then keep paddling through the cut to the cays on the other side. The second beach is north another mile. Park where you can see the beach to wade.

Fishing Information

As mentioned previously, a boat or kayak is essential to make the most out of a trip to the Exumas. Boat rentals are available in George Town,

Exuma Island (South)

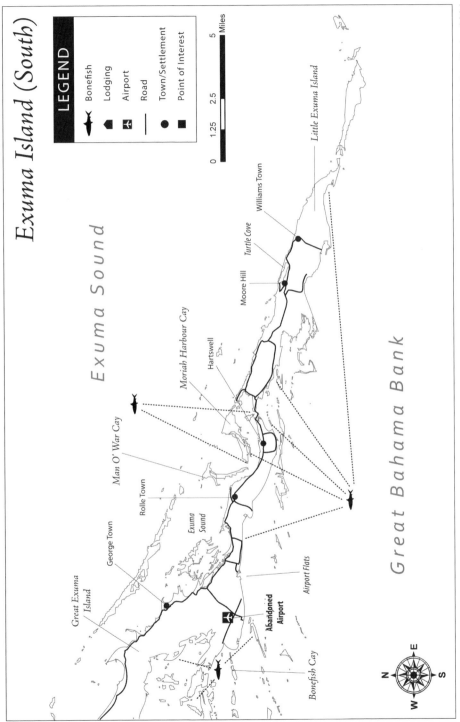

LEGEND

Bonefish
Lodging
Airport
Road
Town/Settlement
Point of Interest

0   1.25   2.5   5
Miles

Exuma Sound

Great Bahama Bank

Little Exuma Island

Williams Town

Turtle Cove

Moore Hill

Hartswell

Moriah Harbour Cay

Man O' War Cay

Rolle Town

George Town

Exuma Sound

Great Exuma Island

Airport Flats

Abandoned Airport

Bonefish Cay

N
E
S
W

Rod Hamilton Design 2014

but there are restrictions on how far you can take them and there are only a few vendors that rent kayaks. The simplest approach is to determine if your rental accommodations come with a kayak or to bring your own inflatable kayak that you can comfortably paddle up to one mile.

The tides on Great Exuma can be a wonderful help to fishermen. Much like those in Eleuthera, the tides differ by as much as three hours, north to south, and two hours from the eastern to the western shore. That means, with a little planning, you can fish the tides you want virtually all day.

The fish on Airport Flats don't have their PhDs, but let me tell you, they are well on their way to getting their master's degrees. They get pressured and have seen most of the flies in Dick Brown's book. When fishing the middle section of the flats in front of the homes, use long leaders with at least four feet of fluorocarbon and lean toward smaller flies. Flies that move on their own without a retrieve are best, such as something with rubber legs or rabbit fur that will create motion based on the cur-

One of several that morning from Airport Flats, Great Exuma

208

rent rather than a retrieve. For the tailing fish you often have to go with weightless flies that can be cast right on top of the fish without making a sound. The fish in the other areas listed above don't get anywhere near the pressure as those on Airport Flats and the bonefish react the way they're supposed to. Most of the usual flies in your box will work.

There are some big fish in the Exumas. The average fish is typical of the Bahamas, ranging from three to six pounds, but over the course of a week you're sure to see fish close to double digits.

There are a number of very good guides on Great Exuma and it's hard to pick the best two, so my advice is to contact the Exuma Bonefish Guides Association through their website (exumabonefish.com).

There are a limited number of places that rent boats or kayaks:

Minns Water Sports in George Town, boat rentals. info@mwsboats.com

Out-Island Explorers in George Town, kayak rentals. www.outisland explorers.com

Where to Stay

Great Exuma is a long island and to stay on either end means you could be driving while you should be fishing. I prefer to stay centrally, specifically in the Airport Flats area. There is no beach on Airport Flats, so it may not be suitable for a nonfishing spouse or children.

The options for accommodations are endless; you can find whatever you want on Great Exuma from high-end oceanfront villas and resorts to budget-friendly cottages. Do a little homework on VRBO or HomeAway and you should be able to find whatever you are looking for.

If you are looking specifically at waterfront homes on Airport Flats, contact Michael Joyce (michaeljoyce71@hotmail.com), who manages a number of locations that are perfect for couples and fishing groups.

Getting Around

The Exumas major airport, Exuma International Airport, is located 10 miles north of George Town. It is one of the easiest islands to get to with a number of flights each day to and from Nassau, the United States, and Canada.

Bahamasair, several flights per day. www.bahamassair.com
American Eagle, daily from Miami. www.aa.com
United Express, daily from Fort Lauderdale. www.united.com
Air Canada, direct from Toronto on Sundays. www.aircanada.com
A rental car is necessary and there are many agencies to choose from.
Don's Rentals. donsrentacar@hotmail.com
Airport Rental. www.exumacarrental.com
Thompsons Rental. thompsonsrental@hotmail.com

Seven-Day Sample Trip

Rent one of the homes on Airport Flats that comes equipped with kayaks and you are good to go. Hire a guide for the first day to get a good look at the leeward side of Great Exuma. Always be home two hours before sunset for the tailing fish in front of your house. Dinner is never before 9:00 p.m. on Great Exuma anyway! On the second day take the 15 steps out your

Kim Hamilton with a nice bonefish caught on the southern end of Great Exuma

front door and launch a kayak to cross the narrow channel onto Airport Flats and fish the six miles of sparkling white sand that lies before you. Day three, load the kayak on the car and head south to Hartswell to fish the endless flats, creeks, and mangrove cays found just off the road. Hump day, launch the kayak north of the abandoned runway to fish the flats and cays of the northern section of Airport Flats. Day five, head to Rolletown and put in at the boat ramp and fish the ocean side of Great Exuma. There is a lot of territory to cover here, but fish the leeward side of Moriah Harbour Cay and Man-O-War Cay. Day six, put the kayak in at Bullard's Landing to fish both Almgreen and Tarpum creeks. Make the most of the last day and take the dirt road north of Rolletown to the southern section of Airport Flats. No kayak needed here, just a quick walk and wade.

Spousal Rating: 6

I found Great Exuma to be a difficult place to rate. My wife loves it there and gives it a solid eight, whereas the wives of some of my fishing buddies wouldn't go back. What you will find are beautiful Atlantic beaches and exactly the accommodations you want, but there is limited shopping and no restaurants or nightlife.

Nonfishing Activities

Not surprisingly, you can find almost any water-based activity on Great Exuma. Boating and sailing are the most popular activities here, but options like kayaking, diving, and snorkeling can make it hard to choose what to do next! Hiking and cycling are good if you want something on terra firma.

A short ferry ride from Elizabeth Harbour will get you to Stocking Island, which features spectacular views from atop its high bluff. Beautiful white sandy beaches face the Atlantic, and there are brilliant turquoise water and coves on the flip side. Enjoy something to eat at the Lunch Shack known for the best burgers in the islands, go to the Chat and Chill for something a little more uptown, or book the Sunday pig roast for an all-day event!

If you have the use of a boat, visit the Exuma Cays Land and Sea Park, known for its pristine beauty, outstanding anchorages, and breathtaking marine environment. At 176 square miles it is the largest marine preserve of its kind. Nightlife is on the quiet side, but the residents are friendly and there always seems to be a place open to have a beverage and meet a fellow explorer!

Bits and Pieces

My wife and I stayed for a month in a cute little cottage called Sea Biscuit on Airport Flats. We would wake up each morning, take our coffee out onto the deck, and enjoy the warmth of the sun and the enchantment of the sparkling tropical water dancing over the flat. We walked the flats for miles everyday, made it home at dark, had dinner then rolled into bed, tired but happy. As I find happening more and more frequently with advancing years, nature called and I groggily made my way to the bathroom. Two steps onto the cold tile floor, a shooting pain, and a scream: "Not again!" (expletives removed). I knew that I had stepped on a scorpion. The searing pain was familiar because I had been stung in Cuba the year before! I mean really, how many fishermen do you know who have been stung twice by scorpions? Now I wear it like a badge of honor and figure it's like being struck by lightning. It's happened to me twice; surely that is my allotment for life . . . isn't it?

CHAPTER 5
SOUTHERN YUCATAN, MEXICO

Lay of the Land

The Yucatan land mass is huge, encompassing the Mexican states of Yucatan, Campeche, and Quintana Roo. While there are fishing opportunities in the northern regions of the Yucatan, other than some bonefishing in Cozumel, bonefishing is concentrated from Akumal south to Xcalak.

From Cancun, drive 90 minutes south on a new highway to reach Akumal, Mayan for "place of the turtles." Sea turtles come to lay their eggs in this beautiful community of white beaches and beautiful bays. With plenty of restaurants, housing options, gift shops, grocery stores, and other services, this is a good home base if traveling with family or nonangling partners.

Tulum, 30 minutes south of Akumal, is the site of a pre-Columbian walled city and a popular tourist destination. It is one of the last cities built and inhabited by the Mayans, dating to the third century BC. The town comprises three sectors: Tulum Pueblo, Tulum Playa, and Tulum Ruinas. Most of the workers servicing the tourist industry call Tulum Pueblo ("El Pueblo" as the locals call it) home. Dotted with local fruit and vegetable stands, bus stations, and small hotels and hostels, it has a modest nightlife and provides a noncommercial flavor. Tulum Playa follows the coastline, showcasing boutique and spa hotels with a good selection of restaurants, the brand-new Chedraui Supermarket, and some nightspots. Tulum Ruinas is the archaeological site where the Mayan ruins of Tulum stand (and they are not to be missed).

Ten minutes down the coast road is the entrance to the Sian Ka'an Biosphere Reserve, an incredible 1.3 million-acre reserve whose name means "Origin of the Sky." About 30 miles from the reserve's entrance is Punta Allen, a small Mayan lobster fishing village with 469 residents, located at the tip of the Boca Paila Peninsula. One side of the village borders the Caribbean, the other Ascension Bay. The village has several blocks of sandy streets, palm trees, and small homes. Two generators run electricity to the village twice daily, so it is wise to bring a flashlight. Although there is no gas station, there are a few small markets, a cantina, and a couple of restaurants.

Back on the main highway and an easy three-hour drive from Tulum on a jungle-bordered highway is the small fishing village of Mahahual, which has also become a cruise ship destination. Located on the beautiful turquoise Caribbean Sea with white powdery beaches, the town has two distinct personalities. When cruise ships are in, thousands

Entrance sign to the Sian Ka'an Biosphere, Mexico

come ashore, changing the peaceful waterfront to one of high energy with packed beaches, water sports, and vendors selling wares. But it is very quiet when the ships aren't in port, and you can get a good feel for the locals' friendly nature and the natural beauty of the area. Everything is scaled down a notch or two here compared to Tulum, which is why many people want to visit. The road system ranges from paved streets to dirt paths riddled with potholes. There are no banks, but credit cards are widely accepted. Everyone has a cell phone, and wi-fi can be found without too much hunting.

Xcalak, just north of the Belize border, is about 35 miles from Mahahual and the most southern town in the state of Quintana Roo. With 400 residents and few tourists, this destination is a rustic road much less traveled. Cars are the way to get around although you need to get gas in Mahahual, as it is not readily available in Xcalak. It's also a good idea to shop in Tulum for food if you haven't planned to eat at a local lodge or the restaurant in town. There are no banks, clinics, or landlines, but cell phones and Internet coverage are available depending on where you stay.

Taco stand in Xcalak, Mexico

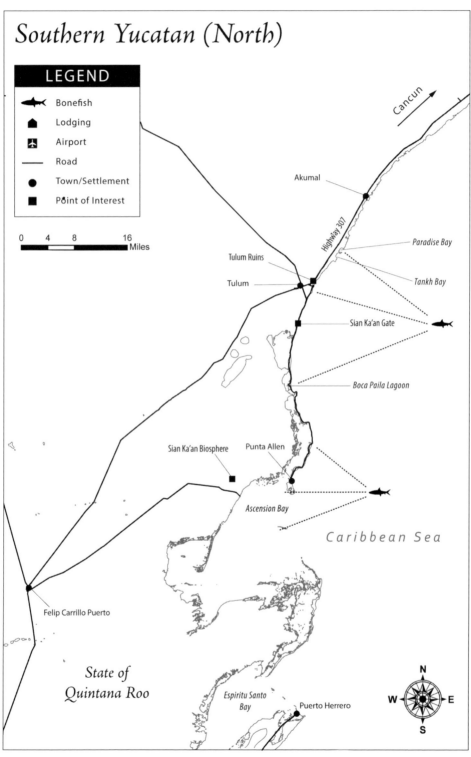

Southern Yucatan (North)

LEGEND

- ⤛ Bonefish
- ⬠ Lodging
- ✈ Airport
- — Road
- ● Town/Settlement
- ■ Point of Interest

0   4   8   16
Miles

Cancun

Akumal

Highway 307

Paradise Bay

Tulum Ruins

Tankh Bay

Tulum

Sian Ka'an Gate

Boca Paila Lagoon

Sian Ka'an Biosphere

Punta Allen

Ascension Bay

Caribbean Sea

Felip Carrillo Puerto

State of
Quintana Roo

Espiritu Santo
Bay

Puerto Herrero

N
W · E
S

Rod Hamilton Design 2014

Where to Fish

The area from Akumal south to Xcalak offers the fly fishing enthusiast some of the most diverse fishing habitats found anywhere in the world. This book is about bonefishing, but it wouldn't be fair not to mention the other species that can be caught when fishing the southern Yucatan's Caribbean coastline, estuaries, and interior lagoons. I can't think of another destination where the self-guided angler has a better shot at the grand slam or super slam of bonefish, tarpon, permit, and snook. Boca Paila and Ascension Bay are famous for their lodges and world-class fishing, but if you want to do it yourself, there are plenty of DIY opportunities.

Akumal to Punta Allen

Akumal. The two main bays in Akumal are closed to fishing, which is slightly irritating to the diehard angler. Most days, it's easy to spot bonefish happily digging away in Akumal Bay, oblivious to the swimmers. On a couple of occasions I have been snorkeling with the turtles, only to see a 15-pound permit cruise past. North of Akumal are the canals of the gated residential area, Puerto Aventuras, which have good fishing, but access now is limited.

Xcacel Bay. Approximately 4.6 miles south of the Akumal turnoff is the road to Xcacel with its beautiful white beach that at times has bonefish and often other species cruising the shoreline. You should be aware that both Xcacel and the more southern bay, Xcacelito, are turtle nesting beaches, so they may be closed for fishing at times.

Xcacelito Bay. Adjacent to and immediately south of Xcacel is another gorgeous beach called Xcacelito that can be fished in the early morning and late afternoon.

Soliman Bay. This beautiful crescent-shaped beach holds bonefish, jacks, barracuda, and triggerfish. There are several private residences along the shore, and fishing is discouraged in front of the homes. Both the south and north ends of the bay hold fish. To get to Soliman Bay, travel 2.45 miles south on Highway 307 past the entrance to Xel-Ha. Follow the side road toward the water until you reach the guard, then tell him you are going to have lunch at Chamico's. Once past the guard, continue on the road south to the end of the bay and park where you see the small cooking hut and a few scattered picnic tables. Tell Chamico you would like to have lunch at noon and ask if it would be OK to fish for a few hours before and after lunch. What could be more Mexican? The fishing on the southern end of the bay can be good for a variety of species, and you will often find bonefish. After lunch walk to the north end of the bay to fish the small cove.

Paradise Bay. This secluded bay is north of Soliman Bay, but it's easiest to access by parking at Chamico's and walking north around the point. Paradise Bay has bones, permit, jacks, cudas, and other species to target. The entire shoreline holds fish, but one of the best spots is in the far northwest corner where you will find a couple of cenotes.

Tankah Bay. You can reach the northern corner of Tankah Bay, which is located to the south of Soliman Bay, by either walking south from Chamico's or driving south on the highway 2.3 miles from the turn-off to Soliman Bay. There are a number of private homes along the beach, but you will find some decent fishing on both the north and south ends.

Tulum Beach, North. Once you reach the town of Tulum, take the left-hand turn toward the water. At the Y veer left and head toward the Tulum ruins. Along the coast road are several public sand roads providing access to the beach. These are perfect, pristine white-sand beaches and are a great place to walk early in the morning and late in the evening when the beaches are virtually deserted. You never know what will take a fly—bones, jacks, cudas, or a bunch of other finny creatures.

Tulum Beach, South. At the Y in the road turn right toward the Sian Ka'an Biosphere gate. The road meets the ocean almost immediately, providing access to the next couple of miles of sand and rock beaches. It is best to arrive early in the morning when you will be sharing the sea with locals fishing and netting baitfish.

Centro Ecológico Sian Ka'an (CESiaK). Three miles from the Sian Ka'an Biosphere entrance is the eco-resort CESiaK. The ocean beach both north and south of here is nothing short of magnificent. When the wind and seas are calm, this stretch of beach can be walked for miles in either direction as you look for bones and jacks.

Boca Paila Bridge. Boca Paila is world famous for its fishing and lodges, but there are several areas for the self-guided angler as well. One of the most obvious is at the bridge, where the road crosses the Boca Paila Lagoon outflow to the ocean. There are several spots to fish, and the targeted species include bones, tarpon, permit, snook, and jacks. The easiest access is via a trail located on the north end of the bridge. Park in the pullout, walk the trail toward the mouth, and where the trail meets the water, walk and wade west back toward the bridge. You can't wade all the way to the bridge, so turn around when it's too deep and fish back toward the inlet's entrance. Once back at the mouth, blind cast your Clouser into the channel and surf—you never know what you might catch. From the mouth start wading north, looking for snook and jacks in the waves and bones closer to the beach. The fishing north is good for almost two miles. There is a less-defined trail on the south end of the bridge, providing access to the entrance and beach to the south.

Boca Paila Bridge Flats. There is a series of three flats to the west of the bridge, with an entry point about 200 yards north of the parking area. It's possible to wade around the entire mangrove cay looking for fish as they come out of the deep water. It's very likely that you will get a shot at a permit if you hit the tide right, so have a crab pattern handy. But keep your eyes open—there are crocs in that area.

Boca Paila Road. As you continue south from the bridge toward Punta Allen there are a number of spots to pull over and fish the beach. Approximately 1.2 miles south of the bridge is a nice bay with a rocky point. The southern end of the bay often holds bonefish, and the rocky point is an excellent spot to intercept permit. After rounding the point the road returns to the water, and for the next 2.5 miles there are several places to pull over and walk the beach. The next curve in the road takes you to a side road, providing access to the southern end of another nice bay and rocky point. From here south to Punta Allen the road follows the ocean closely, so pull over and fish when you see a likely looking spot.

Punta Allen. This area is not known for DIY fishing, but there are a few places to fish, including a small flat at the lighthouse and the lagoon side, close to the mangroves.

Punta Herrero to Xcalak

The fishing opportunities from Punta Herrero south to Xcalak range from beaches on the Caribbean coast to landlocked inland lagoons, from "rivers" that flow in and out with the tide to enormous bodies of water like Chetamul Bay. In a single day self-guided anglers can catch bonefish, tarpon, permit, snook, jacks, and barracuda. I don't know anywhere else that can be done in a single DIY day.

Caribbean side of Xcalak, dock at Tierra Maya Resort

Punta Herrero. Punta Herrero is the "end of the road" for Costa Maya and the southern entrance into the Sian Ka'an Biosphere. Reached by taking the road north from Mahahual, it takes about two and a half hours to arrive at this small Mexican fishing village. The 47-mile road is paved to the military checkpoint, after which it turns into a passable dirt and sand track. The DIY opportunities around Punta Herrero are limited, with the exception of some interesting flats on the lagoon side, but there are local fishermen that can be hired to take you out for the day. They don't know anything about fly fishing, but they know where the bonefish are.

Costa Maya Beaches, North. Heading north from Mahahual and passing mile 29, the road finally approaches the Caribbean, skirting the shoreline for the next 20 miles. This section of coastline provides some of the most exciting fishing in the southern Yucatan. Miles of deserted white sandy beaches with small ocean flats interspersed with rocky points provide an ideal environment for bonefish, permit, and jacks. You will not see another fisherman, and the fish you cast to have never encountered an artificial fly. Be prepared to cast to bonefish, permit, monster jacks, and oceangoing barracuda the size of small fishing boats.

Northern Lagoons. The road from Mahahual to Punta Herrero passes by a large number of inland lagoons. Connected to the ocean by underground caves and tunnels (cenotes), most of the lagoons hold sizable populations of bones, tarpon, and snook. Mosquitero, Bugle Boy, Aeropuerto, Murky, Papas, Cenote, and Blood are just some of the lagoons you pass on the way to Punta Herrero. Most are open to the public with varying degrees of accessibility. They can be fished by kayak or canoe with some wading in places. The lagoons hold tarpon to 50 pounds, some monster snook, and bonefish, if not netted out by the locals.

Mahahual. The vibe and dynamic of Mahahual has transformed over the last 10 years from a sleepy Mexican fishing village to a cruise ship port. The dichotomy is interesting; when a cruise ship is not in port, it's a small, quaint town, but when a ship arrives, the Mahahual overflows with 2,000 to 4,000 tourists. Surprisingly, the fishing is quite good off the beach in town and continues for the next few miles both north and south. North of the cruise ship terminal there is excellent fishing for bonefish, permit, jacks, and barracuda by walking the rocky coastline and wading the intermittent sandy beaches. The coastal beach road south of Mahahual also provides excellent fishing for bones and permit.

Mahahual, South. Following the coast road south from Mahahual presents a wide range of opportunities for bones, permit, and jacks. Once connected to Xcalak, the road now stops at mile 23 where the bridge at

Nick Denbow with a nice Mexican bonefish from the shore of Mahahual

Rio Hauche is washed out. Much like the coastal road north from Ma-hahual, the road south passes by inland lagoons, rocky shorelines, and sandy beaches. Anglers can often find permit around the rocky points, and the sandy bays are excellent places to wade for bonefish. Many of the flats along this section of road are covered with turtle grass, providing an excellent habitat for the bonefish but making it harder to sight fish. The river and lagoon system of Rio Hauche can be reached either by driving south from Mahahual or north from Xcalak and offers something differ-ent for the adventuresome angler. It's a long paddle in your kayak from the mouth to the lagoon, and once you arrive there the terrain can be quite confusing. If you want to fish the Rio Hauche system, my recom-mendation is that you hire a guide or local fishermen from the village at the bridge; they have fished the Rio Hauche all their lives.

Xcalak. The small fishing village of Xcalak (pop. 400) is reached by exiting Highway 307 toward Mahahual and taking a right turn 2.5 miles before town. From the intersection, the paved road heads south for 37 miles and comes to a T just north of a small airport runway. Take the left-hand turn and continue into Xcalak. There is some fishing in Xcalak itself, including the town's beachfront, the Xcalak lagoon (located west of the small bridge), and Cemetery lagoon south of town. Other than that, most of the fishing is either north up the coast road to Rio Hauche or west on the eastern shores of Chetamul Bay.

Xcalak, North. The coast road used to connect to Mahahual, but the bridge is out at Rio Hauche, approximately 12 miles north of Xcalak. This section of the Caribbean shoreline is a mixture of rock and sand protected by a barrier reef. The fishing starts north of the Terra Maya Resort and continues until reaching Rio Hauche. There are plenty of bones and permit, but the turtle grass–covered bottom provides natural camouflage, making the fish difficult to spot. This is one of my favorite shores to fish from a kayak or stand-up paddleboard, which allows you to cover longer distances as you look for tails at low tide. The road passes a number of productive and accessible lagoons; if you are staying at Casa De Suenos, kayaks are located on a lagoon behind the house.

Chetamul Bay. Drive west out of Xcalak and at the T continue driv-ing straight for 0.5 miles until coming to an intersection. Take the left turn heading toward the abandoned ferry dock and park before crossing the small bridge and creek. From here you can fish Chetamul Bay located

David with a Mexican bonefish from Stinky's Lagoon, Xcalak

Peter with a bonefish from the lagoons of Xcalak, Mexico

First-ever bonefish

to the west or the lagoon systems located to the east. Both places are productive for bonefish, and often your choice will be made based on the direction and strength of the wind. Continuing down the road, you will see a small bay to the south, adjacent to the ferry dock. This bay always has fish in it and is worth an hour's fishing. From this bay, continue walking south and fish the shoreline of Chetamul Bay. Once back in the car, return north, driving away from the ferry terminal, and when you hit the intersection turn left. This overgrown road will take you to a small rock jetty. From here, walk and wade south toward the ferry dock or wade north to fish the first two bays. The water becomes too deep beyond the point of the second bay, making a kayak necessary. One of my favorite kayak trips is to the flats north of the rock jetty. I have fished as far north as five miles, but it looks inviting even beyond that.

Fishing Information

Laws and regulations for sport anglers are a little vague in Mexico, but you do need a sports fishing license, which can be purchased online at www.bestbajafishing.org/fishing-permits.php.

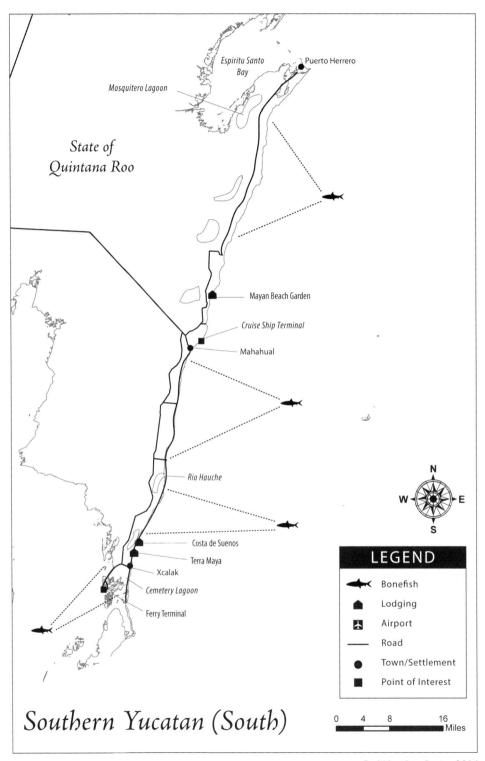

Espiritu Santo Bay

Puerto Herrero

Mosquitero Lagoon

State of
Quintana Roo

Mayan Beach Garden

Cruise Ship Terminal

Mahahual

Rio Hauche

Costa de Suenos

Terra Maya

Xcalak

Cemetery Lagoon

Ferry Terminal

N
W E
S

LEGEND

Bonefish

Lodging

Airport

Road

Town/Settlement

Point of Interest

Southern Yucatan (South)

0 4 8 16
Miles

Rod Hamilton Design 2014

Crocodile looking at a school of bonefish in the Sian Ka'an Biosphere

The Sian Ka'an Biosphere Reserve is a 1.3-million-acre nature reserve with an entrance south of Tulum beach. Upon entering the Sian Ka'an Biosphere it is necessary to stop at the gate, pay your entry fee, and register. I have gone to great lengths to find the printed rules and regulations pertaining to self-guided sports anglers in the biosphere but to date have come up empty. Provided you have a Mexican fishing license, you are allowed to fish within the biosphere, but I have been unable to verify if a kayak is allowed. At this time, I believe you must get a special permit to use your kayak there, but I don't know how you apply for it.

The road from the biosphere's gate to Punta Allen is at best a crap shoot. I have been on it when making the eight miles to the bridge took 90 minutes, loosening every tooth in my mouth, but when the road was graded I have made the 30-mile drive to Punta Allen in virtually the same amount of time.

All beaches in Mexico are public and open to fishing. Providing you have gained access to the beach legally, there is no problem. The major resorts and many homeowners prefer you don't fish in front of their property, so it's best to fish where it's a little more private.

There is no gas available inside the biosphere, so gas up in Tulum, and carry cash because credit cards won't do you much good.

Bonefish flies in Mexico are smaller than those used in the Keys, Bahamas, or Cuba. The typical sizes are #6 to #8 with some, like the Pop's Bitters, dropping down to #12. In most places, the bottom is darker than the crystal white sand of the Bahamas, so flies should tend toward the tans, browns, and greens with cream being the lightest color. Often, the fishing is over turtle grass, rocks, and coral, requiring a weed guard on the fly. If you're with a guide and fishing the flats of Ascension or Chetamul bays you won't need weed guards, but the flats off the Caribbean coast from Mahahual south to Xcalak require them. Usual patterns like Charlies and Gotchas tied with rubber legs work well as do patterns tied with rabbit fur. Small mantis shrimp and a variety of crab patterns should be included in your bonefish fly box. When fishing the Caribbean side of Mexico, you need to carry flies for other species like jacks and cudas, and, no matter where you are, always have a permit crab ready to be tied on.

Bonefish average two to three pounds with the occasional five-pounder caught on every trip. The size of the bonefish means a seven-weight rod handles the fish fine, but the wind still howls, so an eight-weight is easier to cast.

On the famous waters of the biosphere, Boca Paila, and Ascension Bay, there are any number of guides to choose from. My recommendation is you contact John Earles of Tulum Fly Fishing; he is not a guide but matches guides to the fisherman.

Making sure I have everything before a day on Chetamul Bay, Mexico

For Mahahual north to Punta Herrero, the guide to contact is Nick Denbow of Western Caribbean Fly Fishing School.

In Xcalak, there are a number of local guides, including Captain Victor of Xcalak Fly Fishing.

It's virtually impossible to find a boat or kayak to rent outside of Tulum, but a number of the resorts and rental homes have kayaks for use by customers. In many cases they don't let you take kayaks off the property, which really limits their usefulness. My advice is to bring your own inflatable watercraft with you. In small fishing villages like Xcalak, Rio Hauche, and Puerto Herrero there are local fishermen that will take you out for a day. If your Spanish is as pathetic as mine, part of the adventure is trying to communicate and negotiate a day's trip. You can be assured they know nothing about fly fishing, but they know where the bonefish are.

Where to Stay

Accommodations are plentiful in Akumal and Tulum, but there are significantly fewer as you move south to Mahahual and finally Xcalak. There is lots of information on the web, but below are some options that I can recommend.

Akumal has something to fit every budget and travel group, ranging from all-inclusive resorts to beachfront condos to private villas.

To make the choice simple contact Rhett Schober, owner of **Akumal Villas** (www.akumal-villa.com).

Tulum has become more popular as a tourist destination over the last ten years and has something for everyone. My recommendation in Tulum is the **El Pez Resort** at Turtle Cove (www.tulumhotelpez.com).

In Punta Allen, **Serenidad Shardon** offers a beach house and two cabanas that can sleep ten, six, four, or two (www.shardon.com). Ask them about providing kayaks for local exploration!

In Mahahual, tourists stay on the "mall" or boardwalk area of town running north and south along the coast. There are far more options here than in Xcalak with choices ranging from hotels to boutique resorts and private homes. My recommendation is **El Hotelito** (www.elhotelito mahahual.com). If you'd like to stay out of town, I recommend **Mayan Beach Garden Inn** (www.mayanbeachgarden.com).

Xcalak has a few options to investigate. With the traditional feel of a fishing lodge, **Costa de Cocos** has 16 private cabanas, a restaurant, and a bar (www.costadecocos.com).

Kim and David Calkins's **Hotel Tierra Maya** has six spacious ocean-front suites and one private apartment (www.tierramaya.net). They provide a complimentary breakfast as well as the use of ocean kayaks and bicycles. Enjoy a beverage along with dinner over "fish tales" at the Maya Grill, which is open every evening.

Five miles north of Xcalak, **Casa de Suenos** (www.casadesuenos xcalak.com) offers a two-bedroom oceanfront apartment and two one-bedroom apartments.

Getting Around

What can I say—getting to the Yucatan is easy—simply fly into Cancun! Renting a car is a must and is easy to arrange. The rental cars in Mexico

Gassing up in Xcalak, Mexico

are generally clean and well maintained, but they are usually smaller than rentals found in North America. They can be on the expensive side, but discounts are often available when booking a week or longer.

I have had good luck with **America Car Rentals** (www.america -carrental.com), and their free shuttle service will take you from the airport to your rental.

Taxis are plentiful in Akumal, Tulum, and Mahahual. To see the town in a different way, bikes are a good option; they can be rented and are often included with your accommodations.

The drive from Cancun Airport to Tulum is around 2.5 hours. Stick to the speed limit and drive carefully over the speed bumps; there are a lot of them and they're big. Tulum to Mahahual is closer to three hours and then another 45 minutes to Xcalak. Times are dependent on your speed, but take it easy, stop for some fruit along the way, and enjoy the trip. You will get stopped at military checkpoints along the way, but I've never had any issues. The language barrier at the checkpoints becomes interesting at times, but it's just part of the adventure.

Seven-Day Sample Trip

This trip is a little different then most, splitting the southern Yucatan between two locations. Spend the first three days at El Pez in Tulum, then move to Mahahual for the last four days. On day one, travel north toward Akumal and fish Soliman, Paradise, and Tankh bays. For the second day hire a guide to fish the world-famous Ascension Bay. Day three drive through the gates of the Sian Ka'an Biosphere south of Tulum and head to the "bridge." Take the trail on the north end to sight-fish the shallows for bones, then the mouth for snook, finally walking north on the beach, looking for bones close to shore and snook farther out. Returning to the car, walk north on the road 200 yards to where the Boca Paila Lagoon meets the water. Walk and wade the three flats surrounding the mangrove cay, targeting bones and permit. Leave Tulum early on day four and make the three-hour drive to Mahahual, checking into El Hotelito, then meeting up with Nick Denbow of Western Caribbean Fly Fishing for a day's fishing on one of the inland lagoons. Day five, drive north on the coast highway toward Punta Herrero, stopping along the road anywhere from mile 29 to mile 40 to fish miles of deserted beach for bones and jacks.

Day six, head south on the coast road to fish the bays and rocky points from Mahahual to Rio Hauche. On day seven, make the 45-minute drive to Chetamul Bay to fish the bay's eastern shore and lagoons for bonefish.

Spousal Rating: 7

The spousal rating for this trip is really two sides of a coin. If staying in Tulum or Akumal, the nonfishing spouse and family are going to have a terrific tropical vacation, with lots to do, sites to see, beautiful beaches to lie out on, and great meal choices throughout the day. When you travel farther south to Mahahual and Xcalak, the amenities drastically reduce and are more suitable for either an adventurous spouse or someone who just wants to lie quietly on the beach.

Nonfishing Activities

Akumal was established in 1958 as a community for scuba divers. Three major reef formations make this a smorgasbord of water activity for individuals and families alike. Explore some of the incredible underground river and cave systems or one of the many cenotes, natural fresh or brackish water sinkholes perfect for snorkeling and swimming. Whether you rent a kayak or bike or visit rescued monkeys at the Jungle Place, Akumal can keep you busy all day long.

Lined with commercial enterprises, the town of Tulum is fast growing, filled with the usual water sports, restaurants, spas, and yoga retreats. The Tulum ruins are less than 25 minutes from Akumal. Sitting atop a rocky bluff overlooking the shoreline, Mayan history could not come with a better view! Deep in the jungle, the Mayan ruins of Coba are located about 45 minutes from Tulum. The site, which is well worth the drive, was built in the Mayan Classic period and includes the tallest pyramid, El Castillo, at 100 feet. Remember to bring good walking shoes and insect repellent.

The Sian Ka'an Biosphere Reserve is a 10-minute drive from Tulum. Spanning 120 kilometers north to south, it was established in 1986 to preserve vast tracks of marine habitat, coastal reefs, savannas, mangroves, and tropical forests. The eight-mile, dirt-road drive from the entrance to the bridge can take anywhere from 30 to 90 minutes, depending on when the brutal potholes have last been smoothed out. From the bridge it is another 60 to 90 minutes to the fishing village of Punta Allen.

Mahahual is all about the water, the beach, and relaxing with a beverage along with some good food. Not a fly fisher, but would like to learn? Take a casting lesson with Nick Denbow of the Western Caribbean Fly Fishing School on the beach of Mahahual while the rest of the group paddleboards or chooses any of the other usual beach and water pastimes.

Located within the Xcalak National Reef Park, the village of Xcalak is small and quiet, coming slowly to the 21st century. Off the beaten track, this is a place to chill on the beach, walk, or read a book!

Take a look at www.locogringo.com for tourist services in Akumal, Mahahual, and Tulum.

Bits and Pieces

Nick Denbow and I were exploring the inland lagoons and beaches north of Mahahual, hoping to catch a variety of fish including tarpon, bones, permit, cudas, snook, and jacks. In this area a day like that is not as far-fetched as it might seem. We pulled the car over at mile 34 and before us was a spectacular sandy beach with a gentle sloping bottom covered by the crystal clear Caribbean. Not a soul or footprint in sight for a mile north or south.

I was carrying my eight-weight bonefish rod rigged with a Clouser, a good saltwater reel, and 200 yards of backing. Immediately we saw some frantic bird activity to the south, and away we went. Soon I was staring at a marauding group of jacks attacking a school of minnows that were pinned to the shore. One cast and I was hooked on to a torpedo. We laughed, we ran, doing everything we could do to stay with a fish that was totally out of control.

All was good until Nick said, "You better take a look at your reel." Glancing down in the midst of this frantic activity and excitement I saw there were only two more wraps of backing and then panic struck. The story turned comical after that, but in the end I landed a beautiful Jack Crevalle in the 15- to 18-pound class that had given me the fight of my life.

CHAPTER 6

CAYMAN ISLANDS

Lay of the Land

The Cayman Islands, located in the western Caribbean Sea, are the peaks of a massive underwater ridge known as the Cayman Ridge, situated about 430 miles south of Miami, 225 miles south of Cuba, and 300 miles northwest of Jamaica. Grand Cayman is the largest of a trio of islands that also includes Cayman Brac and Little Cayman. Grand Cayman is 22 miles long and 8 miles across at its widest point. Christopher Columbus was the first to chronicle this area on May 10, 1503, during his fourth and final voyage to the New World. He named it Las Tortugas for the large number of sea turtles in the area.

Sir Francis Drake arrived in 1586, subsequently naming the islands "Cayman," meaning alligator. Largely uninhabited until the 17th century, since that time a variety of settlers with various backgrounds made their home here, including pirates, refugees from the Spanish Inquisition, shipwrecked sailors, and army deserters! Today the Cayman Islands are a British overseas territory, listed by the UN Special Committee as one of the last non-self-governing territories. The governor is appointed by the queen and can exercise all legislative and executive authority granted in the constitution.

As of 2011, 56,000 residents, representing more than 100 nationalities, find employment in one of 600 banks, tourism, or shipping, providing the highest average standard of living per capita in the Caribbean. The Caymans offer an attractive tax environment, as there are no taxes on income, capital gains, or corporations. There are more registered businesses found here than there are people!

George Town is the capital of the Cayman Islands, the largest city, and home to half of the population. The other four districts of Grand Cayman are West Bay (situated north of George Town), Bodden Town, the North Side, and the East End. The Owen Roberts International Airport is located a mile and a half outside of George Town, and the city also has good hospitals and health care. The coastal roads are in decent condition, wide and properly signed, but side roads leading to the interior can be another matter. Cell phones and Internet are in wide use, and obviously banking is not an issue.

Where to Fish

Special thanks to Davin Ebanks of Fish Bones Guide Service located on Grand Cayman for providing virtually all of the fishing information on the Caymans. I have fished Grand Cayman in the past, but there is nothing like having a true professional and local to help shorten the learning curve. Most of the fishing is on Grand Cayman, but Davin has highlighted a few spots on Cayman Brac and Little Cayman as well.

Underwater shot of approaching bonefish (Photo courtesy of Pat Ford)

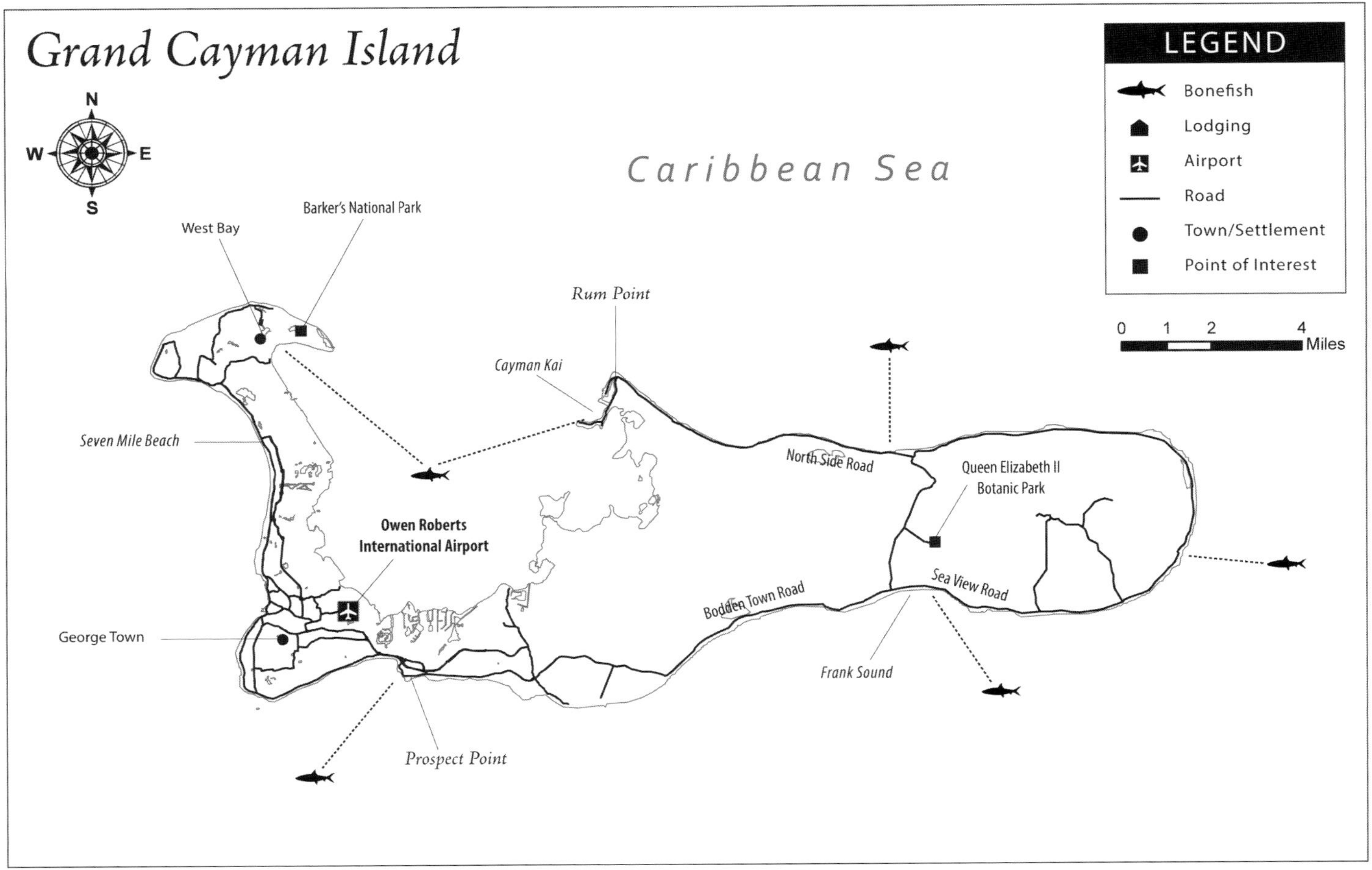

Grand Cayman Island

Caribbean Sea

N
E
S
W

LEGEND

Bonefish

Lodging

Airport

Road

Town/Settlement

Point of Interest

0 1 2 4 Miles

Barker's National Park

West Bay

Seven Mile Beach

George Town

Owen Roberts
International Airport

Prospect Point

Rum Point

Cayman Kai

North Side Road

Bodden Town Road

Queen Elizabeth II
Botanic Park

Sea View Road

Frank Sound

Rod Hamilton Design 2014

Prospect Point. The western side of Grand Cayman has many popular areas, including Prospect Point, off Prospect Point Road, which is the first major point east of George Town Harbour. The flat is pretty small but quite protected, making it ideal for those windy days that shut down the rest of the flats. A reef runs into shore here, providing the perfect habitat for a variety of interesting species like jack, snapper, barracuda, and the occasional tarpon. Bonefish are in evidence on both the grassy flat to the north and, when the tide is out, among the scattered corals nearer the reef. These fish can be very aggressive to the fly, but all the corals make the big ones difficult to land. Use barbless nonstainless hooks here, as you'll break off a lot of fish.

Frank Sound. This body of water is about 25 minutes farther east from Prospect Point. The flats here are narrow and probably the softest you'll encounter on the whole island, but they are protected for most of the year, making it an ideal place to find tailing fish. Be warned though, it is a fairly popular DIY area and the guides also use it in bad weather, so the fish are the closest to "educated" that you'll find. Nevertheless, they'll happily take a well-presented fly if they don't hear you coming. The calm conditions usually call for longer leaders up to 12 feet long and very light flies.

East End. This area is east and curving north as you head around the island. It is usually unfishable in all but the calmest weather as its easterly face is unprotected from the constant trade winds. There are bonefish here, as there are around the rest of the island, but unless the winds have been calm for a couple of days you'll find the water muddy and the flats blown out. However, if the weather conditions are right, it's definitely worth a look.

North Coast. There is a sharp change on the shoreline as you head along the north coast road and then back to the west. Most of the sandy beaches disappear, replaced by harsh, rocky "ironshore." The flats here are narrower and deeper, and there are lots of coral heads. The north coast running from about Morrits Tortuga Club west to Rum Point is ideal for blind casting around coral heads for jacks, snappers, and cudas. While there are bonefish here, there aren't as many as on the southern flats, and the bottom is often much too hard to find them tailing. However, in summertime when the winds turn southerly this can be a great area to walk with a fly rod, and when you do find bonefish they willingly take a fly.

You'll also find cruising jacks pushing water on the incoming tide, baby tarpon, and the occasional shoreline snook.

Rum Point and Cayman Kai. Here are a couple of beautiful beaches to hit with the family; just make sure to throw your fly rod in the car. Like other popular beaches in the Caribbean, these get busy with swimmers, kayakers, day-trippers, party boats, and jet skis, making the fish here ultra spooky. The fish aren't particularly educated by anglers but are extremely wary of people and will simply ease off the flat as you approach. However, they can certainly be caught, and the advantage of fishing here is that you'll be in more classic bonefish water. Rum Point is almost the only sandy flat on Grand Cayman, and while the fish don't tail often, they can be very easy to see cruising over the hard sand.

West Bay. This bay is due west from Rum Point across the North Sound. The northernmost tip of that peninsula is Barkers National Park. This is another great DIY area and probably has the highest turnover of fish on the island. Many of the other flats have "resident" fish that live on or near the area. The Barkers flats have excellent access to the deeper water of the North Sound, and bonefish use them as a highway between the deep water to the north and south. To reach the Barkers flats, which are only about a 20-minute drive from George Town, simply drive north along Seven Mile Beach and follow the signs for Restaurante Papagallos. A quick search of Google Maps will also show the appropriate route. Once you reach Papagallos, keep driving and take the left fork when the road splits. Pull off whenever you feel like it. The whole shoreline is productive, depending on tide conditions.

Cayman Brac. Information is scarce for Cayman Brac. This is truly a place for the adventurous DIY angler to figure it out on his or her own.

Little Cayman. Little Cayman has the longest tradition of flats fishing in the Caymans, and the Southern Cross Club has been there since the beginning. The Little Cayman Beach Resort also caters to those who want to fish, and both establishments have guides on staff. It's fun to hire a guide for a day or two; however, Little Cayman is truly a place where the self-guided angler can be successful. The eastern half of the island, particularly the southern coast, is ringed by flats, and bonefish are everywhere. Smaller than Grand Cayman's fish, these bonefish run about two pounds, with the occasional five-pounder thrown in to keep things interesting.

Fishing Information

Once again my sincerest thanks to Davin Ebanks for providing most of the information on the Caymans found in this section.

Bonefish are definitely the most reliable of the flats species in the Caymans and can be found all around the islands. Grand Cayman has the largest fish, with schoolies averaging three to four pounds, and six- to eight-pounders in evidence most days. Since all three islands run east-west instead of north-south like many Bahamian locations, the tides are fairly consistent. And, while there are no extensive flats like those of the Bahamas, the Cayman Islands offer a unique chance to simply drive to a flat, wade out, and encounter tailing bonefish. The flats are easily accessed by foot, making them sensitive to fishing pressure. So keep moving, give the fish a rest, and explore the miles of coastline waiting to be discovered.

The Cayman bonefish have an undeserved reputation for being spooky and picky. This simply isn't true; they are just like bonefish in other Caribbean locations, and they're far more aggressive than many of the bones you'll find in hard-hit locations like the Florida Keys or the popular DIY flats on Eleuthera and Abaco in the Bahamas.

The reason bonefish in Cayman have this reputation is simple. Unlike most of the Bahamas, Cayman flats are covered in a thick layer of turtle grass, yet many anglers insist on fishing as if they were on a sandy bottom.

Nervous water. This is what you are looking for. (Photo courtesy of Pat Ford)

The bonefish have a limited field of vision in the grass, so the fly has to be right in front of them or they won't see it. That calls for accurate casting and retrieving only when the fish can see your fly. The main mistake most DIY anglers make with bonefish in the Cayman Islands is to strip too soon, too much, and too fast. You've got to feed the fish. Let them see the fly and then let them catch it. Start off with small strips, no longer than three inches. That will usually get it done.

Cayman bonefishing usually requires lightly weighted flies and longish leaders that turn over gently. Typical, heavy bonefish flies tend to sink into the grass and get lost. Weed guards are also critical to success here.

Standard bonefish patterns work—Crazy Charlies, Gotchas, Veverka's Mantis Shrimp, and Del Brown's Bonefish Fly (small Merkin) tied on #8 and #6 hooks—but they need to be weighted lighter than usual with reliable weed guards.

The usual rules of color apply here: match the bottom, and if that doesn't work use a contrasting color. On a daily basis some tan or brown version of a shrimp or crab will get it done, but don't stick to drab colors in your selection. Local anglers have had great success with orange, hot pink, and chartreuse as well. DIY anglers will do best to have a variety of patterns so they can switch if they get refusals.

A quick picture and then gentle release (Photo courtesy of Pat Ford)

As of this writing you don't need a fishing license, but that might change as the islands upgrade their marine parks laws. Also, note that only catch-and-release fishing is permitted from shore for visitors. If you want to keep your catch, you'll have to charter a local captain for some reef or bluewater fishing.

Like any mature Caribbean tourist location, the Caymans have a variety of vendors offering all the equipment necessary to enjoy a day on the water. Here are a few that rent kayaks and stand-up paddleboards.

Action Watersports. www.ciactionmarine.com

Empty Suitcases. www.emptysuitcases.com

The bonefishing guide I recommend is located on Grand Cayman.

Davin Ebanks. www.fish-bones.com

Where to Stay

Accommodations are ample but tend to be expensive. There are several luxury resorts that include all the bells and whistles, but there are budget-friendly options as well. Many visitors stay in condos and take advantage of the quality grocery stores by shopping and preparing their own meals, but there is no shortage of places to eat for those days you don't feel like cooking. The main hotel strip is Seven Mile Beach, home to several major hotel chains and numerous condominiums. The Internet is your best resource to find a hotel or resort that fits your needs. There are hundreds of homes and condos available on VRBO and HomeAway.

Getting Around

Owen Roberts International Airport (GCM) of Grand Cayman is served by a number of international airlines that can get you from just about anywhere to GCM. Here are a few to check out:

Air Canada. www.aircanada.com

Westjet. www.westjet.com

British Airways, which departs from London Heathrow. www.british airways.com

US Airways, from Charlotte, Boston, and Philadelphia. www.usair ways.com

American Airlines. www.aa.com

Delta. www.delta.com

Between the Cayman Islands:

Cayman Airways. www.caymanairways.com

Do you need to rent a car here? It depends. If you are happy to hang out on your backyard beach, take a tour or two during your stay, or make use of the public bus system, then a car is unnecessary. If you want to explore more of the island and head off fishing while the family goes jet skiing, you need to rent a car. All major car rental companies are within walking distance of the airport. Pricing depends on the time of year, with the highest rates levied from mid-December to mid-April. If you decide to rent a car, confirm the age requirement for the agency you choose. For some, the minimum age is 21 and for others it's 25.

Avis. www.avis.com

Budget. www.budgetcayman.com

Cayman Auto Rentals. www.caymanautorentals.com.ky

Scooters and bikes are another great way to explore the area and rentals are easy to arrange. Many hotels provide bikes for the use of their guests—ask first!

Cayman Cycle Rental. (345) 945-4021

Taxis are readily available at the airport with fixed rates to all island areas.

Thirty-eight minibuses serve as the Grand Cayman public bus system with daily service starting at 6:00 a.m., getting you to all districts for $1.50 to $3.00 a ride.

Seven-Day Sample Trip

The seven-day trip on the Caymans is a little different then most. You don't travel to the Caymans for seven days of nonstop fishing. I suggest you fish a couple of full days with a guide, fish a few mornings and afternoons on your own, and spend the rest of the time with your family. Before you leave from home, book the first and last day of your stay with Davin Ebanks of Fish Bones Guided Fly Fishing. On day two head out early in the morning to fish Prospect Point and Frank Sound, then back to the hotel to join the family at the pool. On day three pack up the "gang" and head to Rum Point and Cayman Kai for a picnic lunch, water sports, and some casual fishing. On day four leave the hotel early and drive to West Bay to fish the Barkers flats. If you feel like a journey, drive to the East End and around to the north shore to explore and throw a line wherever it looks good. To put it all together, meet up with Davin for your last fully guided day.

Spousal Rating: 8

This is a quality tropical vacation destination. You can book Grand Cayman knowing that the family will have a great time with something for everyone. The self-guided fishing opportunities are good and provide ample reason to pack your equipment. It may not be the best fishing destination, but the flats around Cayman offer a pleasant opportunity to casually wet a line early in the morning while the family sleeps or to stalk some tailing bonefish as the family lounges on the beach.

Nonfishing Activities

Grand Cayman is a hard place to beat! The atmosphere is laid back, wrapped up beautifully in all the modern amenities. Though the island is known for its world-class diving conditions, you may want to try something a little different. The island's most famous excursion is to Stingray City where you can feed the friendly southern rays and get a picture alongside them.

Rent jet skis or try kite surfing along Seven Mile Beach, which stretches from just outside George Town Harbour to West Bay. It's one of the world's great beaches and has public access its entire length, making it easy to find your own piece of heaven on earth.

The Botanical Park Nature Reserve, located on the eastern end of the island, is home to several blue iguanas and local flora, along with information regarding their medicinal properties. While you are in the area, take a look at the East End Light, the first lighthouse in the Caymans.

Hike the Mastic Trail through the old-growth forests of the island's interior and don't miss the Boatswain's Beach Turtle Farm where turtles are bred from hatchlings and released in the island's waters. Head inside, out of the sun, to tour the Cayman Islands National Museum, which has an emphasis on maritime heritage, or the National Gallery of the Cayman Islands, which houses traditional and modern works of art and culture.

When you're in need of sustenance, relax and refuel at one of the many restaurants and cabana beach bars dotting the island, and, if you're up to it, take advantage of the great duty-free shopping!

Bits and Pieces

The last time I was on Grand Cayman I had one of my more memorable fishing trips of the last 20 years. What's burned into my memory bank aren't the bonefish but instead the baby tarpon that inhabit the lagoons and canals. An offhand remark by a local steered me to canals in the interior of the island loaded with three- to seven-pound tarpon that just couldn't say no to a surface popper. I got up every morning at 5:00 a.m., drove the 30 minutes to the canals, walked the dikes, and cast poppers into the most god-awful tangle of bushes and downed trees you can imagine. And on virtually every cast one of those "babies" would smash the popper. I only landed three or four each morning, but the action was unbelievable. No GoPros or YouTube in those days, but if there were, you would have seen a tarpon smash a popper every five minutes. Each morning I returned to the condo on Seven Mile Beach for breakfast, wondering if life could get any better.

CHAPTER 7
TURKS AND CAICOS ISLANDS

Lay of the Land

The Turks and Caicos Islands (TCI) are a British Overseas Territory under the jurisdiction of the United Kingdom. They consist of the larger Caicos Islands and smaller Turks Islands, and are located 50 miles southeast of the closest Bahamian island, Mayaguana, and approximately 550 miles from Miami. Only 8 of the 30 islands are inhabited. All combine to make a total land area over 200 square miles consisting of low, flat limestone with extensive marshes and mangrove swamps, surrounded by a continuous coral reef.

For almost 700 years, the Taino and Lucayan Indians were the sole residents, settling mainly in Middle Caicos and Grand Turk. Shortly after Columbus arrived in 1492, the Lucayan civilization disappeared, leaving the islands sparsely populated for 30 years. Modern-day residents known as "Belongers" are descendants of slaves from Bermuda, the Dominican Republic, and Cuba, as well as of Loyalists after the American Revolution; they were brought to rake salt ponds, giving birth to an important industry.

Sovereignty exchanged hands for many years, starting in 1706 when the French and the Spanish briefly captured TCI. Four years later the British reclaimed the islands for Bermuda, with Britain ultimately retaining them, placing them under the Bahamian government umbrella by the end of the century. Attempts to integrate these two communities failed, and after the "Great Bahamas Hurricane" in 1866, the Turks and Caicos Islands became dependencies of Jamaica, another British colony.

When Jamaica won independence in 1962, TCI became a British colony on its own, which it continues to be today. Tourism, commercial fishing, and benefits realized as a zero tax jurisdiction are the primary means of maintaining a fairly steady economy. "Beautiful by Nature" is this country's motto, and it is well deserved. The stunning 12-mile-long Grace Bay found on the north shore of Providenciales has been named the world's leading beach four years running. Cockburn Town, the capital since 1766, is found on Grand Turk. Turks Island Passage, also known as the Columbus Passage, is a 22-mile-wide, 7,000-foot-deep channel that separates the Turks Islands and the Caicos.

Our focus will be specifically on Providenciales (known as Provo), North Caicos, and Middle Caicos. The country has a total population of about 40,000 with half residing in Provo, the hub of TCI tourism. Developed in the 1980s, upscale Provo offers many modern conveniences, including luxury hotels and villas, a wide variety of restaurants, well-supplied grocery stores, shopping, and golf. The US dollar is the offi-

Welcome to Providenciales, Turks and Caicos (Photo courtesy of Marta Morton, Harbourclubvillas.com)

cial currency; most hotels, restaurants, and taxis accept credit cards, and banks, ATMs, Internet, and cell phone coverage are widely available. Provo is also home to a modern medical facility, medical and dental clinics, and an international airport. Highways serving Providenciales are generally in good shape, but exploring that dirt road you just have to see can get a little rough with major potholes that never seem to get filled in!

The Caicos are collectively called "the family islands," and the farmer in the family is North Caicos—41 square miles of lush beauty, known for tall trees and small farms of corn, cassava, beans, and okra. The island, home to 1,400 residents, is located 12 miles northeast of Provo, just a 20-minute ferry ride away. The ferry will get you to the Sandy Point dock where most residents live. Whitby and Bottle Creek are the other two main settlements, and all three towns offer taxi service, car rentals, and bike rentals.

Middle Caicos is the most ecologically oriented of the brood and the largest of the islands at 48 square miles. The three settlements—Conch Bar, Bambarra, and Lorimers—boast a total population of 300. Limestone cliffs with long sandy beaches are found in the north, contrasting with swampland and tidal flats in the south. Vividly green and ideal for agriculture, Middle Caicos is home to the largest cave network in the Bahamian Archipelago. Both islands have small grocery stores, nurse-staffed medical clinics, gas stations, a few casual restaurants, car rentals, and accommodations ranging from basic to luxury. Count on using cash for most transactions outside of Provo.

Where To Fish

Of the 30 islands that make up TCI, I've fished and explored Providenciales, North Caicos, and Middle Caicos. Take note that at the time of this writing it was illegal to sport fish within the boundaries of any national park or nature reserve in TCI. This means that well-known locations like Bonefish Point and Silly Creek on Providenciales are closed to fishing. Virtually the entire south shore of North Caicos and Middle Caicos falls within the boundaries of the North Middle and East Caicos Nature Reserve and are closed to fishing. Bottle Creek itself is open to fishing, but the cays of Bottle Creek are in the East Bay Islands National Park. The boundaries can be found on the Department of Environment and Coastal Resources website (www.environment.tc/Protected-Areas-Division.html).

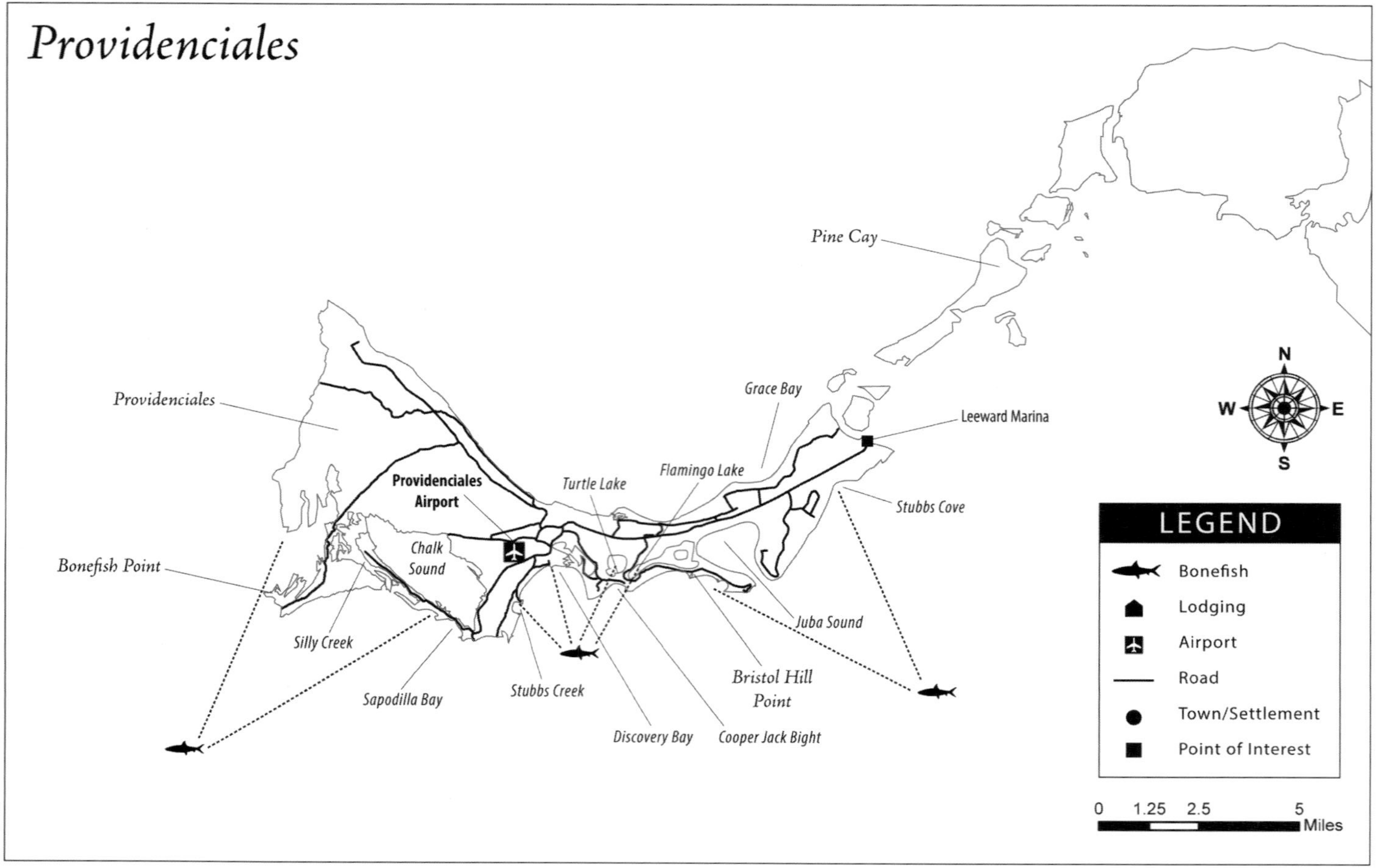

Providenciales

Pine Cay

Leeward Marina

Stubbs Cove

Grace Bay

Juba Sound

Flamingo Lake

Bristol Hill Point

Cooper Jack Bight

Turtle Lake

Discovery Bay

Stubbs Creek

Providenciales Airport

Chalk Sound

Sapodilla Bay

Providenciales

Silly Creek

Bonefish Point

LEGEND

Bonefish	
Lodging	
Airport	
Road	
Town/Settlement	
Point of Interest	

N E S W

0   1.25   2.5   5
Miles

Rod Hamilton Design 2014

Providenciales

Flamingo Lake. This lake is found where Venetian Road turns into Turtle Tail Drive. A consistent producer and easy to wade, it's best to drive beyond the culvert separating Flamingo and Turtle lakes and park on Turtle Tail Drive anywhere past the Harbour Club Villas' driveway. Most of the fishing is done from the west end, through the narrows and up to the small mangrove island seen in the middle. These fish see their share of flies but are definitely catchable and always present.

Turtle Lake. Across Venetian Road from Flamingo Lake is Turtle Lake. It's completely dry at low tide and fills from the boat channel on each incoming tide. The fish arrive on the tide, feed up the middle of the flat, and spread out into the mangroves lining the shore. The fishing can be good, but the wading is tough. Either take a kayak or stand-up paddleboard in, or wade out to the entrance, pick a spot, and wait for the fish to come to you. At low tide you can always cast heavily weighted Clousers on long leaders into the depths of the boat canals. The bones hang out there with lots of jacks and the occasional large cuda on patrol.

Bristol Hill. Toward the end of Turtle Tail Drive, past Bristol Hill Drive, is a beautiful oceanside flat. Park in the large undeveloped area adjacent to the dugout boat channels and walk into the bay. In front of you will be a group of small cays, known as the Five Cays. There are always fish here during the low and incoming tides, and it's a pleasure to wade. At low tide the flat extends a long way west, and it's known to hold some very large ocean bones. This is a nice place to bring the family for an afternoon.

Juba Sound. Drive another quarter mile past the Bristol Hill parking area and pull your car over to the side of the road. To the north is Juba Sound, which feeds Flamingo Lake and deserves more attention than it gets. Walk from the road north until you find the channel of deeper water that connects Juba Sound to the ocean. Bonefish use this channel on every tide, and it's a great place to wait them out.

Turtle Tail Road. At the end of Turtle Tail Road is the ocean outlet for Juba Sound. There is a small flat on the inside of the outlet that fish use as they exit to the ocean. Following the channel into Juba Sound will also get you into some nice water.

Discovery Bay. Drive down Cooper Jack Road and turn right on Doubloon Close, then follow it to the gate and park. Walk the trail

Jay Majhanovich with a nice bonefish from the shores of Providenciales

down to the deserted Cooper Jack Marina development. The large bay to the west is Discovery Bay and an excellent location to find large singles and schools of bones. This is a big piece of water, so you can expect to spend an entire tide fishing. The flats themselves are easy to wade, and oftentimes just walking the shoreline is the best way to ambush fish. The creek system you see in the back is fed through an opening about halfway around the bay. Take the time to fish the entrance and flat around the creek opening.

Cooper Jack Bay Road. The entrance to the boat canals that feed Turtle Lake is at the end of Cooper Jack Bay Road. The beach to the west of the canal entrance has some excellent fishing at dead low tide when the fish move out of the canal.

Bonefish Drive. Off Cooper Jack Road and Bonefish Drive is the creek behind Discovery Bay. This creek is seldom fished but is where the bones end up at high tide, entering from Discovery Bay. The better fishing in the creek is toward the opening to the bay.

Industrial Road. Just before Industrial Road meets the roundabout and turns into South Dock Road you will see the back of the creek that feeds Discovery Bay. This is another easy access, and it is simpler to get to the mouth from here than via Bonefish Drive.

Five Cays Road. Take the left off South Dock Road onto Five Cays Road. Fifty yards before the cemetery is a dirt road to the beach. This is a beautiful long beach that forms the west side of Discovery Bay. Depending on the wind direction, your best strategy may be to fish the beach walking north all the way to the creek opening. Moving south along the beach takes you to the cove in the corner and the fish plant. Fishing either from the beach or wading the flat is good in both directions.

Stubbs Creek. Where Five Cays Road turns to dirt, stay to the right and follow it for 0.4 miles. On your right is a steep rock road and on the left is a faint trail into the creek and bay. Excellent fishing is to be found in both the creek and flats of the small cove.

Sapodilla Bay. This is a nice bay used heavily by the sun worshippers, so it is only good for fishing in the early morning and evening. Turn right onto Chalk Sound Drive and pull over 100 yards past the police station.

Taylor Bay. Continue past Sapodilla Bay for another 0.75 miles on Chalk Sound Drive to find the beach path to Taylor Bay. This small isolated beach is used extensively during the day but can hold fish in the early morning and late afternoon.

Silly Creek. Located in the Chalk Sound National Park, this is a well-known bonefishing area, but it is illegal to fish here at this time.

Bonefish Point. Located off the Millennium Highway and then 3.8 miles down Lightbourne Road, this famous bonefishing flat and creek system is within the boundaries of the Pigeon Pond and Frenchman's Creek Nature Reserve. As off this writing it is illegal to fish within a nature reserve.

Juba View Lane. South off the Leeward Highway across from a cell tower is a dirt road posted as Juba View Lane. Follow the road south as far as you can and then park. The water in front of you is Juba Sound and is a good way to fish the northern shore without having to cross the entire bay from Turtle Tail Drive. The best fishing is to the west toward the narrows of Flamingo Lake.

Long Bay Beach. Located directly across the island from Grace Bay, this beautiful beach typifies what Providenciales is known for, but without the crowds, making it a great spot to spend a full day with the family. The fishing is only so-so, but there are bones cruising the shore and it gets better as you move north toward Stubbs Cove.

Ferry from Providenciales to North Caicos

North Caicos and Middle Caicos

Sandy Point Ocean Side Flat. The ferry lands at Sandy Point and, as you enter the cove, you can't help but wonder if there are bonefish around. The answer is yes. Just north of the ferry landing is the community of Sandy Point, surrounded by a beautiful beach, with great walking flats sprinkled throughout. At times the entire area can be good, depending on the wind direction. When calm, fish at low tide starting at the point and make your way northeast, walking the entire shore. This is an ideal spot to bring the family for a day of water sports.

Parrot Cay Channel. Some caution and understanding of the nature reserve's boundaries are required before fishing this area. The mangrove system south of the ferry dock is called Dick Hill Creek and is within the boundaries of the Dick Hill Creek and Bellefield Landing Pond Nature Reserve. The channel and flats on the outside are in Parrot Cay Channel and are outside the reserve. Fishing the flats here is excellent, as the fish stage outside in the channel in preparation to enter the creek on the flood tide. To get there from Sandy Point, take the right-hand turn at the T and head toward the settlement of Kew, turn right at the small sign to Wade's Green Plantation, and then turn right again at the next stop sign. Pass Wade's Plantation on your way to Bellefield Landing. Park at the dock and walk the shoreline to the north. At the mouth of Dick Hill Creek the channel is fairly deep but can be crossed at low tide. This is a low tide fishery since the fish will enter the creek as the tide rises.

Bottle Creek. Without a doubt, this is one of the most beautiful flat and creek systems I have ever fished. It's so large a group could fish it for a week. A channel follows the western shore of Bottle Creek for its entire length, making it necessary to have kayaks to reach the flats. Fortunately, there are many places to put in from Major Hill Road south through the settlement of Bottle Creek. It's an easy paddle from shore, due east for one mile, where you can anchor the kayak and walk for the rest of the day. Be advised that the northern mouth of Bottle Creek and the eastern cays lie within the boundaries of East Bay Island National Park.

Bottle Creek, South. Once past the settlement of Bottle Creek and before the sharp right-hand turn heading to the causeway, you will find an excellent lagoon and shoreline to fish. Park the car at the top of the hill and find the rough road or trail to the water. Pass through the mangroves and out into a small lagoon. The best fishing is in the larger lagoon to the right.

Bottom of Hill Bay. After the sharp right-hand turn south of Bottle Creek Settlement, the road heads downhill toward the causeway. As it

Howard Gibbs of Last Chance Kayak Rentals ready to drop off the "fishermen" for the day

Kim on a Native Watercraft Versa Board after landing a Bottle Creek bone

flattens out, there is a large mangrove creek on the left and a view of open water. This is a small but excellent bay that connects to Bottle Creek. Continue to drive toward the causeway and, just as the road straightens, you will see a small canal on the north. Park here and walk up the left (west) side until you reach the bay. Once you reach the point, fish to the west, toward the mangroves.

Causeway. If you have fishing in your blood, it's impossible to cross the causeway to Middle Caicos without scanning the water for fish. There are flats both north and south of the causeway where you can often see fish tailing and feeding. If you park on either the west or east ends of the causeway there is a full day's fishing to the south. Be aware of the nature reserve boundary located approximately one mile south. On the northeast corner of the causeway is a dirt road ending at a boat launch. This is an excellent place to put in kayaks to paddle north and fish toward the large ocean opening known as Crossing Place Channel.

Lorimers, Middle Caicos. There is a massive creek system on Middle Caicos that can be effectively fished by launching a kayak at Lorimers. It is five miles long, has great tidal flow in its southern section, and could be as good as Bottle Creek. It can also be reached by turning left on the

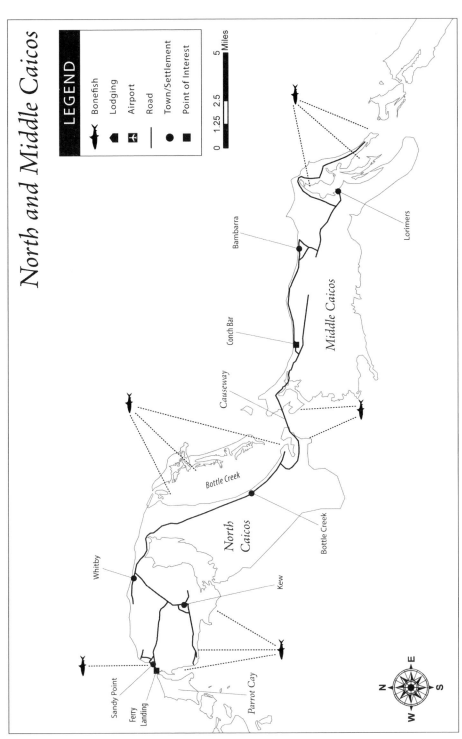

North and Middle Caicos

LEGEND

⫸	Bonefish	
◀	Lodging	
✈	Airport	
—	Road	
●	Town/Settlement	
■	Point of Interest	

0   1.25   2.5   5
Miles

Rod Hamilton Design 2014

Bambarra

Conch Bar

Causeway

Lorimers

Middle Caicos

Bottle Creek

Bottle Creek

North Caicos

Whitby

Kew

Sandy Point

Ferry Landing

Parrot Cay

N
W   E
S

dirt road just before the "Welcome To Lorimers" sign, then following the road until you reach the small roundabout. Take the road to the right and follow it through the deserted real estate development, parking at the end. Continue walking for a half mile until reaching the canal connecting the ocean and creek system. From here either walk or kayak up the creek or fish the ocean flats out front.

Fishing Information

If you are looking for a destination to combine a traditional Caribbean vacation with a few self-guided days, TCI is the place. On Provo there are a number of easy-to-reach spots where the fisherman can hit a flat in the morning and be back in time to share breakfast with the family.

TCI is known for big fish, and on average they tend be slightly larger than a typical Bahamian bonefish. If you are fishing the south shore of North Caicos and Middle Caicos with a guide, it's not unreasonable for most fish to be five pounds and bigger. Fishing on your own, you are sure to catch fish from five to seven pounds and may very well cast to the largest fish of your life if fishing the oceanside flats.

The fish on Provo in Flamingo and Turtle lakes receive enough pressure to be wary, but in other locations typical tactics and flies work fine. The big fish will often break your heart. In Discovery Bay and the oceanside flats, larger flies like the Bonefish Junk or rubber-legged Gotchas in size #4 are the ticket. Where there is more pressure, go with longer leaders and lighter flies. Bring along some heavily weighted tan-and-white Clousers to fish the boat channels.

Provo has a lot of ocean beaches on the south shore that don't get fished. Fishing on those beaches is not like fishing a traditional flat, but if you are with the family, take them to the more deserted south shore and bring your fly rod along.

North Caicos can be a one-day trip from Provo. Book the first ferry, have a rental car waiting for you, fish the entire day, and catch the evening ferry home. Better yet, book the first ferry and have a kayak waiting for you from Howard of Last Chance to fish Bottle Creek. That's guaranteed to be a terrific day.

There are a number of very good guides on Provo; here are a couple:
Darin Bains. turksandcaicosbonefishing.com/

Arthur Dean. www.silverdeep.com/fishing/bonefishing.htm

When fishing North and Middle Caicos, rent either a traditional kayak or stand-up kayak.

The Great Bonefishing Company. www.greatbonefishing.com

Where to Stay

Provo is a true tourist destination and has been developed to offer everything that you would expect from a high-end tropical vacation. Grace Bay tends to attract most of the tourism dollars and offers hotels, resorts, and condos. To see a wide range of private accommodations, visit the websites for VRBO (www.vrbo.com) and HomeAway (www.homeaway.com). North Caicos is the complete opposite of Provo and is more like a Bahamian Out Island with fewer choices for accommodations and meals. There are some nice oceanfront homes in Sandy Point and a few boutique resorts on Whitby Beach.

Whether your choice of accommodations in North Caicos is a small hotel, guesthouse, or private villa, rentals come in a range of prices and many provide meal plans. Decide where you want to hang your hat—Spring Point, Whitby, or Bottle Creek—and search online from there.

Check out the Turks and Caicos Islands tourism website for a wide range of options (www.turksandcaicostourism.com). In Provo I can recommend the terrific **Harbour Club Villas**, and bonefishing is at the end of the driveway (www.harbourclubvillas.com).

Aliston Terrace Apartments, which is owned and operated by Conrad Higgs (conradhiggs@yahoo.com), is the place to stay on North Caicos. The apartments provide accommodations that are simple and priced right for the traveling fishermen or group.

Getting Around

It doesn't get easier! The Providenciales International Airport is able to handle the largest passenger planes, with major carriers flying daily from Miami, New York, Boston, and Dallas.

American Airlines. www.aa.com
US Airways. www.usairways.com
Delta Airlines. www.delta.com

JetBlue. www.jetblue.com
Air Canada. www.aircanada.com
Westjet. www.westjet.com
Bahamasair. www.bahamasair.com

Most major rental companies are active on Provo and easy to book online. A couple of the local companies include the following:

Scooter Bob's. www.provo.net/scooter
Caicos Wheels. www.caicoswheels.com

Rental cars are available on North Caicos and will meet you at the ferry.

Pelican Car Rentals. 946-7122
Al's Rent-a-Car. 331-1947

Taxi service is very good on Provo and plenty are available at the airport and Grace Bay. There are also several taxis on North Caicos if you need to be picked up at the ferry.

TCI Ferry Service (www.tciferry.com) departs regularly from the Walkin Marina on Provo to Sandy Point, North Caicos. The 25-minute ferry runs multiple times daily and on public holidays.

Seven-Day Sample Trip

Book into Harbour Club Villas for the first four days and then the Aliston Apartments on North Caicos for the last three. After checking in, string up your rod and walk down the driveway to fish Flamingo Lake. Start at the rock point on your left, then wade east toward the narrows. If you have time, cross the road and fish Turtle Lake. On day two head to the deserted marina project off Cooper Jack Bay Road and fish Discovery Bay. The next day fish the channel of Juba Sound at the end of Turtle Tail Road and then jump across the road to Bristol Hill Flat to catch the low and incoming tide. For the last day on Provo, run over to Five Cays Road to fish Stubbs Creek, finishing up on the west side of Discovery Beach, walking north to the creek mouth. Early the next morning, have Scooter Bob drop you off at the ferry and rent a car on the other side. Drive to Aliston Apartments and check in, then you're off to Last Chance where you can rent a kayak from Howard and cross the channel of Bottle Creek for a full day's fishing. Day six, fish the southern shore off the causeway, either the east or west end, depending on the wind. On the last day, rent a kayak again from Howard and fish Bottle Creek to pick up where you left off.

Spousal Rating: 8

If you are looking for a destination that offers the full tropical resort and beach treatment, as well as good fishing, look no farther than Providenciales. Your spouse and family will have a great time and not feel like they got dragged somewhere so you could fish. In fact, they may not even miss you when you're gone.

Nonfishing Activities

In Provo, most people start with famous Grace Bay Beach for fun in the sun or air-conditioned shopping. From midday to the wee hours of the morning try your luck at Casablanca Casino or the Royal Flush in Turtle Cove. Finding food is not a problem in Provo. Restaurants presided by talented local or international chefs are plentiful, but make sure to try some conch at least once! Explore Princess Alexandra Marine Park, the world's first conch farm.

Conch Salad, Turks and Caicos (Photo courtesy of Marta Morton, Harbourclubvillas.com)

Is your dream to ride a horse down a beautiful secluded beach? You can do it in Provo! Get lowered down 80 feet by rope to find a swimming hole at the bottom of a naturally formed limestone hole! Cheshire Hall, a 200-year-old cotton plantation ruin carefully preserved by the Turks and Caicos National Trust, is one of the key attractions in Provo.

In North Caicos, the shallow waters of Bottle Creek are perfect for kayaking, bird-watching, or quiet picnics. Look for flocks of pink flamingos at Flamingo Pond and Mud Hole Pond. Straw work crafts are still practiced on this island, widely known as the "breadbasket" of the Turks and Caicos Islands. Tour one of the Loyalist plantation ruins, the largest of which is Wade's Green, and don't miss the caves near Sandy Point where Lucayan artifacts have been found.

Explore the huge limestone cave system of Middle Caicos or the spectacular seascapes of Mudjin Harbour and Crossing Point bluffs. Miles of paved roads make biking a great way to see this island, but if you want to go off road, hike along the high cliffs and empty beaches in the company of seabirds and cacti.

Beautiful flat on Providenciales (Photo courtesy of Marta Morton, Harbourclubvillas.com)

The historic walking trail between North Caicos and Middle Caicos provides access to the protected western shore of Middle Caicos and opens up to breathtaking views. Of course there is snorkeling, swimming, and kayaking on and around pristine deserted beaches too! If you don't want to figure it out for yourself, guided tours are available.

Bits and Pieces

Bottle Creek is one of the most beautiful flats I have ever fished. My wife and I had a memorable day, each using a new VersaBoard from Native Craft. Kevin Styles and Howard Gibbs of www.greatbonefishing.com have developed the perfect plan for a day of DIY fishing on Bottle Creek. They drop you off with a kayak or stand-up paddleboard on one of the world's great flats and pick you up at the end of the day. We paddled over seven miles that day, stopping and fishing where it looked good and enjoying the spectacular scenery the rest of the time. On that trip we fished for 60 days on five different Caribbean islands, and that day stands out as one of the best.

CHAPTER 8

THE UNITED STATES

BISCAYNE BAY

Lay of the Land

In 1513, Juan Ponce de Leon sailed south from St. Augustine and found a "bright nameless great bay." There are a number of stories about how Biscayne Bay, a lagoon 35 miles long and up to 8 miles wide, was named, but one thing for sure is that it has always attracted explorers and adventurers. The bay is divided into three regions—North Bay, Central Bay, and South Bay—and the North Bay separates Miami Beach Barrier Island from Miami and the mainland.

The largest part of the bay is the central region, buffered from the Atlantic by the Safety Valve, a series of shallow flats broken up by tidal flow channels. The largest estuary on the coast of southeast Florida, it connects to the Everglades and Florida Bay, encompassing a marine ecosystem of approximately 428 square miles. It is home to the 173,000-acre Biscayne Bay National Park in the central region and to the Port of Miami, one of the largest passenger and commercial ports of call in the world. Supporting industries directly related to bay activities create over 130,000 jobs each year in hospitality, construction, and commercial and sport fishing.

Residents and visitors participate in recreational pursuits like sailing, boating, snorkeling, and diving. Because it is close to Miami, there is an eclectic feel to the area, offering everything you might want in a city,

Cruising bonefish in shallow water (Photo courtesy of Glenn Pittard)

including the arts, great shopping, and dining in addition to spectacular outdoor pursuits. Good highways, cell and Internet service, banking, ATMs, medical services, and all the consumer goods you want are easy to find in this area.

Where to Fish

Let's call it the way it is: Biscayne Bay is best fished from a boat and better yet with an experienced guide that knows the area well. Of all the places I have fished on my own, Biscayne Bay is one of the toughest. The reasons are twofold: Access to quality wading flats is poor, and the bonefish here are the smartest fish you are ever going to face. On the bright side, they are there, they can be caught, and chances are good that the fish you land will be the largest of your life. To increase your chances and dramatically expand the fishing range, the DIY fishermen is better off to use a kayak, canoe, or stand-up paddleboard. If you don't live in the area, it means renting from one of the many vendors available. With the exception of a few locations on Key Biscayne, the self-guided fishing areas are concentrated on the western shore of Biscayne Bay.

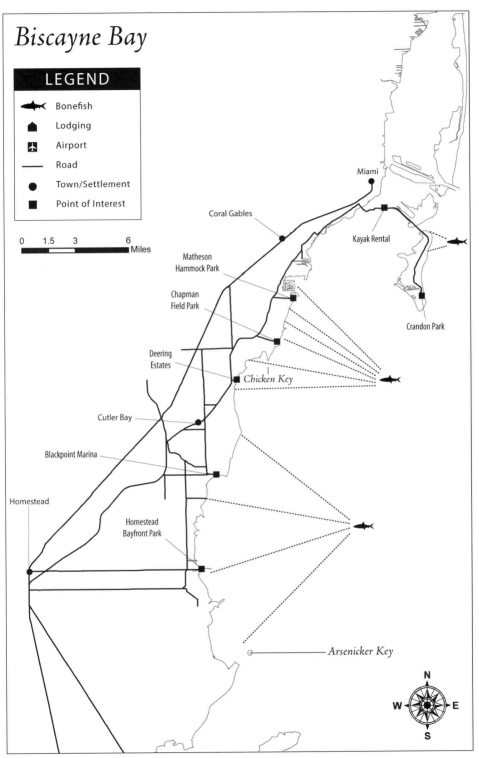

Biscayne Bay

LEGEND

- ➤ Bonefish
- ⌂ Lodging
- ✈ Airport
- — Road
- ● Town/Settlement
- ■ Point of Interest

0   1.5   3   6
Miles

Miami

Coral Gables

Kayak Rental

Matheson
Hammock Park

Chapman
Field Park

Crandon Park

Deering
Estates

Chicken Key

Cutler Bay

Blackpoint Marina

Homestead

Homestead
Bayfront Park

Arsenicker Key

N
W   E
S

Rod Hamilton Design 2014

Underwater shot of a nice fish cruising by (Photo courtesy of Pat Ford)

Key Biscayne

Rickenbacker Causeway. On the way out to Key Biscayne, there is some fishing on either side of the causeway. Kayaks are available to rent from vendors adjacent to the causeway.

Key Biscayne. There is a wadeable flat located on the northeast corner of Key Biscayne that can be good at times. It's best to fish here early in the morning or late in the day.

Crandon Park. Located right on Key Biscayne, this is an ideal place to launch your canoe or kayak to fish the flats to the north. Kayaks and canoes can be rented at the park. This area gets busy, so fish both early and late on a low tide.

Matheson Hammock to Turkey Point

The 20-mile stretch of Biscayne Bay from Matheson Hammock to Turkey Point is by far the best section for the self-guided angler to concentrate on. Most of the guides fish the eastern shore of Biscayne Bay so you won't see many anglers but you will see fish. It is best fished from a canoe, kayak, or stand-up paddleboard as there are only a few access points where you can park your car and enter the water to wade. There are a surprising number of large bonefish in this stretch of water and it may be your best shot at catching a fish on your own.

Matheson Hammock. This county park, located off Old Cutler Road, has nice beaches, picnic areas, and a large marina. There is a small flat directly north that can easily be waded, but the majority of fishing is south from the marina. There are canoe and kayak rentals at the park, which expands the size of the area available to fish.

Chapman Park. This park can be reached off Deering Bay Drive, where fishing is productive both north and south. The park is an excellent launching point for a canoe or kayak and from here you can paddle north to Matheson Hammock or south to Deering Estates.

Deering Estates at Cutler. This 444-acre county park provides excellent access to the west shore of Biscayne Bay. Off the parking lot is a nice trail to the People's Dock where you can launch a kayak or canoe. It is situated on a beautiful part of Biscayne Bay with good fishing if paddling either north to Chapman Park or south to Black Point Park.

Black Point Park and Marina. Located off SW 87th Avenue, this beautiful park is the ideal launching point to fish the undeveloped shoreline north to Deering Estates. Paddle 2.5 miles north along the shoreline to a stretch of flats that can be waded at low tide. If the wind is coming from the north, you will find more protection launching in the canal south of the marina and paddling toward Homestead. To reach the canal, follow

Night fishing for bones under the night lights of Miami

the road around the marina and park your car beside the canal. Launch your canoe or kayak and paddle into Biscayne Bay. It is one continuous flat south to Bayfront Park. Along this stretch, the shoreline is undeveloped and provides ample solitude considering its proximity to Miami.

Homestead Bayfront Park. Located in Homestead, this county park is located on the southern end of Biscayne Bay and is the gateway to the Florida Keys. This is an excellent put-in for access south to Turkey Point and the Arsenicker Keys or north to Black Point Park.

Arsenicker Keys. This is a long five-mile paddle to the south, but it is one of the most productive fishing areas in Biscayne Bay.

Elliott Key. For a little more adventure, why not camp for a few days at the designated campground and fish the surrounding flats? The bottom tends to be a little soft, so it is best to fish from either a stand-up kayak or paddleboard. To save the seven-mile paddle, find a friend with a boat or have the concessioner from Biscayne Bay National Park in Homestead run you out by boat. If you camp later in the year than March, bring your bug spray.

Fishing Information

Biscayne Bay is not a destination I would plan a pure DIY fishing trip around, but it's a wonderful location to fish one day with a guide and a couple days on your own. So if your spouse wants to go to Miami or South Beach, book it.

For those days without a guide, plan to hit one of the access points mentioned above in order to fish the outgoing tide, the low tide, and half of the incoming tide. There are some flats that are easily waded, such as Key Biscayne and Matheson Hammock, but most are best fished from a stand-up kayak or paddleboard, which can be rented from a number of vendors.

The fish in Biscayne Bay are big and smart, averaging close to seven pounds. Catching a Biscayne Bay bone on your own is a trophy worth pursuing. They have seen a lot of flies, so you may have to shake it up a little. I like larger flies, usually size #2 to #4, including Greg's Flats Fly, Cordell Baum's Electric Dread, Bonefish Toad Fly, Borski Slider, EP Crab, Bonefish Bunny, and Spawning Shrimp. The flies should be heavy as the water is typically two to three feet deep, and carry flies with weed guards.

A nice bonefish enticed out of the mangroves

Fishing can be very good during the winter months and into the spring even though Florida is subject to cold fronts moving through. You need a Florida state fishing license, and if you fish in the evening, bring your bug spray.

Kayak, canoe, and stand-up paddleboard rentals abound in Miami, Biscayne Bay, and Coconut Grove. Consider looking at one of the national parks, whose vendors do a great job providing equipment rentals, or bring your own. Many companies will deliver and pick up the equipment you rent from them.

Biscayne National Park. www.biscayneunderwater.com

Stand Up Paddle Board Center. www.standuppaddlekeybiscayne.com

Matheson Hammock Kayak Rentals. www.miamidade.gov/eco adventures/rentals-matheson_hammock.asp

Crandon Park Kayak Rental. www.miamidade.gov/Parks/Parks/crandon_beach.asp

Cordell Baum. www.bonefishwhisperer.com

There are a number of guides that fish Biscayne Bay, but here are a few I can recommend:

Captain Rich Smith. www.captainrichsmith.com
Captain Raul Montoro. www.biscaynebayfishing.com
Cordell Baum. www.bonefishwhisperer.com

Where to Stay

As you might imagine, whatever you want to find here, you can! Start with the needs of the travel party. Your needs will vary depending on whether you are a couple with a nonfishing partner, a family with small children, or just anglers. Once you pinpoint a location central to your needs and interests, you can then set a budget! Everything from price conscious basics to five-star luxury can be found through the usual avenues. The Internet will be your best friend to find just what you are looking for in a motel or hotel, or check out something like VRBO or HomeAway for a condo, cottage, or home experience.

Getting Around

If you are arriving by air, Miami is the obvious choice for proximity to the area, and it services the world.

Renting a car is a must here. It's easy with an endless number of rental agencies available at the airport and in most towns. If you have a GPS, consider bringing it or rent one with the car—it's worth it!

Seven-Day Sample Trip

For the self-guided angler, I'm assuming you are not in Miami on a "guys" fishing trip but instead on a holiday with your spouse and looking for a couple of full days of fishing combined with a few hourly outings. Stay at any of the numerous hotels or condos on South Beach and book your first two days with Captain Rich Smith. A day or two with a guide will be your best shot at landing a Biscayne Bay bonefish and help you to learn what's necessary to boat one of those trophies. On day three take your spouse to Key Biscayne to enjoy Crandon Park and the surrounding area. Rent a kayak from the vendor and paddle north to fish the flat on the northeast corner of Key Biscayne. Day four, head to Matheson Hammock to fish an evening low tide, walking the southern flat, then head back home for dinner in South Beach. Day five, rent a NuCanoe from Cordell Baum and have him meet you at Black Point Park to fish the flats to the north. Day six, take a drive to Bayfront Park in Homestead, visit the Biscayne Bay National Park visitor center, then rent a kayak to fish the area north. Day seven, chill out on South Beach to look at all the other "fish in the sea."

Spousal Rating: 8

Why wouldn't it be an eight? There are a million things to do here; it's the perfect spot to take the family if you are looking for an active vacation.

Nonfishing Activities

Within sight of downtown Miami, the diversity of Biscayne Bay is staggering. Outdoor enthusiasts can boat, snorkel, camp, dive, observe wildlife, or just hang out on the beach. Rent a stand-up paddleboard, windsurf, play tennis, golf, or take the South Beach Food and Walking Tour. Spend the day at the Miami Seaquarium or experience Florida alligators up close and personal on an Everglades airboat tour. Take a glass-bottomed boat or snorkeling tour to really see Biscayne National Park. If you need to get out of the sun, visit the Dolphin Mall, home to over 240 value-focused designer stores ranging in scope and price from Coach, to Nike and Sony. The options are truly endless!

Bits and Pieces

On every trip I usually fish with a local guide for a day or two, particularly if it is a new location. I was visiting a good friend in Miami when I decided to try something new, fishing from the front of a canoe on Biscayne Bay. I was skeptical at first, but I had heard about Cordell Baum, who has an international reputation as the bonefish whisperer, and decided to give him a try. We met at Black Point Park and unloaded his canoe, then he poled us into the bay. I didn't know it could be done, but I stood in the front of his canoe for seven hours and in the end had a really enjoyable day. Cordell poled the boat the whole day and we covered several miles north from the put-in. It was an absolutely hypnotic way to see and fish the western shore of Biscayne Bay. With the skyline of Miami in view the entire day, juxtaposed with the quiet approach of a poled canoe, it turned a day on the water into a very intimate experience in a big city.

THE FLORIDA KEYS

Lay of the Land

The Florida Keys start at the southeastern tip of the Florida peninsula about 15 miles from Miami. Most consider Key Largo to be the start of the Keys, which extend south and then head westward to Key West. The islands lie along the Florida Straits, neatly dividing the Atlantic Ocean to the east from the Gulf of Mexico to the west. In addition to stunning coral reefs, you'll find wide expanses of sea grass beds, mangrove forests, lush tropical hardwood hammocks (closed canopy forests), rocky pinelands, and a variety of freshwater and saltwater wetlands.

In 1512 Juan Ponce de Leon, former governor of Puerto Rico, received permission from the king of Spain to search for land north of Cuba. He "discovered" the Keys in 1513, meeting members of the Native American Calusa and Tequesta tribes, the region's first inhabitants. He named the islands Los Martires, "the Martyrs," as they looked like suffering men from a distance. The Spanish brought Christianity, cattle, horses, sheep, and the Spanish language to this area. The Spaniards were indifferent to colonization of the rocky, mosquito-infested islands; instead, they enslaved or killed many of the Indians, leaving most of Florida untouched for hundreds of years.

The total land area of the Keys is 137 square miles with a current population just over 73,000, down 8 percent from 10 years ago. As the rest of Florida grew by 15 percent in the same period, the Keys' numbers were kept in check in an environment of strict building regulation, high cost of living, and few lucrative jobs. Located in the subtropics, the climate is considered closer to that of the Caribbean than the rest of Florida. It is the only frost-free place in Florida; it is hot, wet, and humid from June to October but a little drier and cooler the rest of the year.

The Overseas Railway, which was constructed in the 1910s to connect the islands, stopped service as a result of damage incurred dur-

What a real fisherman looks like

ing the Labor Day Hurricane of 1935. Today US 1, a 110-mile-long, two-lane highway built parallel to the Overseas Railway running the length of the Keys, services transportation needs. Though there are over 1,700 islands in the Keys, very few are populated and most are quite small. Bridges connect 43 of the islands, with the Seven Mile Bridge the longest. It is really 6.8 miles—but let's give it to them. For discussion purposes, they are divided into four main groups: the Upper Keys, the Middle Keys, the Lower Keys, and the Outlying Islands, which are accessible only by boat. Addresses are noted by mile markers, or MM, starting at MM 126 in Florida City and counting down to MM 0 in Key West. The addresses sometimes indicate the side of the highway as well, with "ocean side" indicating the south side of the highway and "bay side" indicating the north.

Key Largo is the first port of call in the paradise we collectively call the Keys. An hour's drive from the Miami International Airport, it is a world away from the big city, with two state parks: John Pennekamp

Coral Reef State Park and Dagny Johnson Key Largo Hammock Botanical State Park, a national marine sanctuary. It is sandwiched between the watery wilderness of the Everglades National Park to the west and fish-covered coral formations to the east.

Half an hour down the road is the village of Islamorada, Spanish for "Purple Island," referring to a purple-shelled snail that once lived here and to the brilliant colored orchids and bougainvilleas of the area. Incorporated in 1997, it has a total population of 6,119 and, though it bills itself as the "sportfishing capital of the world," truly has the feel of a village. The 36-mile stretch encompassing the Middle Keys to Lower Keys starts with Marathon, a 10-mile-long family-oriented community reflecting the old Keys lifestyle. The name Marathon dates back to the origin of the Florida East Coast Railroad. The workers, who were laboring day and night to complete the project, said, "This is getting to be a real marathon." Key West is the southernmost location in the continental United States, offering Southern charm and Caribbean flavor in a laid-back island nation called the Conch Republic. Banking, medical services, supplies, Internet, and phone coverage (check with your cell provider to see what's best) can be found up and down the Keys.

Where to Fish

I love the Florida Keys and they contain many of my favorite fishing locations. The fishing can be tough, and any bonefish caught here while DIY fishing is a trophy. The habitat is spectacular, and the variety of species available means you can always catch something.

This is one destination where a kayak or watercraft really helps to expand the fishing territory, and I wouldn't visit the Keys without access to one.

The bottom tends to be firmer on the oceanside flats and a stand-up paddleboard, kayak, or canoe is pretty much mandatory for most of the bayside areas.

During the winter months the temperature of the water on the bay side can be too cold for bonefish, so focus on the oceanside flats and keys. Around the middle of March the water begins to warm and the bay side becomes the place to target bones.

Florida Keys (North)

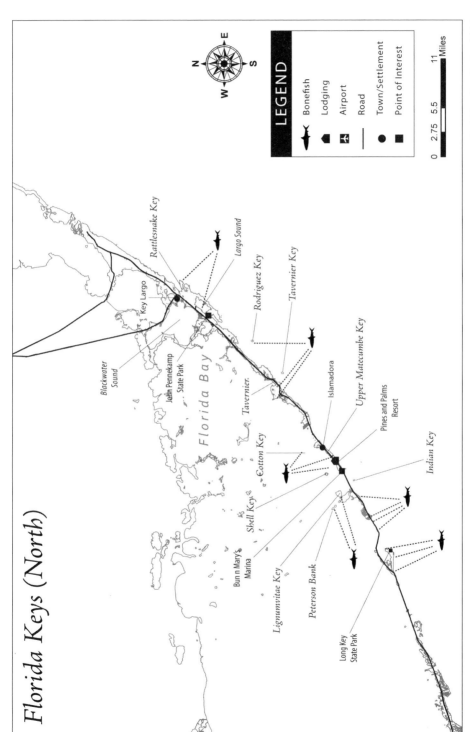

Rattlesnake Key

Largo Sound

Key Largo

Rodriguez Key

Tavernier Key

Blackwater
Sound

John Pennekamp
State Park

Florida Bay

Tavernier

Islamorada

Upper Matecumbe Key

Cotton Key

Pines and Palms
Resort

Shell Key

Indian Key

Bun n Mary's
Marina

Lignumvitae Key

Peterson Bank

Long Key
State Park

N
W   E
S

LEGEND

Bonefish

Lodging

Airport

Road

Town/Settlement

Point of Interest

0   2.75   5.5   11
Miles

Rod Hamilton Design 2014

Upper Keys

Rattlesnake Key. This is one of the best oceanside flats in the Upper Keys and an easy one-mile paddle from the Garden Cove put-in. From the north tip of Rattlesnake Key south is a three-mile stretch of fishable water.

Largo Sound. A canoe or kayak is necessary to fish this area; they are available to rent at Florida Bay Outfitters. Launch your canoe or kayak at John Pennekemp Park, mile marker 102.5, or rent a kayak or canoe and maneuver through the connecting channel along the western shore of Largo Sound. This provides a nice paddle in protected waters and better than expected fishing, close to Key Largo.

Harry Harris. Monroe County Park at mile marker 92.5 offers access to some interesting oceanside areas. It is a 2.5-mile paddle from the park to Rodriquez Key.

Rodriguez Key. This is a well-known oceanside bonefishing area, with very good fishing on the south and east side. The distance to paddle is between one and two miles, depending on where you put in.

Tavernier Key. There are plenty of nice flats on the north, east, and south sides of Tavernier Key, and it's a simple 1.5-mile paddle from Tavernier Creek Marina located at mile marker 90, bay side.

Captain Rich Smith casting from the Diablo stand-up kayak

Whale Harbour Flats. There are good flats on both sides of the canal; the oceanside flat has historically been fished best on the south side. It is accessed from Smuggler Cove at mile marker 88.5, bay side.

Cotton Key. This beautiful little bayside key has some nice flats on the eastern shore as you approach the western shore. It is a 1.75-mile paddle from the highway bridge.

Bud N' Mary's. The oceanside flats north of Bud N' Mary's at mile marker 80 can be good. If you are staying along this section of Islamorada, don't be afraid to fish out in front with your stand-up paddleboard.

Pines & Palms. This is a nice family style resort located on the ocean side at mile marker 80.4. There are two docks for guests to fish off and kayaks for them to use. The two flats just north of the resort fish well and can be waded at low tide.

Shell Key. This is a well-known bonefishing area on the bay side, providing consistent fishing along the key's eastern and northern shores. It is a three-mile paddle from Robbie's or 1.3 miles from World Wide Sportsman.

Shell Bank. This bank is a bit farther to paddle than Shell Key but has excellent bayside flats. Makes for a long day, but it's an ideal destination for a kayaker who wants to get some extra exercise.

Football Field. This is the local name for the flat located west of World Wide Sportsman at mile marker 81.5. It is a nice flat to get to with an easy 250-yard paddle and would be an excellent choice with a stand-up paddleboard.

Teatable Key. There are flats surrounding this small oceanside key. If you want to pick an easy one-tide spot, it's a quick paddle from Bud N' Mary's or Robbie's at mile marker 77.5.

Indian Key. Indian Key is another easy key to reach from Robbie's and an excellent one-tide choice. There are flats all around the key, but watch for fish coming out of the channel and onto the northside and eastside flats.

Lignumvitae Key. Rent a kayak or launch your own from Robbie's and paddle east to this nearby key. There's good fishing on the southern flat and along the eastern shore.

Peterson Bank. This bank is for the more adventuresome paddler as it's another 1.5 miles beyond Lignumvitae Key. It's been a favorite for years.

Looking for tails as the sun sets (Photo courtesy of Glen Wonders)

Sea Oats Beach. On the ocean side at mile marker 74, this beach's flats are located right beside the road, making it simple to fish. Obviously, it gets lots of pressure for this reason, but the fish are there. It has a nice firm bottom and is easy to walk and wade at low tide.

Anne's Beach. Located at mile marker 73, this is another spot where you can park the car and fish. Get here for the last half of the outgoing tide and the first half of the incoming tide. It's a nice place for the nonfisherman to pull up a lawn chair and read while you wade for a couple of hours.

Craig Key. This key is located at mile marker 72. There is a medium-sized flat on the ocean side with a firm bottom that you can wade.

Middle Keys

Long Key State Park. The entrance to the park is at mile marker 67.5. If you are only a day user, check the park's hours of operation. If you are camping, this is an excellent choice, allowing you to fish the flats both in the early morning and late evening. There are several areas within the park to fish, including from the day-use beach and near the camping area. Get there as early as you can since swimmers use the beaches. For those with a kayak, the northern end of the park's peninsula and Long Key Bight are both consistent producers of bonefish. The paddle is no more than a mile to good flats and slightly longer if fishing the bight.

Mile Marker 66.5. This small flat is on the opposite side of the road from the park and can be fished at low tide. It's a nice spot to fish the evening tide and take pictures of the sun setting.

278

Grassy Key. There are some nice oceanside wadeable flats at mile marker 58.

Curry Hammock State Park. The entrance to the park is at mile marker 56.2 on the ocean side. A nice flat right in front of the campground can be walked, but it's a little soft in places.

Mile Marker 55.5. On the bay side, park at the bike trail and walk east past pole 1255 looking for a trail access sign. Follow the trail to the water and walk past the deep hole to the west to find the flat. Take a few blind casts into the hole as you go by.

Deer Key. There are nice flats all around Deer Key, but it's important to be there as the tide fills in the backcountry and empties out of the mangroves. You will find an easy put-in at Curry Hammock State Park at mile marker 56.2 and along Coca Plum Drive.

Lower Keys

Little Duck Key. Located at the eastern end of the Seven Mile Bridge at mile marker 39.9, this small flat in front of Veteran's Memorial Park on the ocean side is worth trying.

Missouri Key. This is a nice oceanside flat to walk at mile marker 39.5.

Ohio Key. Another section of oceanside flats at mile marker 39 that can be waded at low tide.

Bahia Honda State Park. This is a large, well-known park located on the ocean side at mile marker 38. It has an excellent stretch of walk-and-wade flats along the entire oceanside beach. I prefer fishing the northern end of the park, watching for bones coming out of the channel and onto the flat with the incoming tide.

Coupon Bight. This extensive interior flat is reached off Big Pine Key, an easy paddle in protected water off Long Beach Drive. At the end of the road is a path leading to the flats.

Sugar Loaf Key. Fish both north and south along the shoreline of this great oceanside shoreline flat along Sugarloaf Beach. There are a lot of great areas to explore within Lower Sugarloaf Sound.

Saddle Bunch Key. This area is best accessed by following Old State Road 4a, as there are some wonderful interior flats for the kayaker and stand-up paddleboard.

Walking the flats of Deadman's Cay, Long Island (Photo courtesy of Sam Root)

Geiger Key Beach. To reach the beach at mile marker 12.5, turn at the Circle K and follow the road approximately three miles to the end. There is plenty of parking roadside and good fishing from the end of the road south.

Fishing Information

The Keys separate the Gulf of Mexico from the Atlantic Ocean, so the east side is called "ocean side" and the west is "bay side."

For the self-guided angler to find bonefish, the best tactic is to concentrate on the oceanside flats from December to March, then, as the bayside water temperature heats up around the middle of March, begin to shift over to the bay side. I have identified a number of places where you can simply park the car and walk the roadside flats, but most of the productive areas need to be fished from a stand-up kayak, canoe, or stand-up paddleboard. My suggestion is to go online and book your watercraft in advance so that you have it when you arrive. There are many places to rent boats, so rent a boat to get to the flats you want and take a couple of stand-up kayaks or paddleboards along to launch once you are there.

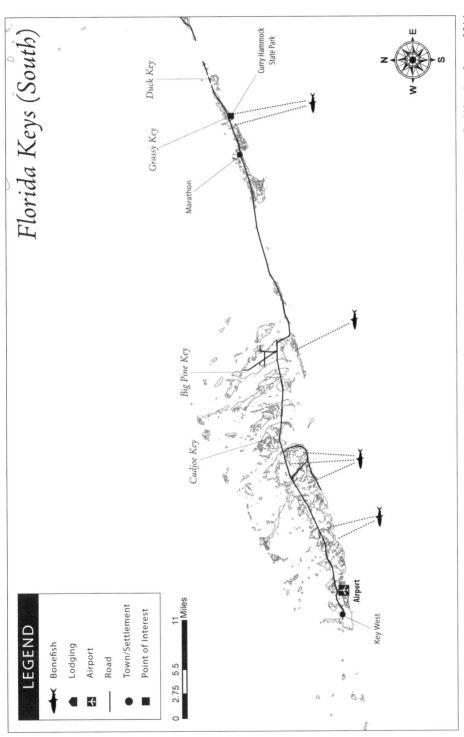

Florida Keys (South)

LEGEND

- Bonefish
- Lodging
- Airport
- Road
- Town/Settlement
- Point of Interest

0   2.75   5.5   11
Miles

Duck Key

Curry Hammock State Park

Grassy Key

Marathon

Big Pine Key

Cudjoe Key

Airport

Key West

N
W   E
S

Rod Hamilton Design 2014

Remember these are big fish, so the flies are some of the largest you will use anywhere in the world. The typical sizes are #0 to #4 with enough weight to get down three feet quickly into swift tidal currents. I like lots of moving parts like bunny fur and rubber legs with a fair amount of flash. I've done well with larger Clousers and use more crab patterns in the Keys than most places. I like the Raghead crab and some of the EP crab patterns.

To have your best shot at catching a Keys bonefish, budget to go out with a guide for two days out of the week. There are lots of guides in the Keys, but I recommend Captain Rich Smith out of Marathon.

Key Largo Rentals

Florida Bay Outfitters. www.floridabayoutfitters.com
Key Largo Florida Boat Rentals. www.flkeysboatrentals.com

Islamorada Rentals

Islamorada Watersports Company. www.islamoradawatersports.com
Robbie's of Islamorada. www.robbies.com

Marathon Rentals

Captain Hook's. www.captainhooks.com
Marathon Florida Keys Rental Boats. www.vacationboatrentals.com
Marathon Kayak. www.marathonkayak.com
Kayak Rentals Marathon Florida. www.kayakrentalsmarathonflorida.com

Key West Rentals

Lazy Dog. www.lazydog.com
Blue Planet Kayak. www.blue-planet-kayak.com
Key West Boat Rentals. www.boatrentalsofkeywest.com

Where to Stay

This area is bursting with an abundance of hotels, motels, resorts, guesthouses, inns, cottages, and condos—you get the picture! Take a little time to determine the vibe you want because everything is available! VRBO and HomeAway Vacation Rentals are good places to start. With choices like these plus supplies and restaurants readily available, meal planning is a piece of cake!

The Pine & Palms Resort is a great choice; we have stayed there several times. It is located in Islamorada at mile marker 80.4. Owner Jim Bernardin, an experienced fisherman, has created accommodations to fit any family or group, offering oceanfront cottages and one, two, and three-bedroom suites, all featuring full kitchens.

Getting Around

Flying into Fort Lauderdale, Miami, or any other major Florida city will provide enough options to fit any schedule. You can also choose to fly into Key West International Airport via connecting or direct flights, and charter companies service the Marathon Airport.

All the major car rental agencies can be found at the airport. While having a car is ideal, there is good ground transportation available from the Miami International and Fort Lauderdale International Airports.

Greyhound Lines makes scheduled stops along the route between Miami International and down the Florida Keys to Key West.

Services such as Keys Shuttle and the Florida Keys Express Shuttle provide door-to-door service between the international airports in Miami and Fort Lauderdale and the Keys.

Car, moped, and bicycle rentals are available at most destinations in the Keys. Make sure to ask if bikes or watercraft are included through your accommodations. Kayaks, canoes, paddleboards, and other watercraft rentals are also easy to find.

Seven-Day Sample Trip

Check into the Pines & Palms in Islamorada so that you are well positioned to hit the flats both north and south. Catching a bonefish in the Keys is tough; take my advice and book Captain Rich Smith on the first and last day. On day two, rent a kayak from Florida Bay Outfitters and paddle to the oceanside flats of Rattlesnake Key. For the third day, drive to Long Key State Park to walk the flats. The next day try the different

School of bones coming straight in (Photo courtesy of Vince Tobia)

flats and areas of Bahia Honda State Park. If the water temperature is right, stay closer to home and, for day five, rent a kayak and fish the bay side around Shell Key and the Football Field. Day six, meet up with Captain Rich so he can calm you down and convince you that the bonefish are catchable. If you have time on the last day, launch one of the Pines & Palms kayaks and paddle north around the point to walk and wade the nearby bays.

Spousal Rating: 8

The Keys are special with lots to do, tons of restaurants, a smorgasbord of places to stay from high-end to budget accommodations, and a laid-back lifestyle, just like a tropical vacation is supposed to be.

Nonfishing Activities

Key Largo locals consider their home to be the diving capital of the world, but proximity to the Everglades makes this a premier destination for kayakers, birders, and all nature lovers as well.

In Islamorada you can take an ecotour, go to Founders Park on the waterfront—complete with an Olympic-sized pool, shallow water beach, water sports rentals, and tennis and basketball courts—or go to Robbie's and buy a bucket of bait to feed the tarpon off the dock.

Snorkeling heaven exists at Sombrero Reef of Marathon, a federally protected area of the United States' only living coral barrier reef. Explore the many trails found on the 63-acre property at Crane Point Museum and Nature Center or go to the Dolphin Research Center and Turtle Hospital, which has the ability to rescue, rehabilitate, and release injured sea turtles.

Key West can be anything you want it to be and everything is within walking distance. You can choose shopping, theater, fine dining, or one of the many entertainment options on Duval Street to fill your day. View treasures from shipwrecks, discover the haunts of your literary heroes, and bask in the midst of Victoria architecture. End the day watching a world-class sunset from Mallory Square where performers, vendors, and artists are on hand to make it a complete Key West experience.

Bits and Pieces

While staying in Islamorada, my wife and I rented a new-style kayak from one of the local companies to try out the boat and see if we could outfox a bonefish around Peterson Bank. The kayak was a dream, it was a beautiful day, and the only thing missing was to hook up with Mr. Bone. As we got to Lignumvitae Key the kayak became a little sluggish and paddling became harder. We tried to keep pushing forward, thinking it was us and not the boat, but sadly the kayak sank lower and lower in the water and we were making less headway. At this point I should tell you that when we rented the kayak, our attendant was quick to inform us he was really hungover from the night before, but really, he asked, "What could go wrong?"

Turns out these particular kayaks have drain plugs, or at least should. Ours didn't, and the shell filled with water. Now the kayak doesn't sink but must weigh 1,000 pounds when filled. It was a long way back, my wife didn't like the way the sharks had begun to circle, and it turned out my waterproof boat bag wasn't so waterproof. After a tough couple of hours getting back to the dock, the rental attendant still wasn't on his game and was less than helpful when we told him, "We could have died!" Ah, laid-back life in the Keys. In the end both smartphones were ruined and the passports were a mess, but on the bright side I did learn how to dry out money.

OAHU, HAWAII

Lay of the Land

Oahu, known as the "Gathering Place" in Polynesian, is the third-largest and most-populous island in the Hawaiian chain. This volcanic land mass measures 44 miles long and 30 miles across with 227 miles of beautiful shoreline. Oahu has a tropical savanna climate and experiences a rain-shadow effect suppressing summer rainfall. Sunshine is predominant with temperatures varying little throughout the year, highs averaging 80 to 90 degrees F and lows 65 to 75 degrees F.

Until the 1890s the Kingdom of Hawaii was an independent sovereign nation, recognized by many world powers including the United States. Threats to Hawaii's sovereignty were made throughout history but were realized in 1893 when the last monarch, Queen Lili'uokalani, was deposed largely by a group of American citizens who opposed the establishment of a new constitution. The Territory of Hawaii existed from July 7, 1898, until August 21, 1959, when it was admitted to the Union as the 50th U.S. state.

The city of Honolulu can be described many ways. As the Hawaiian state capital, it is a major tourist destination, international business hub, and military defense center, all found in a melting pot of culture, cuisine, and traditions from the East, the West, and the Pacific Islands. In the Hawaiian language Honolulu means "sheltered bay" or "place of shelter." Kamehameha III moved the capital in 1845 from Lahaina on Maui to Honolulu, where he and subsequent rulers built their vision of a modern island center. Additional unrest, such as the large fire of 1900 and the Japanese attack on Pearl Harbor in 1941, did not shake the capital.

Today, Honolulu is home to the main airport and seaport of the Hawaiian Islands, and it acts as a natural gateway, bringing in millions of visitors and billions of dollars annually. Federal military spending is the second-largest source of economic activity in this region. Once of para-mount importance, plantation agriculture in sugar and pineapple produc-tion has declined greatly. Farming is still pursued today but with a focus in the biotech world.

One of those flats that seems to go on forever (Photo courtesy of David Lambroughton)

Three-quarters of Oahu's 960,000 residents live in Honolulu, making it the largest city in the Hawaiian chain, offering all the things one would expect in any North American urban environment, island style or not. Downtown Honolulu is the financial, commercial, and government center of Hawaii. The Arts District is on the eastern edge of downtown and Chinatown, the Capitol District is the historic center, and of course the tourist base is Waikiki.

There is a good freeway and interstate highway system in place, but this has not kept Honolulu from having the nation's worst traffic congestion. Gridlock, caused by 600,000 registered cars and 1,500 miles of mostly two-lane roads, can only be avoided by driving between 9:00 a.m. and 3:00 p.m. or after 6:00 p.m. Public transportation is "TheBus," operating over 100 routes serving all of Honolulu and most cities and towns of Oahu. If you are traveling from outside the United States, check into a travel policy to help with any medical emergencies. Review policy conditions carefully to know the terms and limits of your medical coverage. While Hawaii may be separated from the continental United States, it still shares the same technologies, luxuries, and accommodations as most states on the mainland. Many cell phone companies provide service to the Hawaiian Islands, but it's wise to check with your carrier about fees or roaming charges before leaving home.

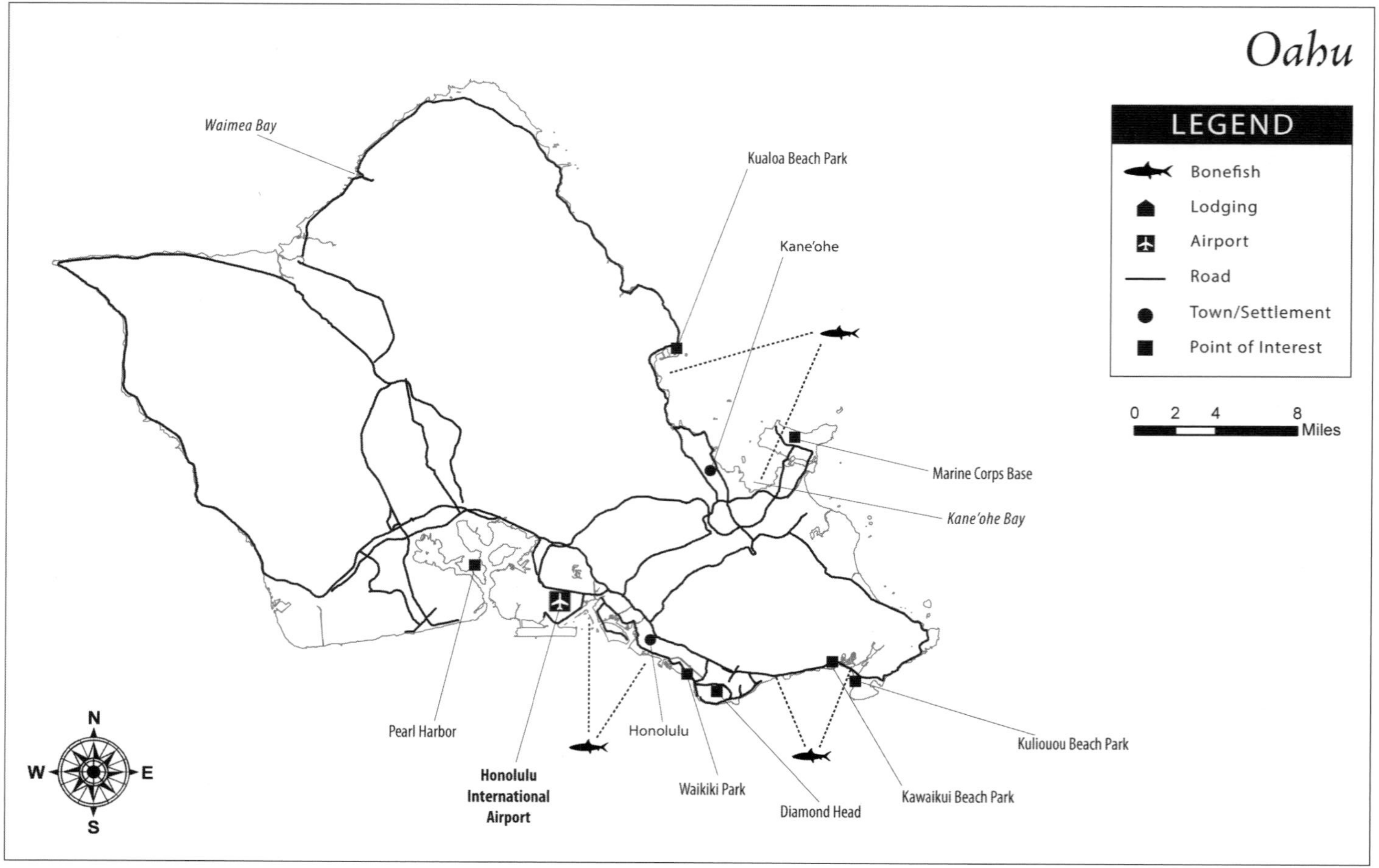

Oahu

LEGEND

Bonefish
Lodging
Airport
Road
Town/Settlement
Point of Interest

0   2   4   8
Miles

Waimea Bay

Kualoa Beach Park

Kane'ohe

Marine Corps Base

Kane'ohe Bay

Kuliouou Beach Park

Kawaikui Beach Park

Diamond Head

Waikiki Park

Honolulu

Honolulu International Airport

Pearl Harbor

N
W   E
S

Rod Hamilton Design 2014

Where to Fish

Special thanks to Captain Rick Lee of Bonefish Hawaii for providing the information on where and how to fish in Oahu.

If you are looking for a DIY bonefishing trip that appeals to the hardcore angler and nonfishing partner alike, look no further than Oahu, home of the tourist mecca Waikiki. A six-pound fish is average here, and the opportunity to hook one in the double digits is possible each time out. However, this is not to suggest that hooking a Hawaiian bonefish is a foregone conclusion. Hawaiian bonefish are some of the largest and most educated you will encounter anywhere, so bring some stout leaders and a good dose of patience.

Many of the flats on Oahu are easily accessed via improved Honolulu City and County beach parks, which offer free parking, restrooms, and showers to rinse gear and boots at day's end. A few offshore flats may be reached with rental kayaks; however, prevailing conditions should be monitored closely as strong trade winds and large surf are normal in the islands.

Ala Moana Beach Park. There are a number of flats located near and around Waikiki that may suit the visiting angler "on foot." Bonefish frequent the reef flats fronting Ala Moana Beach Park, which can be accessed via the oceanside parking lot at Kewalo Basin.

Hilton Hawaiian Village Hotel. Also in the Waikiki area are the flats fronting the Hilton Hawaiian Village Hotel; you can gain access to them via the Waikiki Yacht Harbor parking area adjacent to the Duke Kahanamoku Lagoon. Exercise extreme caution in this area, as summertime south swells and high tides may cause dangerous wave action and currents. Both the flats here and those off Ala Moana Beach Park range from calf to waist deep, so many anglers resort to "blind casting," which is an effective approach. As both these flats are located near Ward Shops and Ala Moana Center, this area has many benefits for a nonfishing spouse or friend.

Waialae Beach Park. Just past scenic icon Diamond Head is the posh residential area of Kahala. Its main thoroughfare, Kahala Avenue, crosses a bridge at Waialae Beach Park. A nice flat extends to the south from the parking area, showcasing some of the most expensive real estate in the world. Look for sandy channels that bonefish use as

Walking the rocky shores at high tide can be productive. (Photo courtesy of Vince Tobia)

"highways" from the outer reef areas onto the inner flats. The prevailing northeasterly trade winds and sun generally favor fishing South Shore flats in a downwind, east to west direction.

Wailupe Beach Park. Traveling east from Waikiki on the Kalanianaole Highway, you will find Wailupe Beach Park near the residential area of Aina Haina. A hard coral flat of approximately one mile stretches southward toward the Kahala Hotel. Wading from the beach's parking lot in the morning hours puts the prevailing trade winds and rising sun at your back. Again, look for numerous sandy channels and slow cruising bonefish.

Kawaikui Beach Park. A mile farther along the Kalanianaole Highway is Kawaikui Beach Park. There is good wading in both directions on a mixed bottom of coral and sand. The flat to the east is a bit deeper with excellent opportunities for blind casting. The shallower southside flat may provide better chances for sight fishing. Lots of parking is generally available, as are public showers and restrooms.

Kuliouou Beach Park. Just before reaching the community of Hawaii Kai, keep a sharp eye out on the ocean side for Bay Street. A couple of blocks in, you will find Kuliouou Beach Park. From here you can access

a large flat extending eastward into Maunalua Bay and southward surrounding Paikoo Lagoon Wildlife Sanctuary. This access will provide you
with lots of water to fish and is a favorite spot for local anglers. Accord-
ingly, these big bones can be very tough to fool but are well worth the
effort. Tailing fish in skinny water may be available early and late in the
day, especially on lower tides.

Kaneohe Bay. A scenic drive around the eastern tip of the island or
a more direct route through the Pali Highway Tunnels will take you to
the windward areas of Kaneohe and Kahaluu. Kaneohe Bay possesses
some stunning scenery as well as some of the most productive bonefish
flats on the island. The majority of these flats require a boat for access;
however, there are a few that may be reached from shore. A large sandbar, Ahu'olaka, is located near the middle of Kaneohe Bay. Access to this
flat, as well as a number of other "pancake flats," is from Hee'ia Pier by
boat. Several companies offer reasonably priced sandbar excursions on
large catamarans that will get you there and back with a few hours to fish.
Very few anglers use these services, so unfortunately you may be the only
fisherman on the boat with a number of frolicking girls in bikinis. If you
prefer to paddle to these flats yourself, you must use extreme caution when
attempting to reach any of this water with a kayak. The paddle is a little
over one mile each way, and very rough seas and strong winds are common. DIY anglers who are not in excellent physical shape may be better
served to fish elsewhere or hire a guide to access these areas.

Kualoa Beach Park. Some interesting flats at the north end of
Kaneohe Bay are accessed from Kualoa Beach Park. This area is adjacent
to the spectacular Kualoa Ranch, where many of the scenes from the
Hollywood film *Jurassic Park* were shot. This area may be challenging for
fly casting, as prevailing northeasterly trade winds blow directly onshore
much of the year. Much of this water lends itself to blind casting, as it is
generally a bit too deep to see fish tailing.

Keehi Lagoon Park. On the south shore of Oahu a system of flats located near the Honolulu International Airport may be accessed via Keehi
Lagoon Park. These flats are all reached by boat, but it is essential to use
caution with regard to wind, surf, and strong currents. At times, tailing
fish are available and there are three large flats to wade. There is enough
water here for a full day of fishing.

Fishing Information

Although there are lots of bonefish in the waters surrounding all the Hawaiian Islands, the availability of traditional flats and shallow water habitat is very limited. The island of Oahu will provide the fly angler with plenty of opportunity, as well as the majority of Hawaii's best water to fish. The general rule that the harder a destination is to reach, the better the fishing must be does not hold true in Hawaii. Oahu has the best fly water by far.

Outfits for Hawaiian bonefish should include a nine-foot, eight- or nine-weight setup with a saltwater taper floating line. A reel with a strong drag that holds at least 150 yards of backing is a must. Leaders of nine feet tapered to 15-pound test fluorocarbon will perform well. A stripping basket may also help to manage your fly line as you wade.

Flies commonly range from size #2 to #8, with the larger patterns generally performing the best. Preferred prey items include a variety of crabs, Mantis Shrimp, and saltwater Gobies. Colors vary from tans to dark browns, depending on the color of the particular flat you are fishing.

Wading in Hawaii is generally over hard coral and marl interspersed with sandy channels. A good pair of flats boots will serve you well. For many traveling anglers, an old pair of running shoes that can be easily packed and discarded at the end of the trip works perfectly. Exercise extreme caution while wading as most Hawaiian flats have live coral areas that can inflict painful wounds on shins and knees. Take it slow and easy because you want to be moving slower than the bonefish you are targeting.

Although Hawaii only experiences a tidal swing of approximately 2.5 feet from high to low, most flats only fish well for a short period during each phase of the tides. Couple this with gusty trade winds, surf, and occasional cloud cover, and you have a lot to manage. Hawaiian bonefish generally do not have to move a great distance to access their preferred flats and thus will wait until the optimum tide phase on any given day to move in. Fishing with someone who knows the water well will give you a significant advantage and save lots of valuable time.

Hawaiian bonefish are available throughout the year in good numbers as water temperatures range between 76 and 81 degrees F. Cloud cover and wind can be much more of a consideration than time of year, as overcast skies make spotting fish quite difficult.

Renting a kayak or stand-up paddleboard in Honolulu could not be easier. There are a number of agencies happy to rent by the hour, day, or week.

Our number one guide for Oahu:

Captain Rick Lee. www.bonefishhawaii.com

Where to Stay

Oahu is a small island, so everything is convenient. Don't worry about a central location or being by the airport; instead, go for the experience you want, whether that's an ocean view, sheer comfort, "peace and porpoises" near the hub of the convention center, or a bed and breakfast. Then start the hunt. Internet sites like VRBO and HomeAway are the ticket!

Getting Around

Honolulu International Airport (HNL), located on Oahu's south shore, is a 10-minute car ride from downtown and 20 minutes to Waikiki. It is the largest airport in the state of Hawaii and is serviced by every major airline. From Honolulu you can fly to all of the Hawaiian Islands.

Though Honolulu is small, the best way to get around is by car. Rent a car at the airport for the best rates, averaging at $70 per day.

Avis. www.avis.com

Budget. www.budget.com

Enterprise. www.enterprise.com

Thrifty. www.thrifty.com

Other transportation options include a good public bus system (www.thebus.org), which serves most of the island and is affordable at $2.50 per trip or $25.00 for a four-day pass you can purchase at any ABC Store.

The 34-seat, open-air **Waikiki Trolley** (www.waikikitrolley.com) is a fun way to travel. It stops at key attractions, restaurants, and some hotels, and there's driver commentary to boot! Tour passes can be purchased for one, four, or seven days at $19 to $50 with discounts for children and seniors.

Taxis are plentiful and convenient but pricey. Fares are fixed, so regardless of the cab company, expect to pay about $30 to get you from the airport to Waikiki or downtown.

Big bonefish from Cherokee Sound

Seven-Day Sample Trip

The fish in Oahu are big, so you owe it to yourself to fish with Captain Rick for two days to give yourself the best shot at hooking one of those behemoths. On day one, meet up with Captain Rick for your introduction to Hawaiian bonefish. Day two, leave the family on Waikiki and head to Waialai Beach Park and then to Wailupe Beach Park. The next day, fish Kuliouou Beach Park, looking for tailing fish at low tide. For the fourth day, pack up the family and head to Kaneohe Bay where everyone will have a great time and you can fish some of the best flats on the island. Day five, fish Keehi Lagoon Park close to the airport, and on the last full day team up with Captain Rick to end the trip on a high note. If you have time on day seven before the plane leaves, fish Ala Moana Beach Park or the flats in front of the Hilton Hawaiian Village Hotel.

Spousal Rating: 9

When you book Oahu, you are going to have a world-class tropical vacation where there is no doubt the entire family will have fun and memories to last a lifetime. The fact that the largest bonefish you are ever going to see happen to be swimming outside your hotel balcony is purely a coincidence.

Nonfishing Activities

The challenge in Honolulu will be deciding what *not* to do! Great restaurants, beautiful beaches, shopping inside or out—the choices are endless. The Bishop Museum holds the state's largest collection of natural history specimens and the world's largest collection of Hawaiian and Pacific cultural artifacts. Visit Pearl Harbor and the USS *Arizona* Memorial, Honolulu Zoo, Waikiki Aquarium (which is a working marine biology lab), or one of the many gardens such as Foster Botanical Garden or Lili'uokalani Botanical Garden. Catch a performance by the Honolulu Symphony, established in 1900, or support one of the many theater venues.

Not enough to choose from? Walk through the world's largest openair shopping center at Ala Moana Center, tour Diamond Head (which is a volcanic "tuff cone" made of unconsolidated ash), see the natural wonder of Manoa Falls, or snorkel at the famous Hanauma Bay Nature Preserve, known for its beautiful horseshoe-shaped sandy beach and clear turquoise waters. And saving maybe the best for last, there are the beaches! Surf, swim, or relax . . . ahhhh!

Bits and Pieces

A friend of mine works at one of the local fly shops and has some great stories about the fish that swim in the waters of Oahu between Diamond Head and Koko Head. Now, he only exaggerates about half as much as other fishermen, which in my eyes qualifies him for sainthood. When you ask him about bonefish in Hawaii, he stammers and then begins to whisper, "There are monster bonefish on the southeast side of Oahu. Big, solitary alphas that don't spook and are smarter than a sixth grader on Google. I found myself there in the fall under perfect conditions. The notorious winds were absent and the waters were calm as I watched what surely was the mother of all bonefish coming at me. Nose down. Three rod lengths away. Standing waist deep in water, that fish was feeding on the bottom with its tail out of the water. The distance from my hips to the ground is 36 inches and the current world record bonefish is 34 inches long. I cast and he looked. I cast and he looked. He never ate. How big was that fish? Why wouldn't he eat my fly? Now I know why people need pacemakers. I'm going back this winter."

INDEX

and Caicos Islands, 256–57; on
  Yucatan, 227–28
Gummy Fly, 138
Gummy Minnow, 132
Gunpowder Creek, 94
Gunpowder Road, 94
Guyana Creek, 109

Half Sound, 134
Halvorson House Villa Resort, 125
Hamilton, Bahamas, 179
Hamilton, Kim, 92*f*, 202*f*, 210*f*, 254*f*
Hamilton, Rod, 88*f*, 164*f*
Harbour Club Villas, 257
Harbour Island, 129–30, 133, 140
Harry Harris, 276
Hartswell Flat, 205
Harvey's Bay, 177
hats, 17
Hawaii, 286–95, 288*f*
Hawes, John C., 116
Hawks Nest: beach, 123; creek, 123
Hawks Nest Cay, 158
Hawks Nest Resort and Marina, 126
Haynes Library, 129*f*
heads, spotting, 29
Hermitage, 116, 116*f*, 127
Hideaway Bahamas, 146, 151
Higgs, Conrad, 257
High Rock, 146
Hill Bay, bottom, 253–54
Hills Creek, 94
Hilton Hawaiian Village Hotel, 289
HomeAway, 72
Homestead Bayfront Park, 268
Honolulu, 286–87, 295
hooks, 58, 70; setting, 67–68
horizontal lines, and spotting, 24
Hotel Tierra Maya, 229

hunting, 34
Hurricane Sandy, 153–54, 153*f*

Inagua National Park, 170–71
Indian Key, 277
Industrial Road, 250–51
inflatables, 14–15
insurance, 80
Islamorada, 274, 282, 285
Island HoppInn, 125
Ivel's Bed & Breakfast, 113

Jack Bay, 135
James Bay, 133
Joe's Sound, 121–22
Johnson, Fedel, 72, 112–13
Johnston, Randolf, 86
Joulter Cays, 189
Joyce, Michael, 209
Juba Sound, 249
Juba View Lane, 251

Kamehameha III, king of Hawaii, 286
Kaneohe Bay, 291
Kaufmann, Randall, 39
Kawaikui Beach Park, 290
kayak boots, 38
kayaks, 14–15, 202
Keehi Lagoon Park, 291
Kerrie, 92*f*
Key Biscayne, 266
Key Largo, 273–74, 282, 284
Key West, xi, 274, 282, 285
Kirwin, Joe, 90
knots, 52–53
Knowles, "Pinky," 180, 185
Kreh, Lefty, 43, 53–54
Kualoa Beach Park, 291
Kuliouou Beach Park, 290–91